The No-Nonsense Guide to Teaching Writing

STRATEGIES, STRUCTURES, AND SOLUTIONS

Judy Davis • Sharon Hill

HEINEMANN
Portsmouth, NH

Heinemann
361 Hanover St.
Portsmouth, NH 03801–3912
www.heinemann.com

Offices and agents throughout the world

The authors and publisher wish to thank those who have generously given permission to reprint borrowed material:

"Dragonfly" from *Creatures of Earth, Sea, and Sky: Poems* by Georgia Heard. Published by Boyds Mill Press (1997). Reprinted by permission of Georgia Heard.

"My Grandmother's Hair" by Cynthia Rylant. Copyright © 1991 by Cynthia Rylant. Reprinted by permission of the author.

"October Saturday" by Bobbi Katz. Copyright © 1990 by Bobbi Katz. Reprinted by permission.

"Too Much" from *TIME for Kids* (January 29, 1999). Reprinted by permission.

"The World of a Child in an Old Chair" by Hank Lubsen. Copyright © 1995 by The New York Times Co. Reprinted by permission.

Library of Congress Cataloging-in-Publication Data
Davis, Judy (Judy A.)
    The no-nonsense guide to teaching writing : strategies, structures, and solutions / Judy Davis,
Sharon Hill.
        p. cm.
    Includes bibliographical references and index.
    ISBN 0-325-00521-4 (alk. paper)
    1. English language—Composition and exercises—Study and teaching (Elementary)—United States.
I. Hill, Sharon (Sharon E.) II. Title.
LB1576.D2373 2003
372.62'3—dc21   2003010359

Editor: Lois Bridges
Production management: Patricia Adams
Production coordination: Abigail M. Heim
Typesetting: David Stirling, Black Dog Graphics; Gina Poirier, Gina Poirier Design
Design coordination: Renée Le Verrier
Interior design: Jenny Jensen Greenleaf
Photographs: Donnelly Marks
Cover design: Catherine Hawkes, Cat and Mouse
Manufacturing: Steve Bernier

Printed in the United States of America on acid-free paper
09 10 11 EB 13 12 11 10

To Tanya Kaufman

Who taught us that to be a teacher is to be a learner

Contents

Foreword

Judy Davis and Sharon Hill are gracious hosts. Visit their homes. Lots of friends stop by to share good conversations and plentiful comforting foods. Know that they are just as gracious to the thousands of visitors who over the years have come to study in their classrooms at The Manhattan New School and before that at P.S. 183, the wonderful schoolhouse, where this dynamic duo originally became professional and long-lasting buddies.

Even more important, Sharon and Judy are gracious hosts to the students in their upper elementary classrooms, creating breathtaking environments that inspire and enable their diverse students to become passionate and competent readers and writers. These classrooms are likewise filled with good friends, rich literary conversations, and comfort that comes in many forms—good morning hugs, the right poem at the right time, the thrill of moving an audience with one's words and artwork, the pride that comes from jobs well done, and the knowledge that you are known, heard, and appreciated. Then, too, in the spirit of being good hosts, there are abundant celebrations filled with toasts and the breaking of bread together. No doubt, there have been many bagel breakfast publishing parties in rooms 305 and 504 at The Manhattan New School.

I am honored to have been asked to write the foreword to this book, *The No-Nonsense Guide to Teaching Writing*. I left the principalship of this very special school four years ago and reading the book has helped me to catch up on what I have been missing. Written in a clear and concise manner, this incredibly practical book will become essential reading for the new upper elementary and middle school teacher as well as the experienced teacher determined to strengthen his or her teaching of writing. I think of Judy and Sharon as "two-hands on the shoulders" kind of teachers who aren't afraid to teach. At one point in the text they offer the response, "No ifs, ands, or buts." Those direct and confident words apply to the question, "Will this book help teachers turn their classrooms into effective writing workshops, ones in which students care about process and product, skills and strategies, as well as one another?" Yes. No ifs, ands, or buts.

Reading the book made it easy to imagine all the staff meetings, grade-level get-togethers, and collaborative studies that Sharon and Judy must have initiated in order to create such a comprehensive and thoughtfully planned approach to their writing workshops. Theirs is a gloriously bold style of teaching, in which they demand great things of their students and of themselves.

I was particularly delighted to read how they "make students famous," handle "loaded entries," ask students to "show evidence" of their learning, offer "pep talks," design "content rituals," provide "flip pads," and encourage "trains of thought." I read with interest about all the assessment, recordkeeping, organizational, and reflective tools they have added to their writing workshops, the attention they pay to storytelling, and the genres they have chosen to elevate. Then, too, I took nostalgic trips down memory lane as I read their crystallized thinking about their classic poetry anthologies, the whole-class journal, and writing in response to literature favorites and carefully selected newspaper clippings.

Readers will especially appreciate how these very experienced teachers have anticipated predictable problems, included powerful and abundant student works in progress, as well as conference transcripts, editing rituals, and detailed descriptions of what you might expect the teacher to be doing and the students to be doing during each course of study.

I used to think that the highest compliment Judy and Sharon paid to The Manhattan New School is that their own daughters were involved in this stellar schoolhouse. Sharon's younger daughter Daniella was a student there and Judy's daughter Meredith was a student-teacher. I now must add an additional and equally important compliment. The writing of this book pays royal tribute to the professional community in which it was written and I am eternally grateful to these splendid colleagues and friends for telling their story so well.

Shelley Harwayne, Superintendent, New York City Public Schools, May 2003

Acknowledgments

"No man is an island." But for so many teachers, that couldn't be further from the truth. They stand bound by the four walls of their classrooms, left to think, to plan, to imagine the possibilities alone. Our story is one of collegiality, community, and mentorship. We will be forever grateful to have been part of many learning communities and have so often relied on the wisdom and guidance of those who have fed our thinking all these years, that it is hard to know where their voices end and ours begin. To these mentors, past and present, we extend a heartfelt thank-you.

To Shelley Harwayne, for being our "jack of all trades, master of all," our role model for everything from her ability to know the name of every child and parent at The Manhattan New School to her ability to serve holiday dinner for 50 and make it seem effortless. Thank you for creating a school that at so many times felt more like home than home itself, for helping us frame curriculum that made sense, for bringing the best out in us at all times, for constantly immersing us in the world of books, for believing in us, and for not allowing us to let go of the idea that we had a story to tell. You have left your mark on our teaching and our lives and will surely leave your fingerprints on the changing face of the New York City Department of Education.

To Jacqui Getz, a kindred spirit if there ever was one, for her friendship, her humor, her sense of style, for the Swedish Fish that brought us to her office for a pick-me-up in the middle of the day, for the endless hours at Starbucks helping us organize and rethink this book, for the retreats that brought us together to think, to organize and structure our work, to redirect our instruction, to laugh, and, of course, to eat and to shop.

To our family at The Manhattan New School who have fed us with a perfect balance of professional support and friendship, who know how to teach and to hug, to plan curriculum and parties, which bookstore has the best children's books, and where to buy the best shoes. We love each and every one of you and are grateful for this extended family. Thank you to Lauren Benjamin, Jennifer Brophy, Valerie Brosnan, Ida Mae Chaplin, Dana Chipkin, Ann Marie Corgill, Neuza Costa, Dora Cruz, Beri Daar, Erica Edelman, Elissa Eisen, Lisa Elias, Juana Firpo, Tara Fishman, Jordan Forstot, Lisa Fuentes, Caroline Gaynor, Mindy Gerstenhaber, Pam Godwin, Julie Greene, Judith Hirschberg, Layne Hudes, Steven Jaffe, Petrana Koutcheva,

John Keaveney, Jayne Kuckley, Diane Lederman, Anita Lee, Rachel Lisi, Jennifer Macken, Amy Mandel, Jill Marino, Cheryl Melchiorre, Melissa Wigdor, Michael Miller, Corinne O'Shea, Giovany Rodriguez, Roberta Pantal-Rhodes, Denise Rickles, Paula Rogovin, Karen Ruzzo, Renay Sadis, Lydia Salavarria, Barbara Santella, Mary Anne Sacco, Pamela Saturday, Marisa Schwartzman, Lorraine Shapiro, James Smith, Mark Stein, Sharon Taberski, Kevin Tallat-Kelpsa, Barbara Wang, Pat Werner, Debby Yellin, Beatrice Zavala.

Special thanks to Steven Jaffe for coming to our rescue with his technology and photography expertise.

To Doreen Esposito, who although a relatively new teacher, is wise beyond her teaching years. You have certainly taught old dogs some new tricks.

To Lisa Elias, Julie Greene, Caroline Gaynor, Jennifer Brophy, Pat Werner, and Amy Mandel for sharing their teaching ideas and their students' work.

To Karen Ruzzo and Mary Anne Sacco for the commiseration and inspiration along this shared writing journey.

To those of you who have left MNS, know you are missed but not forgotten: Eve Mutchnick, Joan Backer, Sungho Pak, David Besancon, Kathy Park, Cindy Michaels, Isabel Beaton, Lisa Siegman, Regina Chiou, Kristi Lin, Tammy DiPaolo, Meggan Towel, Constance Foland, and Pam Kosove.

To Joanne Hindley-Salch who taught us how to listen to our students and to each other, how to manage our classrooms with good humor and grace, and how to bring the good work we were doing in our classrooms to other teachers in a way that made sense. We are proud and thankful to be "in your company."

To the hundreds of young writers whose honest writing changed our lives and will someday help shape the future of the world, and to all the parents who trusted us with their children and allowed us the privilege of spending our careers with those precious gifts: we thank you.

To our friends at Teachers College Reading and Writing Institute. First, to Lucy Calkins for her vision of a learning community that brought teachers from far and wide together to form a network of thinkers and learners that made us proud to call ourselves teachers, for her inspirational speeches that sent us off with a new zest for teaching and learning, and for the gathering of staff developers that included Joanne Hindley-Salch, Georgia Heard, Andrea Lowenkopf, Dorothy Barnhouse, Ralph Fletcher, JoAnn Portalupi, Vicki Vinton, Randy Bomer, Katherine Bomer, and Carl Anderson. To the many educators we met through our association with Teachers College who became our colleagues and remain our friends—Mimi Aronson, Hindy List, Kathy Cunningham, Kate Montgomery, Daria Rigney, Artie Voigt, Sue Slavin, Kathy Doyle, Shirley McPhillips, Laurie Pessah, and Lydia Bellino. Sharon extends her thanks to her many colleagues and friends who supported her work and fed her thinking during her time at the Reading and Writing Project. They include Pam Allyn, Janet Angelillo, Teresa Caccavale, Grace Chough, Kathy Collins, Lynn Einbender, Nick Flynn, Rory Freed, Elise Goldman, Isoki Nia, Gaby Layden, Amy Ludwig, Liz Phillips, Lisa Ripperger, Donna Santman, Kim Tarpinian, and Kathleen Tolan.

To the teachers and staff developers in Boston, Dublin, Corning, Commack, Jericho, Missouri, Kentucky, Smithtown, Winnepeg, Sweden, San Diego, and William Floyd who have welcomed us into their hearts and their classrooms. Special thanks to Ann Deveney, Martha Gillis, Franki Sibberson, Karen Szymusiak,

Linda Trifon, Syd Korsunsky, Arlene Wild, Rigmor Lindo, and Loretta Fowler for inviting us and for making us feel like we made a difference.

To Stephanie Harvey and our friends in Denver who set the bar high and inspired us to think and do our best work always.

To Carl Anderson, a friend, colleague, and remarkable teacher. Thanks for being our strong supporter along the way. Your willingness to read our manuscript long before we were ready to let it go helped us clarify our thinking.

To Don Graves for the quiet conversations on Shelley's couch and at NCTE. You are an inspiration to us and teachers everywhere.

To Georgia Heard, a long-time mentor and friend. Your works gave us the inspiration to forge ahead and trust our instincts.

To Tony Stead, and Katie Wood Ray. We are honored that we think along the same lines and grateful that our paths have crossed.

To Janet Jurist for the library research, and Rae Reyes for the help with the bibliography.

To Ray Coutu, our very first editor and friend. Thank you for lighting the fire that got us going.

To our wonderful supporters and friends at Heinemann for not only the help and guidance with our book but for providing the lifeline for literacy support to thousands of educators the world over.

To Lois Bridges, the heart and soul of this book. It's hard to find the appropriate words for the person who gave us words when we couldn't find them. As every newborn baby deserves a godmother, every new author deserves a fairy godmother, and we have found that in you. Your magic reached across the country and cast its spell on us and our book.

To Kären Clausen, Editorial Assistant, for your diehard pursuit of permissions; to Renée Le Verrier, Special Projects Editor, for the artistic vision that became a reality; to Abby Heim, Production Supervisor, for your hard work in imagining the realm of possibilities and including us in the decisions; to Alan Huisman, Developmental Editor, for bringing order to our manuscript when we lost our way; to Patty Adams, Production Editor, for so graciously giving your time and expertise while copyediting, we forever will be amazed and grateful for your ability to know what we meant when we didn't quite get it right; and to Leigh Peake, Editorial Director, for trusting that we really did have a book in us.

Not only does Judy know she is among the luckiest teachers alive, but she is acutely aware of the web of love and dedication that surrounds her daily. To those who make up this select group of family, friends, and colleagues, she forever will be indebted. Thank you to Ken, my husband and best friend. It seems like just yesterday that we met and yet you have been behind me in everything for 35 years. Thank you just isn't quite enough, I know, for your undying love, unending patience, unrelenting support for my work and for this book, for the tech support and the life support.

To my daughter Meredith, the first and the best writer in the family. Thank you for living up to my expectation of what a daughter could be. I couldn't be prouder of your humanity, your generosity, your dedication to your family, friends, and students. Thanks for following in my footsteps and forging new paths. You give me goose bumps when you talk about your teaching highs. Thanks for the Thursday nights, the buzzes, and the delicious hugs. And although this book isn't dedicated to you, most certainly my life has been dedicated to you.

To my mother Frances Forman for always believing that I could do anything.

To Beri Daar, Jill Marino, and Barbara Wang, my co-teachers and right hands for the last three years. You never will know how much your support has meant to me and to the completion of this book.

To the circle of friends who have become my extended family. Marcia Byalick, my first writing teacher, role model, and friend of 42 years, for teaching me that concentrated hard work pays off; to Bob Byalick, for always making me laugh; to Jane and Barry Schweiger, for the home away from home and the years of celebrations; to Debby and Mike Lubell, for taking me away from the computer and feeding me with barbeque and love; to Jill Benado and Bill Hartman, for the inspiration to find relaxation and fun whenever possible; and to Dennis and Gail Roth for New Year's Eve caviar and Edna Valley.

To Patti Seifert, for teaching me the real meaning of the word "hero."

To Diane Snowball who values teachers and their stories and for helping me see the importance of telling mine.

To Maureen Barbieri, the first one to read anything I wrote. I played your encouraging words over and over again in my head as I struggled with writing.

To Suzanne Lewin and the teachers at P.S. 158M; and to Josh Klaris and the teachers at P.S. 183M for welcoming me into their schools and their classrooms and for asking the smart questions that got me thinking and kept me on my toes.

Sharon recognizes that without the support and understanding of her family and friends, this book would not have come to fruition, and she wishes to express her gratitude to those who made it possible.

My friends from childhood, Carlyn Burke and Kathy Grant, knew instinctively when to give me a call to see how I was doing, when to schedule visits and plan parties that, in spite of how busy I was, I just couldn't miss and ultimately provided just the rejuvenating break I needed. Susan Forrest, you listened and knew how much I needed to be convinced there was an end in sight.

Barbara Wilson, Terry O'Neal, Rochelle Farrington, and my friends at Highland knew when to send up prayers or email me spiritually uplifting snippets to make sure I didn't forget what really matters.

Martine Benarroch is the newfound jewel mined from my busy schedule. Thanks to her, Steve, and Leor for making their home Daniella's second home.

To my brother Al Goldson; thanks for taping music for me to listen to and for baking me cakes of organic grains and honey. They nourished both my mind and spirit. My sister Claudette has the biggest giving heart; nothing is too much to ask of her. She has given me her love, her deepest respect for the work I do as an educator, her admiration just because I am her big sister, and always, flowers. Through the writing of this book, I never had to worry about meals for the family. She rescued me by providing Sunday dinner so, in my absence, the girls were cared for and fed.

From my mother, Doris Goldson, I got the gift of patience and compassion. She has been my long-time supporter and friend and has been my loving oasis in a stressful world. So often, after a long day of writing, I knew I could stop by to listen and be listened to, to hug and be hugged back, long and tight. Then I would go home knowing I had a lot to give Earl and the girls.

My aunt and second mother, Myrtle Webb, has been my supporter and guardian angel from my earliest beginnings. She taught me diligence and perseverance. She gave me the first book I fell in love with, and she taught me to look up in order to reach for the stars. I celebrate her lifetime of support in the writing of this book.

Though at times it seemed that writing took the place of my precious girls, it never really did. I dedicated my time to writing because I knew each weekend away was a weekend closer to the end, when we could resume our normal lives. I thank Dasha for making me stop to listen and participate in conversations that often left me wide-eyed in amazement at her incredible insightfulness; for knowing when a massage was needed to soothe me, replenish my energy, and saturate me with love. Falling asleep was my gratitude then. Now I express my heartfelt love and thanks. Daniella never ceased to remind me of how important it is to play, to laugh, and to sing. She has the strongest arms and the biggest heart. So when I couldn't do, couldn't be, and wasn't there (even at her most important swim meets), she didn't let that stop her. She just went ahead, took charge, and "kicked butt"!! To her I express my love and gratitude for the incredible independence and resourcefulness she possesses.

My husband, Earl, is the one through whom I have discovered the thrill and security found in mutual trusting. His love is a sanctuary that has nurtured my growth over our many years of friendship and marriage, allowing me to reach undreamed heights. From him I receive daily unrestrained affirmation of his love and devotion. My gratitude and love go especially to him.

Introduction

We consider ourselves fortunate to have worked with some of the best known and most accomplished writing teachers in the field of education. Our inspiration to provide the best instruction for our students and our vision for imagining what is possible comes from our mentors. They invited children to write and, what's more, they showed children—and us—what it means to be a writer.

After many years of teaching, we became part of the Teachers College Reading and Writing Project community. We learned to question our practice and reinvent our writing instruction from Lucy Calkins and Shelley Harwayne. We joined the staff of The Manhattan New School and continued to break the molds of old traditions, discarding our red pens and grammar textbooks. We embraced new models as we conferred alongside Shelley Harwayne and Joanne Hindley, and more recently, our principal Jacqui Getz. We learned to listen to our students and honor what they had to say. We have underlined, highlighted, dog-eared, and embraced the teaching-ideas in the books of Carl Anderson, Nancie Atwell, Randy Bomer, Lucy Calkins, Ralph Fletcher, Donald Graves, Shelley Harwayne, Georgia Heard, Joanne Hindley, and Katie Wood Ray. We are now delighted to showcase in our own book the strategies, structures, and solutions that we have learned along the way, not only from these groundbreaking thinkers in the field of education, but from our colleagues and from our students. We hope this book supports you in your classroom, day by day, month by month, as you come to enjoy the teaching of writing. We have learned to trust our students and ourselves and we hope this book, which highlights the precise, explicit (no-nonsense!) details of the successful teaching of writing, helps you to do the same.

Like you, we often struggle with thirty students, some who are fluent and for whom words come easily; others for whom writing is as foreign as walking on the moon. They speak a dozen different languages and hail from diverse families who may have lived for generations in the neighborhood or immigrated thousands of miles from across the Atlantic, Indian, or Pacific Oceans.

As an outgrowth of our daily practice as writing teachers, we have come to understand the importance of direct and explicit teaching for lifting the quality of our students' writing. To accomplish this work we are guided by an understanding of the qualities of effective writing as well as by an overarching structure that frames the writing process, establishes high expectations for superlative work, sets limits, and helps our students produce polished work worthy of publication on a regular basis. We refer to this structure as a "cycle." Each cycle lasts approximately four to five weeks, is tied to clear instructional goals (which we deliver through mini-lessons), and carries our students through a process that goes from collecting ideas in their writing notebooks to producing a polished, published piece that can be shared and celebrated with others.

Our book takes you into our classrooms and invites you to eavesdrop on our teaching practices and our conversations with students. We show you how to:

- develop goals for effective teaching, learning, and writing
- structure and organize your daily Writing Workshop as well as your writing work across the year
- gather tools that will help students get organized and become more reflective about their own work
- design targeted minilessons
- develop supports for effective writing conferences
- engage students in thoughtful conversations about quality writing
- learn from samples of student writing and mentor texts

Part 1: Getting a Handle on the Essentials establishes the foundation of our work and explains the essential components of our Writing Workshop. *Part 2: Helping Your Students Become Writers* outlines our writing curriculum. *Part 3: Extending Writing Possibilities* explains how to conduct genre studies and lays out step-by-step teaching for three genre studies.

How Our Book Can Be Most Helpful

At first glance, you might be tempted to read this book by flipping to the sections that seem most important for your teaching. We know how difficult it is to find time to do everything you need to do: plan for your teaching, read professional literature, and have a life. We suggest, however, that you read the book straight through to get the "big picture," then go back and find the parts that best support your writing instruction.

As classroom teachers ourselves, we know how helpful it is to see real samples of children's writing. To that end, you'll find numerous samples that show our students writing across function and genre including their notebook entries, published personal narratives, poems, feature articles, and typed texts of picture books not only woven throughout the text but also on our website: <www.heinemann.com/davis-hill>. You might consider sharing our students' samples with your own students. Often, the best way to inspire students to achieve their best is to show them what other students have done. And a quick note about the notebook entries: If, when you look at the quality of some of the entries, you think, "This seems too neat to be true" . . . it is! We asked some of the students to rewrite their work to make it easier to reproduce and read; nonetheless, we maintained the authenticity of their original notebook entries, including grammatical and spelling miscues. Since our teaching is a work in progress, keep

WEBSITE

in mind that some notebook entries might not reflect the structures and formats we have put in place as a result of our ongoing reflection about best practice and should only be read for content.

Whether this is the first book you read on the teaching of writing or the fifteenth, the message should be clear: Effective writing instruction begins with specific goals and thoughtful, detailed plans for the year ahead, as well as a clearly-defined structure and organization for each writing day. In this way, quality writing will flourish in your classroom day in and day out, all year long. Writing is akin to thinking; clear, well-organized writing reflects sharp, logical thinking. Let's provide the environment, tools, and informed instruction to allow our students to discover the joy of finely-crafted written expression, and show them how to use it across content, genre, form, and function. In this way, all our students will discover their own thinking, hear their own voices, establish their own authority, and ask the vital questions that transcend our classrooms and shape a lifetime of learning.

Getting a Handle on the Essentials
GOALS, TOOLS, AND MANAGEMENT

"Writing changed Alix's life. Her daily notebook entries made up of observations, thoughts and experiences gave way to writing for real audiences and real purposes. She writes easily and readily. She has found her voice."

–KAREN FEUER, MOTHER OF ALIX LIV
MNS GRADUATING CLASS, 1995

Setting Achievable Goals

A successful Writing Workshop begins with clear goals for your student writers, and an understanding of the teaching that's required to help your students achieve those goals. As experienced teachers of writing, it would have been easy for us to begin one year after another by following the blueprints of our successes and ignoring the failures, especially since reflection and planning are hard work. But as we became more reflective about our practice, we realized the importance of establishing a thorough list of goals for:

• Our students as writers

• Ourselves as teachers of writing

• Our students' writing—making sure it reflects the qualities of effective writing

A turning point in our teaching came when our third-, fourth-, and fifth-grade teaching colleagues at Manhattan New School gathered together at the end of the year and our conversation led us to define our goals for our Writing Workshops by stating them explicitly in writing. In this way, we clearly assessed and fine-tuned our practice.

If our goals were comprehensive, and if we taught toward those goals, we were confident that our teaching and the quality of our students' writing would improve. Our students would then be well on their way to meeting the standards of exemplary writing. We developed three sets of goals. See Figure 1–1.

Goals for Our Student Writers

We want every student to:

• live like a writer, paying closer attention to the world—observing, questioning, wondering, having opinions, and seeing other perspectives

• learn strategies for finding ideas for writing

• develop a sense of themselves as writers, to reflect on their process, and to set goals

• learn to write with clear intentions and purposes

FIGURE 1-1. *Setting goals with students.*

- be active members of a writing community, sharing their writing, giving and receiving feedback
- appreciate the writing process itself—to possess a willingness to write to discover what they have to say
- develop a working knowledge of the qualities of good writing
- create a repertoire of strategies that will lift the quality of their writing
- write with intentions toward audience
- become familiar with various genres as "containers" for writing
- develop an understanding of the purpose of revision
- learn to edit using appropriate writing conventions
- develop strategies for internalizing what is taught in minilessons and conferences
- develop an understanding that what is learned in the Writing Workshop applies to all the writing they do

Goals for Ourselves as Teachers

Too often when our students seem to miss the mark, we point the finger of blame at them. Or we give up and say they are not able to accomplish what we expect of them. Instead, we must be willing to look critically at *our* practice and make the necessary adjustments in *our* teaching to enable our students to meet their goals. To that end, we asked ourselves whether we had provided the necessary structures for ourselves and our students that would enable us to meet our teaching goals:

- Are we guided by a vision of where we need to begin in September and where we want to be in June? (We realized that we needed to consider both short-term as well as long-term plans.)

- Are we planning in accordance with the standards appropriate for our grade level?
- Are we providing tools that help to scaffold our work?
- Do we have a regular conference and assessment system that allows us to check in with all the children on a regular basis?
- Is our teaching responsive to the needs of all our students?
- Do we know what we need to teach?
- Are we helping students discover real reasons for writing?
- Are our minilessons strategic and explicit?
- Are we providing students with appropriate writing mentors?
- Are we providing enough opportunity for practice in the classroom?
- Are we holding students accountable for the work we expect them to do at home and in school?
- Do our students understand the importance of rereading their writing for different purposes? Have we established the expectation they will routinely reread for revision, reflection, and setting goals?
- Are we publishing frequently enough so that children are routinely engaged in preparing a piece for an audience, including revising and editing?
- Are there structures for teacher and student feedback?
- Do we foster writing across the curriculum?

Goals for Student Writing

We created a third list that reflects the qualities of effective writing. We considered these nonnegotiables; in other words, these are qualities we hope all students exhibit in their writing on their way to becoming accomplished writers.

In composing this list of qualities, we not only relied on our experience as writers and our knowledge of what makes good writing, but we also turned to a variety of texts we identified as samples of exemplary writing. We worked very hard to consider what it is that students really need to know about good writing to help them in their formative years, and serve as the foundation for all future writing. We placed the list of the Qualities of Good Writing next to the goals we had established for our writers and ourselves, and felt reassured we had set valid goals and expectations for our students. It was time to help our students achieve them and we set out to do so.

We received proof that our practice was successful when a group of professors from the Journalism Department at Columbia University invited our fifth-grade students to share their writing. Our students sat in circles, five to six students to a circle, reading and receiving feedback about their writing from the professional journalists. The journalists were delighted with the clear intentions of these young writers; their use of language; their effective leads, their ability to organize their thoughts; the variety of structures they were able to use; their overall confidence and ease in speaking about their writing processes. One professor commented that what our students already knew about good writing were the same aspects he taught his graduate students at the School of Journalism. Another professor jokingly suggested that if our students were taller and possessed the life experiences to accompany their knowledge of good writing, he'd enroll them right on the spot. It was an uplifting experience for all and convinced us that we were on the right track.

Qualities of Good Writing

CLEAR INTENTIONS
Audience: Who is the writing for?
Content: What is it saying?
Purpose: What is it supposed to do for the reader? Inform? Persuade? Entertain?

ORGANIZATION
Is the focus clear?
Is the thinking logically developed?

AUTHENTICITY
Is the writer knowledgeable about the subject so the reader develops a sense of believability about the piece and trust in the writer?

CRAFT
Does the writer demonstrate his own unique writing style through the artful use of language, using strong verbs, sensory images, authentic dialogue, repetition, comparisons, lists, effective leads, surprising language?

Voice: Has the writer given the reader a sense of a person behind the piece? Do we understand how the piece should be read and understood?

Genre: Is the container chosen for the writing based on the author's purpose?

Structure: Has the writer organized the piece to give it shape? Has the writer thought about the structure of the entire piece as well as the structure of parts of the piece?

CONVENTIONS
Does the writer use punctuation, grammar, and spelling conventions that help make the meaning clear?

Using the Right Tools

Having the right tools in the writer's workshop is crucial. By tools, we mean any-thing that supports the ongoing work of the writers in our classrooms. These tools fall into two overlapping categories:

1. Tools that serve the students
2. Tools that serve the teacher

Of course we've created something of a false dichotomy here for purposes of expla-nation. In reality, if a tool supports our students as writers, it simultaneously sup-ports us as teachers of writers.

Tools That Serve the Students

The Writer's Notebook

A writer's notebook is a tool our students use to record the things they notice, observe, and think about. We call each recording an entry. The entries can be any variety of ideas. The most common that we see our students writing are:

• memories
• observations of the things happening around them
• descriptions of people and places important in their lives
• opinions
• wonderings
• wishes
• family stories, hobbies, and other passions

   In other words, children write best about the things that are important to them. It is writing that comes from what they know and what they have experienced. For this reason, we usually discourage fantasy, mystery, or fairy tale writing. Instead, we encourage students to be in touch with what's going on in the world, by paying attention to the meaningful, everyday things that may otherwise go unnoticed and unrecorded.

BEGINNING THE WRITING NOTEBOOK

A writer's notebook can be a traditionally bound composition book or the fancier notebooks found in stationery stores. We encourage students to personalize them with pictures or other artifacts that are meaningful to them. See Figure 2-1 (below and on the website, <www.heinemann.com/davis-hill>). We discourage the use of spiral notebooks because they tend to give the message that it is okay to tear out pages.

The important thing about choosing a notebook is that the pages are large enough to support plenty of writing per page as well as space in the margin for writing questions, jottings, and notes. When there is an expectation to fill the larger page, we have found the thinking becomes bigger. Teaching toward "bigger thinking" is especially important for our more reluctant writers who tend to connect "writing more" with the quantity of lines rather than the quality of thought.

With an emphasis on "quality of thought," we ask students to use only the left-hand pages of the notebook for writing entries. The pages on the right are used as students reread their entries, providing space for them to write more. As they return to those entries, we teach students to use new strategies to develop their initial ideas. Such strategies may include getting a new idea from an old one, recrafting an entry, using questioning to push their thinking, or adding more details to the entry. (Please see detailed minilessons in Chapter 8.) This right-hand space makes the notebook more conducive to this revisiting. Our expectation is that students will understand that their thinking may not necessarily be complete because they come to the end of an entry. The right-hand side is a constant reminder that there may be more thinking to be done on any given idea or topic.

The notebook also offers writers the freedom to conveniently collect ideas for writing. We encourage students to not only use it in school, but to see it as a place where they can capture their thoughts about anything at any time. So even though it is a requirement in school, as they begin to take ownership, our hope is that they begin to see it less as an assignment and more as a personal tool for writing about what's important to them.

FIGURE 2-1. *An array of notebooks.*

WHY USE A WRITER'S NOTEBOOK?

In her book *Writing Through Childhood,* Shelley Harwayne, our mentor and founding principal at The Manhattan New School, presents a powerful invitation when she introduces the notebook to children by asking them to "Imagine doing the kind of writing that you will want to save for a lifetime. When you are twenty, fifty, or eighty, you will still keep these beautiful bound books in a special place because you will always want to recall what kind of kid you were, what you paid attention to, and what you thought about when you were young." After such an invitation, it's not unusual to see students go away hugging their notebooks while teachers go away feeling confident that an invitation to students to keep a notebook is an invitation to live like writers—real writers who take time to notice their world and to write about it. See Figure 2–2.

The notebook is a manageable tool in which students keep an ongoing collection of writing. A bound notebook, as compared to a folder or binder, eliminates the worry of losing work and makes the work easily accessible. It houses ideas that writers can return to in order to grow ideas, restructure, rethink, revise, connect ideas, and ultimately choose from a variety of entries to publish for an audience. Our message is that we expect them to publish, and, with that in mind, the notebook is an important tool to support that work.

The following quotes from our students reflect their feelings about keeping a writer's notebook:

"I think writing is like looking for treasure—ideas are everywhere." Alexi

"My writer's notebook is like a timeline of happenings and feeling that happened in my life. I think to myself, 'When I grow up and look back at my notebook, I'll know how I felt when I was a kid.'" Dana

"My writer's notebook is like a long-lost relative. It tells the story of my life and my feelings." Laura

FIGURE 2-2. *Sam on the floor writing in his notebook.*

"My notebook is a carefree place to grow your thoughts and nurture your ideas. And there are no restrictions." Luca

"I love my writer's notebook because it goes on and on and writing is a never ending subject." Julie

"I like using a writer's notebook because it's so organized. I can look back on them and revise or I can leave them the way they are." Nina

Mentor Texts

Shelley not only valued the writer's notebook as a tool for nurturing student writing but also deeply understood that one of the most important tools we use as teachers of writing is literature. When we set out to learn to do anything, we look to others who are expert at what we are trying to learn to do. Learning to write is no different. In teaching our students to be good writers, one of the first things we want them to be able to do is to anchor themselves to authors and texts they admire. A "mentor piece" is a short text or portion of a text used as a support for the work we are trying to accomplish in the workshop. Most of these pieces are read aloud or shared using the overhead projector. When possible, multiple copies of these are also made available for easy reference. We keep them in labeled baskets around the room so they are readily accessible. Very often, our students' published writing will become mentor pieces for other writers in the class. After pieces are published, we put them in plastic sleeves and set them in baskets so students can read each other's work when they need support or we can refer to them in a conference.

What we look for when choosing a mentor text:

- The topic is one the kids can relate to and will spark ideas for their own writing.
- The text not only tells a story, but also addresses an underlying issue that children will be able to readily uncover and write about in relation to their own lives.
- The text is well written and provides many opportunities to teach the qualities of good writing.
- The text is written in a specific genre we are focusing on in a genre study.

As students become more proficient writers with clear intentions for their writing, we expect that students will continue to refer to the mentor pieces we have chosen, as well as seek out published writers on their own for support.

By surrounding ourselves with possible mentor texts, we become informed about which ones will best serve our students' needs. After some practice, we seem to know the right ones when we see them.

Magazines and Newspapers

We order magazine subscriptions to *Time for Kids* and *Junior Scholastic* for each of our students and weave them into lessons throughout the year. We find these timely articles help broaden the possibilities for ideas to write about. Newspapers are also subscribed to and used regularly throughout the year.

Writing Partnerships and Response Groups

We would like to meet the needs of all of our students at all times, but the reality of our 30-student classrooms makes it almost impossible. What we can do, however, is set up structures that allow us to manage this task of providing support: writing response groups and writing partnerships. These structures help students realize that the teacher is not the only source they can turn to for help. As shown in Figure 2–3, they can rely on each other for support. Of course, informal pairings frequently occur and are encouraged after minilessons for students to process the strategy learned in the minilesson and talk about the writing work they will do that day. This quick discussion with a neighbor is getting them ready for the work they might do later in a more structured partnership. There are many different ways for forming partnerships and response groups. They include:

Permanent Writing Partner

• The person who reviews your weekly writing and comes to know your notebook work very well. This partnership should be formed based on the supports one writer in the group can give to the other. Since it takes time to get to know the writers in your class, early partnerships are most often formed based on what you notice about work habits. Once you get to know the students better, you can be more informed in creating alliances and base partnerships on writer's strengths and needs.

Writing Focus Partnership

• This arrangement is usually formed by simply saying to a student, "I think you need to talk to Jennifer. She is an expert at what you are trying to do, I know she will help you."

FIGURE 2–3. *A writing response group.*

Study Groups to Research Some Aspect of Writing

• Two or more children work toward a similar goal and come together to research, support each other's attempts, and share their knowledge of an area of writing they may be studying.

Response Groups

• Students get together in small groups to share their writing and provide feedback that supports the work the writer is attempting to do.

Editing Checklists

We want our writers to understand the difference between writing and editing. Although we do not want them to be bogged down with spelling, punctuation, or proper sentence structure during the process of getting their ideas down in the notebook or in a draft, we do want them to understand that properly edited writing is what we ultimately expect. We use an editing checklist, shown in Figure 2–4, to help our stu-

---

Editing Checklist

SPELLING

1. I have found misspelled words and tried spelling them in the margin.

TRICKY WORDS

2. I have checked to see if I used the correct homophone.

   • there, their, they're   • to, too, two
   • your, you're   • weather, whether
   • used to   • past, passed
   • which, witch   • except, accept
   • then, than   • its, it's
   • could have

DOES IT MAKE SENSE?

3. I have reread my work to make sure I have not left out any words I intended to write.

4. I have checked to make sure my sentences are not too long. If they were, I have either rephrased them or made them into more than one sentence.

PUNCTUATION

5. I have placed **periods, commas, questions marks,** and **exclamation marks** in places where they belong.

6. I began each sentence with an uppercase letter.

7. I have used **uppercase** letters for names of people, places, and proper nouns.

8. I have indented each new paragraph as my thoughts shifted.

FIGURE 2-4. *Editing checklist.*

dents become more accustomed to rereading their work with a lens toward editing, we need it to become a ritual, something they do on a regular basis. We copy an editing checklist for each student and laminate it. Students clip them to the right side of their notebooks, moving it along from page to page as they would a bookmark. The margin of each left-hand side of the notebook is marked with the numbers 1 to 8, to coincide with the tasks on the checklist. Each time the students write, they go back to reread their work, checking for each of the items on the checklist and making the appropriate changes. In the case of spelling, they use the margin for attempts at spelling the word correctly. They check off each completed task in the margin. (See Figure 2–5.) When we take notebooks home to read, we also look to see how students are working with the checklist and talk to them about it during our regular conferences. After a few cycles of this work, spelling, punctuation, and sentence structure in the notebook are notice-

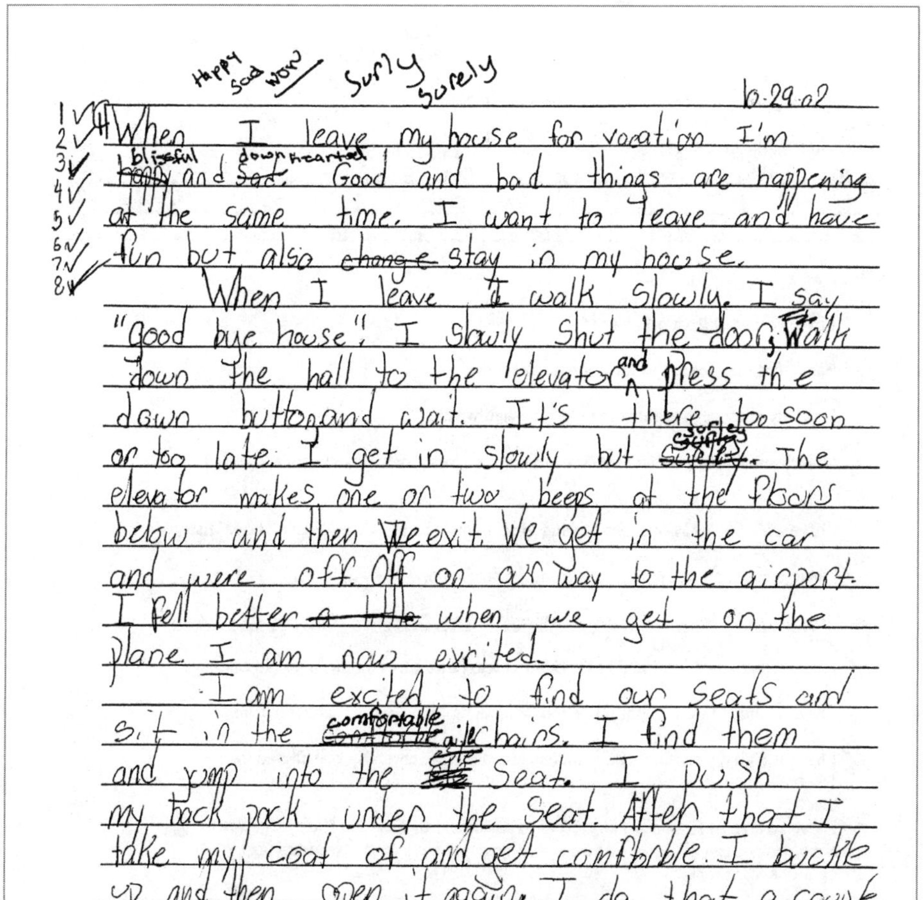

FIGURE 2–5. Alex's notebook page.

ably better, and when students are editing a piece to be published, they tend to catch more of their own errors and errors when they edit their partner's work. (See Figures 2–4 and 2–5 and Appendices A, B, and E.)

Student Assessments

Taking time to reflect on their writing is part of the process that helps students grow as writers and thinkers. While the mentor piece provides a model of good writing, the assessment provides an opportunity for reflecting over their commitment to writing during the previous week and for setting goals for the coming week. For this purpose we have designed a weekly assessment that students complete each weekend (see Figure 2-6 and Appendix B) of the collecting stage of every cycle. On

---

STUDENT WEEKEND WRITING ASSESSMENT

Name _Alex_   Week of _11/11/02_

Reflecting on the goal I set last week, I can say _I did a pretty good job. I really made sure I read them aloud to my self. There were a lot of things wrong. Since I read my entries aloud I was able to fix the mistakes._

This week:

G̶ I have written at least 6-8 entries.

✓ Each of my entries are **at least one** page long.

✓ I edit my entry each night when I am finished writing.

G̶ I have **at least three different** types of entries. (memories, observations, opinions etc)

✓ I have added **at least two** new writing ideas to my "Things I Can Write About" list.

✓ I have worked on improving my writing. I worked on _thinking about how strong verbs and realistic comparisons can make my writing better._

✓ I have reread my entries and have found **at least one** new idea from an old one.

✓ I have written more thoughtfully about something I have written about before.

✓ I have shared my writing with someone else and have carefully considered their feedback.

✓ I have written **at least one** entry off an article I read in *Time for Kids* or *Junior Scholastic* or any other magazines or newspapers I have read.. (wonderings, opinions, questions)

I am using this coming week to focus on _writing three different types of entries. I am writing different types of entries. Mostly everything I can relate to, my family. Thats what I do. I will try not to make many entries on my family._

I plan to do this by:

✓ speaking with peers _____ conferring with teacher _____ finding a mentor piece

Parent's Signature _[signature]_ Peer Signature _[signature]_

FIGURE 2-6. *Weekly Assessment—Alex's filled-in sheet.*

Monday morning we ask students to share their assessment work with a partner. They are not only being held accountable for doing the work but insuring they have an additional pair of eyes, aside from the teacher's, to give feedback and suggestions for achieving their goal.

After students have published, there is a Writer's Reflection assessment. This requires students to comment on what they have learned as they moved through the process from notebook entry to published piece, and asks them to reflect on their learning and how it will carry over to all future writing they do. See Figure 7–7k and Appendix C.

The students keep these assessments in their writing folder. At the end of each writing cycle, all assessments are removed from the writing folders and transferred to the writing sections of their portfolios. Before each marking period, we must meet with students individually to review their assessments and our conference notes and to talk about accomplishments and set goals.

Dual-Pocket Folders

To help organize the Writing Workshop, we ask that the students keep all loose papers in a plastic dual-pocket folder that we purchase for them at the beginning of the year. We collect the money from the parents later on. Parents are delighted to have us take the responsibility of ordering supplies since we can buy them much cheaper by ordering a large quantity from a local stationery supplier. Of course this is in the best of all possible worlds. Certainly you can buy less costly folders that you purchase from local vendors or ask students to buy them as part of their school supplies. When the folders begin to look shabby by the middle of the year, replace them in the same way. On one side of a folder the students keep copies of excerpts from mentor pieces we are using for that cycle and the current issues of the magazines. On the other side, the students keep the weekly assessment and any writing drafts they are currently working on.

Portfolio Binders

In addition to the folder, each student has a portfolio binder containing dividers labeled with each academic subject area. This three-ring binder is meant to display their growth over time in each academic area. We will deal only with the contents of the writing section here. For each published piece of writing, there is a cover sheet. We copy these on different-colored paper so that the reader can know when the work of one cycle is complete and a new published piece begins. This introduces the piece that follows and explains what it is about and why it is included in the portfolio. Next comes the published piece of writing, then the notebook entry/entries from which the piece originated, the drafts, and finally, the assessment that reflects on the work the writer did for that publishing cycle.

Writing Supplies

In order to establish an environment that supports our young writers, we make sure that each table is equipped with a basket that contains a supply of pens, pencils, staplers, tape, sticky notes, glue sticks, and paper. In order for our students to be engaged in the work of writing, it is important that the lack of tools does not become an issue. The baskets are always out and available. We assign the responsibility of keeping them stocked to students.

Tools That Serve the Teacher

Organization is the key to a smooth-running classroom. We have emphasized the importance of the availability of tools for our students. It is also true for us as teachers. It is of utmost importance, particularly during minilessons and conferences, to have easy access to markers, chart tablets, overhead projectors, sticky notes, and texts. The flow of a minilesson should never be interrupted because tools are unavailable or not conveniently placed.

Planning Sheets

We have already written about the need for teachers to plan. We know we must have a vision of where we need to begin in September and where we want our students to be in June. When Jacqui Getz succeeded Shelley Harwayne as principal of The Manhattan New School, she inspired in us a greater urgency to develop thoughtful, realistic plans based on the expectations and standards put in place by our state curriculum, district mandate, school philosophy, and colleagues on our grade level. Long-term plans must be put in place before we can plan the minilessons necessary to carry out our day-to-day goals in service of meeting those long-range plans.

In order to help us scaffold that work, Jacqui helped us design a number of different planning sheets that help hold us accountable for the work we have set out to do in each cycle. (See Figures 5–1, 5–2, and Appendices F and G.) Although each cycle is planned—knowing where we will start, where we will end, and when we will end—we are constantly taking cues from our students and allowing our conferences to inform our minilessons. This allows us to be flexible enough to rethink our plans so that we are stepping in tune with the needs of our students. This means allowing teachable moments to take over and slowing down when our students are not ready to move on.

Whether you consider using the planning sheets included in this book, adapt them to fit your own needs, or use ones you have created that suit you better, the point is, you *must* plan. A wise principal in our district prominently displays this sign pinned to her bulletin board: *"If you fail to plan, you plan to fail."*

Conference Sheets

When we sit down to conference with a student, we have all the necessary tools with us. We carry sticky notes, a text or two that might help us model a strategy for the writers we plan to confer with that day and, of course, our recordkeeping materials. (See Figure 2–7, and also Figures 6–7, 6–10 and Appendix D.) Many of the writing teachers we know who have been at this for some time have tried many different forms of conference sheets. Keep in mind that it is not so much the format of the sheets you use, although easy reference is always a key factor, but that you do keep the records and do refer to them. The recordings about particular students not only help with the work you do with that child, but inform your teaching and help you design your minilessons accordingly. The conference sheet we have included not only provides easy reference for each child in the class, but a space for us to make quick notes on ideas for minilessons based on our observations. In September, we design these sheets, filling in each student's name, then photocopy and bind a quantity into a portable, spiral bound book that we can carry with us to jot notes in as we move around the room conferring with our students about their writing progress. Seeing all the boxes in front of us helps keep us honest. If, during the course of a writing cycle, we see that there are particular boxes blank, we cannot in good conscience ignore the fact that we haven't yet conferred with a particular student. Our goal, of course, is to get to as many students as many times during a cycle as possible.

Teacher Writing

We have mentioned before how much we value opportunities to bring our own experiences as readers and writers to help enrich our teaching. When we share our writing with our students, we are not only giving them a glance into our lives as literate adults, we are modeling the experience of writing and the process of writing. Sometimes we purposely compose a piece of writing that will help us accomplish the goal we have in mind for our students. Other times, we simply select appropriate entries from our notebooks. Over the course of time, we keep returning to these pieces of writing for different purposes.

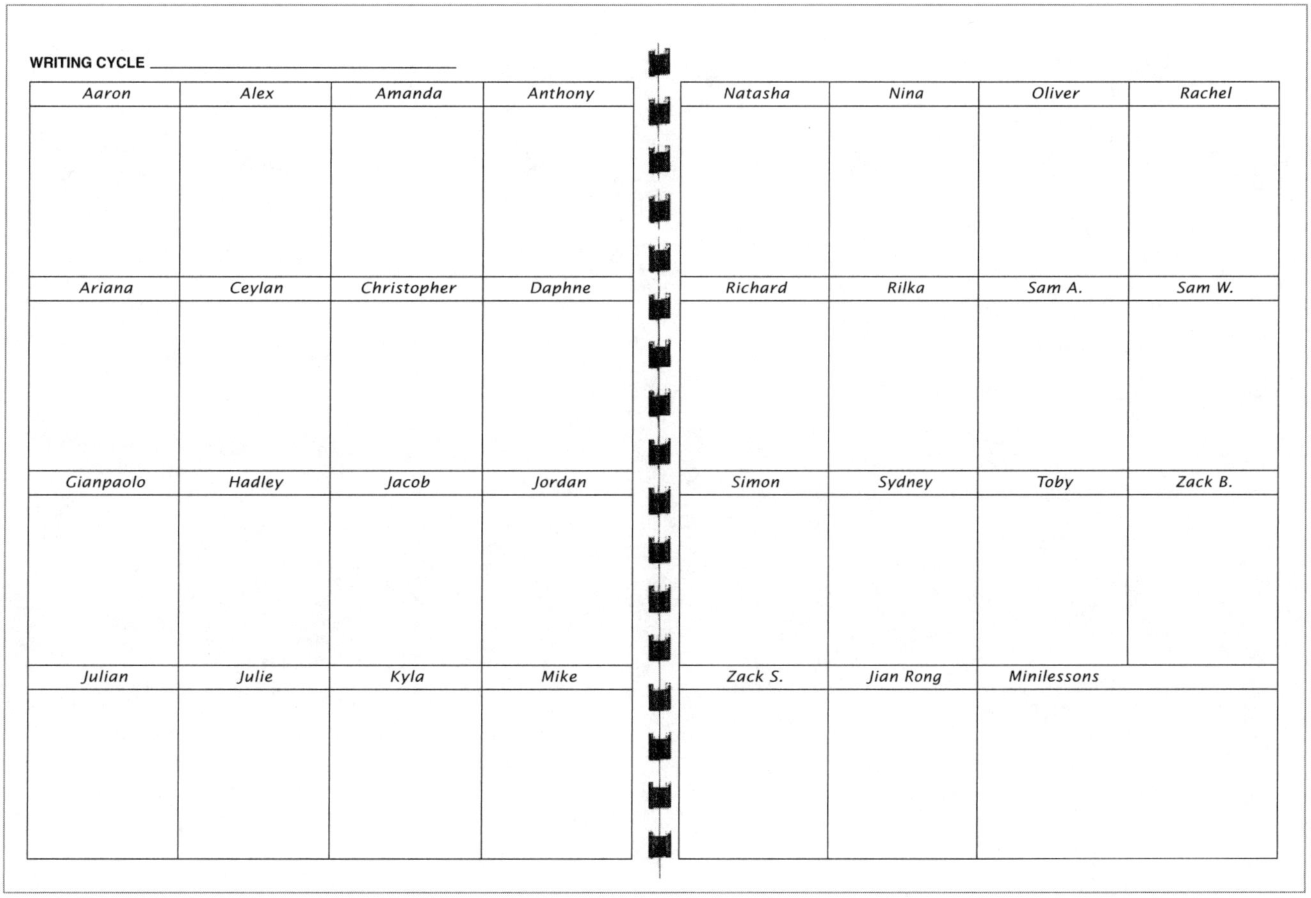

WRITING CYCLE _____

Aaron	Alex	Amanda	Anthony		Natasha	Nina	Oliver	Rachel
Ariana	Ceylan	Christopher	Daphne		Richard	Rilka	Sam A.	Sam W.
Gianpaolo	Hadley	Jacob	Jordan		Simon	Sydney	Toby	Zack B.
Julian	Julie	Kyla	Mike		Zack S.	Jian Rong	Minilessons	

FIGURE 2–7. *Blank Recordkeeping Sheet.*

Sometimes we get together with colleagues on our grade level and each teacher will write a different type of entry for the purpose of demonstrating the different ways people might respond to a text. For instance, at the beginning of the year when we first began to use literature, we noticed that so many of our students would write entries directly related to the content of the text we had read. We got together with our colleagues and asked each of them to write entries after having heard the text, keeping in mind that they needed to push their thinking in order to demonstrate for students some possibilities of where our minds can take us. We shared the entries with our students and identified the different ways in which different teachers were inspired to write. We named the strategies and taught them to use those strategies in their own writing. At other times, we have carefully chosen entries from our notebooks, circled the part of the writing that we would like to work on to accomplish a particular goal, and, through a shared writing minilesson, demonstrated what we wanted our students to practice with their own writing.

As you read further into this book, we will explain in greater detail how we use our own writing to help students develop trains of thoughts, to help them dig deeper into memories and family stories, and how we help students master a variety of writing strategies.

3

Providing Structure and Organization

Our writing curriculum is organized across the year as well as day by day in the following ways:

1. Our writing year is built around writing cycles.

2. Our writing day is structured around a Writing Workshop.

Figure 3–1, The Year at a Glance, gives you a quick overview of the way we have structured the work of the Writing Workshop and the different genres we have chosen to study. However, based on your curriculum focuses and the interests of your students, you may select some of the other forms to study, following the steps we outline later in the book. The remaining chapters in the book will spell out in greater detail how we accomplish the goals we set for our students from the beginning to the end of the year.

Writing Across the Curriculum

As a result of our work in the Writing Workshop, our students will learn they have important things to say and how to say them well. Once they learn this, they will have the strategies to write about anything with the same authority and the same attention to detail, and eventually use the same knowledge base about the qualities of good writing in all content areas.

Although this is clearly a book that will help you plan and implement a Writing Workshop in your classroom, it is important that you read these chapters with the understanding that you must also keep in mind that writing, like reading, must be balanced across all the curriculum areas. When you set out in September to plan your year, examine your expectations not only in the Writing Workshop, but in all content areas, as well as the kind of writing students need to practice in preparation for city- and state-wide tests.

Let's begin by thinking about your Reading Workshop. Just as you plan for your read-aloud, shared reading, guided reading, and independent reading instruction, you should be thinking about the kinds of writing you hope your students will be doing throughout the year. Writing is often used as a powerful tool for thinking in

The Year at a Glance: From Notebook to Published Work

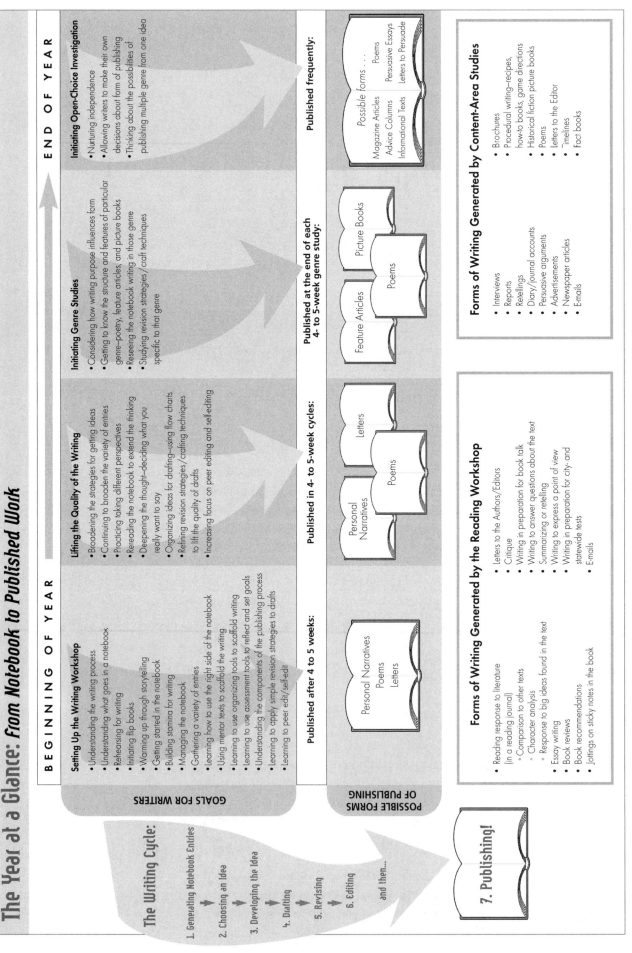

BEGINNING OF YEAR → END OF YEAR

GOALS FOR WRITERS

Setting Up the Writing Workshop
- Understanding the writing process
- Understanding what goes in a notebook
- Rehearsing for writing
- Initiating flip books
- Warming up through storytelling
- Getting started in the notebook
- Building stamina for writing
- Managing the notebook
- Gathering a variety of entries
- Learning how to use the right side of the notebook
- Using mentor texts to scaffold the writing
- Learning to use organizing tools to scaffold writing
- Learning to use assessment tools to reflect and set goals
- Understanding the components of the publishing process
- Learning to apply simple revision strategies to drafts
- Learning to peer edit/self-edit

Lifting the Quality of the Writing
- Broadening the strategies for getting ideas
- Continuing to broaden the variety of entries
- Practicing taking different perspectives
- Rereading the notebook to extend the thinking
- Deepening the thought—deciding what you really want to say
- Organizing ideas for drafting—using flow charts
- Refining revision strategies/crafting techniques to lift the quality of drafts
- Increasing focus on peer editing and self-editing

Initiating Genre Studies
- Considering how writing purpose influences form
- Getting to know the structure and features of particular genre—poetry, feature articles, and picture books
- Reseeing the notebook writing in those genre
- Studying revision strategies/craft techniques specific to that genre

Initiating Open-Choice Investigation
- Nurturing independence
- Allowing writers to make their own decisions about form of publishing
- Thinking about the possibilities of publishing multiple genre from one idea

POSSIBLE FORMS OF PUBLISHING

Published after 4 to 5 weeks:
- Personal Narratives
- Poems
- Letters

Published in 4- to 5-week cycles:
- Personal Narratives
- Poems
- Letters

Published at the end of each 4- to 5-week genre study:
- Feature Articles
- Poems
- Picture Books

Published frequently:

Possible forms . . .
- Magazine Articles
- Advice Columns
- Informational Texts
- Poems
- Persuasive Essays
- Letters to Persuade

The Writing Cycle:
1. Generating Notebook Entries
2. Choosing an Idea
3. Developing the Idea
4. Drafting
5. Revising
6. Editing
and then...
7. Publishing!

Forms of Writing Generated by the Reading Workshop
- Reading response to literature [in a reading journal]
- Comparison to other texts
- Character analysis
- Response to big ideas found in the text
- Essay writing
- Book reviews
- Book recommendations
- Jottings on sticky notes in the book
- Letters to the Authors/Editors
- Critique
- Writing in preparation for book talk
- Writing to answer questions about the text
- Summarizing or retelling
- Writing to express a point of view
- Writing in preparation for city- and statewide tests
- E-mails

Forms of Writing Generated by Content-Area Studies
- Interviews
- Reports
- Retellings
- Diary/journal accounts
- Persuasive arguments
- Advertisements
- Newspaper articles
- E-mails
- Brochures
- Procedural writing—recipes, how-to books, game directions
- Historical fiction picture books
- Poems
- Letters to the Editor
- Timelines
- Fact books

FIGURE 3–1. *The Year at a Glance.*

the Reading Workshop. Will you ask your students to write as they build theories about the characters in the books you read aloud and in those they read independently? How will your students' writing support their literature conversations as they discuss their big questions about text? Will you expect them to answer questions you pose as you are reading aloud? Will you create essay questions that ask the children to conclude how characters change over the course of a story or recall what they remember about the books you read? How much writing will they keep in a reading notebook and what will you collect as an assessment of how competent they are at expressing their thinking about reading?

Likewise, we believe we need to plan for writing that relies on the acquisition of content knowledge. However, we choose to focus on content writing in the Social Studies and Science Workshops. Writing in the content area requires students to research a variety of sources, to gain knowledge and understandings related to the specific content being studied, to synthesize and organize information, and to be able to make generalizations based on their knowledge of that content. The skills learned in the Writing Workshop will impact the writing in the Social Studies and Science Workshops.

In the same ways we teach students to use mentors in the Writing Workshop, we remind them to anchor themselves to texts as they write in the content area. We expect they will apply the strategies they have learned about drafting, revising/crafting, and editing in the Writing Workshop to their writing in the content area, and for that matter to any writing they set out to do. To make this happen, we must expose the students to the different kinds of powerful nonfiction genres we expect them to be tackling in their writing. As children compose their writing, we need to teach them the very specific qualities that make nonfiction powerful. This knowledge, combined with what they learn in the Writing Workshop, will help make their work authentic and well crafted.

If we are clear about the goals of the Writing Workshop and the goals of the work we do in social studies and science, we can make sure the work we do in the Writing Workshop strongly impacts the quality of our students' writing across the curriculum. The qualities of good writing your students acquire through the writing curriculum we lay out in this book will impact their writing work in all content areas.

Writing Cycles

Our writing curriculum is organized around a series of cycles. A cycle is a period in our Writing Workshop, typically four to five weeks, that fulfills specific teaching intentions. Minilessons are designed specifically toward these intentions. The cycle begins with a period of time spent gathering entries in the notebooks and ends with a published piece. The work of every cycle begins with lifting the quality of the notebook entries so that the transition to a published piece comes easily and builds on students' knowledge of the qualities of good writing.

A cycle is structured around:

1. The **writing notebook**
   Students collect entries, build stamina, write on a variety of topics.

A Typical Writing Cycle

- It takes 4 to 5 weeks to complete a writing cycle.

- Children write every day in school and every night at home for the purpose of filling the notebook so they will have a variety of options to choose from when they decide to publish.

- Several pieces of literature are read out loud and a few are selected as mentors because they most closely match the focus of the cycle.

- When texts are longer and more difficult, we introduce them in the Reading Workshop. In so doing, we do not have to spend our writing minilessons reading a text, but rather referring to it.

- We use a variety of our own writings as well as student writings to help us accomplish the work of our minilessons.

- Daily writing, share sessions, and homework are in support of the work of the day's minilesson.

- Over each weekend of the cycle, students use the Weekly Writing Assessment sheet (Chapter 2) to reflect on their accomplishments for that week and to set goals for the next week. Monday morning, children meet with their writing partners to share their assessment sheets and to offer support to each other. Teacher moves around the room taking notes.

- Students choose a notebook entry or entries that contain an idea they would like to work on toward publication. Their focus now shifts from collecting a variety of entries to developing ideas around their chosen topic and making decisions about the genre.

- Students draft, revise, and edit this piece toward final publication.

- Mentor pieces are revisited and studied to help students revise their writing.

- A reflection sheet is completed at the end of each cycle. Students are asked to assess their progress as they work through the writing process as well as identify specific learning they will apply to future writing. (See Chapter 2.)

2. **Publication**

Once students decide to publish a piece for an audience they must:

- stay with that topic by developing more ideas connected to it
- make decisions about the genre to match the purpose
- organize the most important of those ideas into a draft
- revise the draft
- edit
- publish and celebrate the work by bringing it to an audience

The time spent collecting entries in the notebook (as opposed to the time spent on working toward publication) depends on how successful students are at finding and writing about their ideas, as well as the time of the year and the focus of the cycle. Earlier in the year when we are first getting notebooks started, it will be important to spend more time during those cycles helping students develop the strategies that will help them fill their notebooks. Later on as they become more comfortable with the entire process and publish more often, more of the time will be spent on the work writers need to do toward publishing a piece.

Genre Studies

During the first cycles of the year, our work centers on launching the notebooks and lifting the quality of the writing in the notebooks rather than on focused genre studies. The students' published pieces become natural outgrowths of the personal narratives, poems, picture books, and feature articles we use to inspire a variety of entries in the notebooks, knowing we will return to these forms to support our future work in genre studies. Their published pieces reflect their exposure to the mentor texts minus the intensive instruction we offer later about the particular features and structures of these genres. After a number of publishing cycles and sufficient time spent gathering a variety of entries in the notebook, focused genre studies provide the perfect opportunity to dip back into the notebook to begin to write with attention to the features of the chosen genres.

We think of genre as containers for our written thoughts, messages, and ideas we want to share with an audience. A series of planned genre studies help our students begin to make wise choices for their own writing. Although there are many genres we could choose to showcase, the genres we have chosen to study are poetry, picture books, and feature articles. Though writers sometimes choose to write poetry and picture books based on fantasy, the writing we do in our genre studies stems from nonfiction, based on the real-life events and experiences the students have been writing about in their notebooks. When we introduce the feature article study we also relate it to the research needed to support writing in that genre.

In Chapters 10, 11, and 12 we have carefully laid out each study, taking you through each stage of the process, giving suggestions for minilessons, providing samples of scaffolds, and highlighting samples of student work at the end of each study. In addition to these focused studies, we also look for other opportunities for our students to internalize their understanding of different genres. Later in the year, we offer open cycles and invite our students to decide on the genre in which they would like to publish (see Chapter 13 for details). Our instructional priority centers on the understanding that we expect the students to learn as a result of the study and not only based on the product at the end.

The Writing Day

Every day we schedule an hour-long Writing Workshop. The workshop begins with whole class teaching (minilessons) followed by time for students to write. It is during this time that the students receive individual instruction (conferences). We end with time for students to share.

Minilessons: What and Why

The purpose of a minilesson is to provide whole class instruction at the onset of a Writing Workshop. They should be brief, to the point, use language that students can understand, and address one clear objective that the students will then go off and try during their independent writing time, assuming that it fits in with their writing intention for that day.

Minilessons might include anything from management issues surrounding the Writing Workshop to specific strategies to lift the quality of their writing. Keeping them brief maximizes the amount of time available for writing and direct teaching instruction through our individual conferences.

Minilessons must coincide with the long-term and short-term plans we have made and should come as an outgrowth of the skills and strategies we need to teach because we know where we are headed. We cannot afford to be random. Each minilesson must fit in with the bigger picture we have, each one being a valuable piece of the larger vision, like a yearlong jig-saw puzzle we are completing piece by piece over the course of an academic year.

It is also important that we create structures that hold students accountable for what they have been taught. Their work must demonstrate evidence of their practice in response to the teaching that has occurred. As you read further, you will see how we do this in our minilessons, conferences, and share sessions.

Minilessons might also grow out of the need to fix something that we see is going on in the class. As we move throughout the year and confer with more and more students, the work they are doing, or not doing for that matter, must inform our minilessons.

Minilessons come from a variety of sources. We rely on our knowledge and experience as writers, the knowledge and experiences of experts, as well as the mandated standards our school is obliged to follow. We refer to these sources to help us in our day-to-day efforts to become the best teachers of writing. While it seems natural and easy to sit in front of the group and talk our way through a minilesson, we must keep in mind that this is only one way of providing instruction in writing. As practitioners, we know that children learn in different ways. In order to meet the needs of all of our students, we make sure we present our minilessons in a variety of ways.

In summary, good minilessons require careful planning, clear focus, strategic teaching, and structures for student accountability. If we put these and the following practices in place, we stand a much better chance of achieving our goals for our young writers. (See Figure 3–2.)

Minilessons: How

During minilessons we must:

- Rely on our recordkeeping from conferences as a source for informing us about what our students need to be taught.
- Teach according to the needs of the entire class, not toward the needs of a few students.
- Rely on a variety of resources to support and guide our teaching. These may include the following:
  - Children's literature
  - Professional books about the teaching of writing
  - Information from our recordkeeping collected during conferences
  - Mandated standards
  - Samples of student work
  - Our own experiences as writers—samples from our own notebook
  - What we know about the qualities of good writing
  - Our knowledge about the teaching of writing
  - Suggestions from our colleagues
- Present material in a variety of ways:
  - Orchestrate an interactive writing experience by composing a piece of writing together with the students based on some common experience or shared knowledge.

FIGURE 3–2. *A minilesson in action.*

Sample Flow of the Writing Workshop

Minilesson: 10-20 MINUTES

Writing Time/Conferences: 30-45 MINUTES

Share: 5-10 MINUTES

Minilesson (10–20 minutes)

After conferring with a number of students, we notice the lack of detail in several pieces of writing. We notice as a reader it is difficult to create an image of what the writer is trying to say. We know we need to focus our minilesson around strategies to help students slow down the moments.

We prepare an overhead of one example of a notebook entry that needs this type of work and say to our class, "Boys and girls, I have noticed that many of you, like Sam, rushed through your writing and failed to give the reader the detail they needed to create an image. As I read Sam's piece, I want you to think about places where you think he could have taken more time to develop the image." With our class, we read the writing. Together, we decide on *one* idea to further develop. We underline the part of Sam's writing that needs further development, lifting the line and rewriting it on the right-hand side of the notebook page. As a class, we brainstorm ways of slowing down the writing to create the image. We direct the students to reread their notebooks to find an entry where they can do similar work. Before the students begin their writing, we ask the students to turn to someone and articulate their plan for working in their notebook that day. We reinforce the assignment and send them off to find a comfortable place for writing.

Student Work (30–45 minutes)

Student work during the Writing Workshop is in direct response to the work of the minilesson. We move around the room conferring with 2 to 4 students and taking notes in a recordkeeping system that matches our teaching style. These notes serve to inform our future conferences and overall planning.

Share Time (5–10 minutes)

Students share the work they did during independent time that day. We facilitate the conversation by deepening children's understanding of the strategy at hand. This conversation also informs us about future minilessons and gives us the opportunity to direct the writing homework for that day.

- ◆ Demonstrate strategies by writing in front of children on a chart tablet or overhead transparency. They are not contributing ideas here, rather they are following your thinking.
- ◆ Use teacher or student writing that has been prepared for the purpose of demonstrating the strategy being taught.
- ◆ Using overhead acetates, prepare excerpts from texts students have previously read to demonstrate a writing or craft strategy.
- ◆ Just tell the students what you want them to do. Some minilessons may just require a brief explanation before students go off to write.

- Check to make sure our teaching is clear before the children return to their work areas by doing any of the following:
  - ◆ Have student restate the task by asking: "Can anyone tell in your own words what it is I want you to do when you go off to write?" This will help us to determine whether our minilesson focus was clear and also bring clarity to students who didn't get it the first time.
  - ◆ While still in the meeting area, students talk in small groups or partnerships about the work they plan to do that day. The teacher eavesdrops on as many conversations as possible and sets her plans to confer with those who seem to be stuck or are not clear.
  - ◆ Ask a few students to quickly share their plan for writing with the whole class. This might help to clarify or provide ideas or a plan for struggling writers.

- Carefully plan our minilessons:
  - ◆ Know the specific strategy we are going to teach and why.
  - ◆ Know what we are going to say and why.
  - ◆ Be sure materials we will need for the minilessons are available and accessible.
  - ◆ Make sure there is a sense of continuity. Minilessons should follow in a connected and focused way. We should stay with a focus for a series of minilessons and not jump around from one strategy to another as if they were a series of activities.
  - ◆ Understand how the writing our students are doing fits with our plans. Ask, "Do we need to slow down, or move on?"
  - ◆ Each minilesson must fit into the larger context of our current focus (short-term as well as long-term plan).

- Make sure students have more time to write than the time they spent sitting in the meeting area.

Minilessons: Across the Process

The focus and content of our minilessons is determined by the stage of the writing process in which the students are working. Let's examine the focus of our minilessons during each stage of the writing process.

GENERATING NOTEBOOK ENTRIES

During this stage of the writing process we are helping students to find ideas for writing and to learn how to use their notebooks for helping them think about those ideas. We hope that our students will not only record what they know in the notebook, but that there will also be times when they are surprised by what they have come to know as a result of having written in the notebook. Ultimately we want them to be able to write about what matters to them. So first we teach them *how* to find ideas for writing. One of the first things we do together is to generate a list of things they could write about.

In our minilessons we want to think about teaching children to:

- Write about their personal life experiences
- Write about "everyday" happenings in their world
- Express opinions in addition to writing about incidents that have actually happened
- Choose to be descriptive in their writing
- Use senses to describe what they see, hear, feel, etc.
- Write what they are thinking or feeling
- Write from the specific to the general
- Write from the general to the specific

CHOOSING AN IDEA

While children are collecting entries in their notebooks, they are not yet writing for an audience. They are writing for themselves. We want them to, however, get in the habit of publishing for audiences. So, we teach them how to choose ideas from their notebooks that they would like to develop and publish for others to read.

In our minilessons we teach how to choose ideas to work on for publishing. They include:

- How to reread the notebook for the purpose of choosing an idea
- How to decide between several possible choices
- What influences their choice

DEVELOPING AN IDEA

Notebook ideas are not often well developed. The entries are the beginnings of ideas that need to be explored and developed. One of the things we hope to help the children do is become more critical about what is inside their notebooks so they develop an awareness of entries that seem to hold the potential for further exploration. If they learn to do this while they are generating entries, they will be more inclined to return to these entries to dig deeper during this exploration stage. If they are able to do this, then they can move more quickly into drafting and make the process less tiresome. In our minilessons we teach them how to:

- Revisit entries to write "more" (quantity as well as quality)
- Ask questions that will allow them to explore ideas
- Develop trains of thought

- Search the writing to see where they have written in generalities and need to be more specific
- Write so readers will not be inclined to say, "So what!"

DRAFTING

During this stage, the children are ready to use what they have written in the notebooks on a particular topic or idea and begin composing a draft on loose leaf paper.

In our minilessons we teach them how to:

- Reread the writing they have done around the idea and use that information in their draft.
- Make decisions about the most appropriate genre for the writing they are doing.
- Organize their ideas using flowcharts or other graphic organizers.
- Recognize when they need to return to the notebook to further develop thinking.
- Know what they are trying to say, but also realize that sometimes as the draft develops they can become more focused or come to new realizations.

REVISING AND CRAFTING

During this stage of the writing process, writers work on improving the quality of the writing. They can improve the content, the organization, and the ways in which they have used language to get meaning across.

In our minilessons we show how students how to:

- Develop, organize, and make deliberate changes to the writing to make it the best it can be.
- Use the notebook as a safe place to practice or develop their writing craft. The right side of the notebook is a perfect place to try out saying something in a different way. If children are working on drafts, they need to know how they can try things out before making final decisions about the writing. They may do so using the available space in the notebook or looseleaf paper.
- Name, understand the purposes, practice, and internalize the crafting strategies we teach to help students lift the quality of their writing. We expect to see this pay off in their drafts and final published pieces.

EDITING

During this stage of the writing process, we teach children how to make sure they have used the conventions of spelling, grammar, and punctuation to make their writing easy to read and understandable by the reader.

In our minilessons we teach our students how to:

- reread their writing for editing purposes
- insert punctuation
- determine when new paragraphs begin
- apply our word study, punctuation, and grammar investigations to their writing

PUBLISHING

During this stage, children learn about the importance of presentation when preparing a piece for an audience. In our minilessons we teach them how to:

- make choices about the kind of artwork that will accompany the piece
- decide whether their piece will be handwritten or typed
- read the piece to an audience

Conferences: What and Why

This is probably the hardest part of our job as writing teachers. It is the time during their independent writing time that we sit alongside our student writers to see how we can help. It is the time when we are expected to meet the needs of our students, each with individual abilities and learning styles. And, to boot, we are expected to be brilliant on command, to talk to kids, to decide what they need, and to figure out the best way to teach it in the shortest amount of time possible. We're supposed to resist the temptation to over-teach by trying to teach more than one thing, to meet with as many children as we can in a relatively short amount of time, and then to figure out how to make sure we get back to them soon enough to support the work they did. It is the time when we are obliged to check that they are trying the strategies we taught in our minilessons and that we are deftly moving them from one point in their process to the next.

At the heart of every good conference is careful listening. In his book *How's It Going?* Carl Anderson reminds us that "the payoff for this 'deliberate act' of listening is this: we nurture the genuine connections between us and our students, and those connections have so much to do with the success of our conferences." Successful conferences must also be balanced with thoughtful questioning and strategic teaching. This requires us to build in the structures for holding ourselves accountable for planning for our teaching and our students accountable for doing the work we teach. At the heart of that accountability is good recordkeeping. Students are more likely to hold themselves accountable for doing what we have asked, if, in future conferences, we are able to refer to previous conversations and expectations we've laid out for them. It is the time to strike up the kind of conversations that, at the same time, supports the writer's work and teaches something that will move the writer forward.

We think of Lucy Calkins who taught us to teach the writer and not the writing. When we read a child's writing, we can always tell what needs to happen to the piece to make it better. If we were to do just that, help the student make this piece better, we will have changed the writing and not the writer. It is our job during these conferences to teach the writing strategies that will help the *writer* not just for this piece, but for all future writing.

Regular conferring should help students come to the realization that as writers they need to have specific plans for their writing and we as teachers must be prepared to teach them strategies that will help them carry out their plans. So, during our conferences, as outlined by Lucy Calkins in *The Art of Teaching Writing,* we must *research* by asking questions that help writers uncover their plans for their writing, *decide* what they need to learn, then *teach* the writer accordingly. (See Figure 3–3.)

Conferences: How

During conferences, the questions we ask are crucial in helping us know and understand our student writers. Questions must be purposeful, allowing time for the student to respond. Moments of silence should not be quickly arrested with further questions or filled in with teacher commentary. Sometimes students need these silences to think. If they prove to be unfruitful, then we may proceed by asking them to tell us what they are thinking, restate the question, or give examples that help to bring their thoughts to the surface or clarify their thinking.

The following is a list of what we believe summarizes the most important aspects of good conferences.

Think about our best teaching practice:

- ◆ Ask students the kinds of questions that get them talking about their writing.
- ◆ Be willing to share *our* life experiences. As we share they will become more comfortable talking about theirs.
- ◆ Encourage students to talk about their intentions for their writing by helping them learn to use writing discourse.
- ◆ Listen carefully.

FIGURE 3-3. *Conferring with a student writer.*

- Set clear expectations for the work we want them to do—be prepared to teach it.
- Teach the writer one thing at a time—be clear and strategic in your focused teaching.
- Provide mentor texts and opportunities to use them.
- Create structures/templates whenever necessary to help support the work students need to do.

Be a good recordkeeper:

- Take notes—incorporate convenient and effective recordkeeping systems.
- Refer to conference notes from previous conferences with the student to help hold the student accountable for the work you have asked him to do and to make sure there is continuity and consistency in your learning plans for the student.
- Use the information gathered in conferences as sources for minilessons.

Involve other students:

- Allow them to eavesdrop on conferences so the teaching you do with one student filters through to others.
- Use student achievements in shares and minilessons (make students "famous") as a way of helping students gain greater understanding of the strategies you've taught.
- Set up structures for giving and receiving feedback from buddies and writing support groups.

Give appropriate feedback:

- Compliment something they have done well so they continue to do it well.
- Help them focus on their work.
- Teach a particular strategy the student needs to know.
- Help them form a partnership with another student writer who can support the work.

Conferring Across the Process

During the research stage we ask questions that build on our knowledge of who our students are as writers and how they go about doing their writing, as well as their intentions for the writing they are currently doing. Of course in any one conference we may not be researching all of these aspects because we already bring to each conference information we have gathered from past conferences. We use all of the information we have to help us determine what we need to teach the writer at this point in time. While the questions we ask are guided by the knowledge we bring to the conference about the writer and what we know about good writing practice, we must also consider the writer's intentions in relation to the stages of the writing process.

Sharon developed the following list of the kinds of questions that should guide our thinking as we confer with students along the stages of the writing process.

GENERATING NOTEBOOK ENTRIES

- How does the writer notice or pay attention to her/his world or her/his life in support of finding ideas for writing?
- What strategies does s/he rely on for finding ideas?
- Does the writing demonstrate variety of topics?
- Does s/he choose ideas that s/he cares about? Is there thoughtfulness? Does the writing seem to matter to the writer?
- Does s/he tend to revisit ideas to add more information, to dig deeper, to get new ideas from old ones, or does s/he tend to write about an idea once and move on?
- Does the writer convey her thoughts clearly?
- Does her/his writing flow from page to page showing fluidity and stamina, or do the entries tend to be short?
- Do you get the sense that the writer writes for herself/himself or for the teacher?

CHOOSING AN IDEA

- Does the writer seem to care enough about the topic?
- What criteria did the writer use in choosing the topic? (See Chapter 7)
- Does the writer seem to make choices based on the content of one entry or is s/he able to identify ongoing themes that may be threaded through entries?
- Does the writer see the potential for developing the idea to make it worth the investment of time and effort through the process?
- Does the writer consider suggestions from the teacher or peers about ideas that hold potential?

DEVELOPING AN IDEA

- Has the writer explored all possible ideas connected to the topic?
- Has the writer searched through the notebook for any ideas that might be connected to her/his topic?
- Are there people or other students who could help the writer gain deeper understandings about the topic?
- Is the writer ready to move on to the drafting stage of the process?

DRAFTING

- How is the writer accumulating text through the draft? Does s/he get bogged down in details, draft in chunks, or draft quickly to the end and return to fill in the details?
- How does s/he use his notebook to support her/his draft?
- How does s/he use literature to support her/his work?
- Does the writer write with a particular focus or does s/he tend to tell "everything" about the topic?
- How does s/he organize the piece with regard to its structure?
- Does the writer use lists, webs, flowcharts, "T" charts, or other organizing tools?
- Does the writer seem to craft her/his writing as s/he drafts?

- Does the writer write with a particular audience in mind?
- Does the writer compose the draft with a particular genre in mind?
- Does the writer reread her/his writing toward composing the draft?
- How does s/he add to the draft? Is it always at the end?

REVISING

- What is the writer's sense of revision? How does s/he make her writing better? "Fix it up"? Explore new possibilities?
- What revision devices are the writer familiar with to avoid too many rewrites? (asterisks, arrows, etc.)
- Does the writer use the notebook to try out specific strategies that may improve the draft?
- Does the writer select and use mentor texts to help craft the writing?
- Does the writer use texts that might help to define the structure of the piece?
- Does the writer choose to craft and structure the writing with intentions for the revised piece in mind?
- Does the writer compose with genre in mind?
- Does the writer seek out other writers for feedback/support?

EDITING

- What editing strategies does the writer rely on?
- Does the writer appreciate the importance of rereading in editing a piece?
- Does the writer seek the support of other writers in reading/rereading the piece for editing purposes?
- How does s/he use punctuation as a tool for bringing clarity to meaning?
- Does s/he attend to spelling and grammar conventions?

GETTING AN OVERALL PICTURE OF THE WRITER

- Is the writer able to adequately articulate her intentions?
- What does the writer do when s/he gets stuck?
- Does teaching (from conferences and minilessons) stick with the writer? Does the writer build from one experience to the next?
- Does the writer set and work at achieving her goals?
- Does the writer write about things s/he cares about?
- Does the writer allow herself/himself to write to discover meaning?
- Does the writer write regularly in and outside of school without frequent reminders from the teacher?
- Does s/he see herself as a writer?
- Does s/he enjoy sharing her writing and receiving feedback?
- Does s/he seek out the support of other writers?
- Does s/he take the initiative to seek out and use mentor texts to support her/his work and growth as a writer?

Share Time—Why and How

This is the time when we call students back together in the meeting area to share their work, their process, and to give and receive feedback. When we were in school, our only feedback was from our teacher through those dreaded red ink marks all over the page. Creating predictable opportunities for students to share their writing is important. The share is the time for a few students to share the work they did that day and for the others to support their work. Sometimes, the share is open to anyone who feels they have done good work that day and feels their writing demonstrates the strategy focused on in the day's minilesson. At other times, students read their work because they want suggestions from their peers and this is a safe environment to receive that help. It is also an opportunity for the teacher to call on students who have done the kind of work we would like to share with the class and to invite particular students to recall the gist of their conference and make it public to the rest of the class.

Sharing at the end of workshop is not the time for students to simply applaud because a writer has shared. It is not the time for students to ask the writer thoughtless questions with predictable answers. It is not the time for students to be entertained. It is, however, a time for students to listen carefully to a piece of writing and to receive feedback from peers. It is the time for the teacher to ask students to listen with a particular focus in mind, with that focus most often being in support of the teaching done in the minilesson that day. The share time and the minilesson are our best opportunities to reach the whole class and to reinforce successful teaching strategies. We tend to underestimate the value of the share. It is so important for our writers to hear how the strategies taught during minilessons were implemented by the other writers in the community. Unfortunately, it is also the first part of the writing lesson to go when we find ourselves running out of time.

The important thing to keep in mind about the share is that it isn't just a time for congratulations about a job well done, it is more about what others can learn from a job well done. It sure beats the private red pen notes we used to dread from our own teachers that taught us nothing except how to correct that particular piece of writing, if it even did that.

4

Setting Up the Writing Workshop

Providing a Writing Environment

We try to create an intimate environment by setting up a meeting area where the children can come together for minilessons and share sessions. (See Figure 4–1 below and on the website, <www.heinemann.com/davis-hill>.) We set clear expectations early in the year for the proper use of this space. We never want intimacy to be synonymous with lounging or casual behavior during minilessons. Although we are as much a part of that community as the children, we do not want all conversations to be directed toward us. Instead, we want our students to speak to each other with the teacher as part of that conversation. We encourage students to posi-

FIGURE 4–1. *Our meeting area.*

tion themselves so they can see the majority of the class. Too often, meeting areas are set up so that the teacher is the center of any conversation and students speak to the backs of their classmates instead of face to face with them, seemingly more intimate, but not a far cry from the traditional frontal teaching model.

We expect the children to always come to the meeting area prepared with their writer's notebooks and writing folders. While the minilesson is being conducted, students' notebooks are open so they are ready to jot down any ideas that may be forming in their heads. Some jot an idea on a post it, some jot in the margins of their notebooks, some begin the first line while others may jot ideas on their "list of things to write about" (Chapter 5). When students leave the meeting area they are prepared to go directly to the task of writing. In this way, transitions to and from the meeting area are smooth and efficient, making it easy for us to pull up alongside a student and begin our writing conferences.

It is important to set up a ritual for returning to the meeting area for the writing share. We let children know when there is about five minutes of writing time remaining. It is our signal to bring our conference to an end, and for the children to bring closure to their own writing and to return to the meeting area. Once the teacher or several students have physically returned to the meeting area, the rest of the class takes that as a signal to join the group.

We try to create quiet niches with skillful arrangements of tables and bookshelves so that children can find a quiet place in the corner or at a table alongside a writing partner when they go off to write. There are times we confer with individuals in those quiet places as well as with groups of children at the tables.

After we have featured a text to help us teach, we make sure it is accessible for the children. Knowing they will want to return to these texts at a later date, we usually line them up along the ledges, covers facing forward so the children can see the fronts of the books. We make sure many of the texts we use are available in multiple copies, and that there are books organized according to the special text features we are studying. These text features usually include craft and genre. So, when we are studying how authors use comparisons to create images, we make sure we have a collection of several texts that offer great examples in support of our work. These may be displayed together on particular shelves or in baskets around the room.

Many visitors to our classrooms who have observed our Writing Workshops comment about the tone. They admire how willingly and easily the children share their work with each other. They admire the respect children show to each other when they talk about their writing. They love the working hum of the room. Consistency, high expectations, and serving as models who respond in constructive, supportive ways to students goes a long way in helping us create this tone. By making it clear from the very beginning that process and product are equally important in the workshop, children understand that what goes in the notebook will eventually produce a finished piece and that writing is hard yet rewarding work. While we do honor talk about writing, we establish very early in the year that the Writing Workshop is not a time to have conversations with friends that pretend to be about writing. Writers do need to receive feedback, but it is also important that they respect the need to have quiet time for writing.

Keeping Up with Notebooks

Your job as a teacher of writing will be easier if you figure out a manageable way to keep up with the notebooks. We suggest you create a schedule that allows you to review notebooks. If you are conferring regularly, you will most likely be familiar with the notebooks as you sit next to a child and review his/her work. However, in the real world of everyday teaching, you most likely will not get to as many children during the course of a week as you might like and might not be able to spend enough time during these conferences to really get the "big picture" of the child.

What has worked for us is taking home about five notebooks each weekend, reviewing one or two each evening (especially during the busy collecting stage of every cycle and those belonging to students whose conferences might not have gone as well as you hoped). While you are away from the student, you can take the time to reflect on ways to help the student the next time you confer. Although looking at the notebook can be quite revealing, always remember it is in the absence of the writer. You will learn much from the notebook, but it should not be solely what you rely on to make your decision about what to teach a student during a conference. Use what you have learned from the notebook to further help you research your writer, so you will be as well informed as possible about the student before making any specific decisions about what to teach him.

What you notice as you review the notebooks will help you:

• Plan your minilessons as you notice the needs of students.

• Prepare for conferences with those students.

• Inform the student of the entries you are particularly struck by. Leave an encouraging sticky note telling why you found it striking or why you think this might be a valuable idea to continue working on. Many youngsters may not yet have a sense of themselves as writers and choose to work on entries that really have no place to go. If you let them know in advance that you think their ideas are good, you may be providing the kind of affirmation they will recall and heed when the time comes for them to choose ideas to develop for publication. *(Bear in mind, we never write directly in the students' notebooks.)*

• Send students the message that they are being held accountable for the work they do in their notebooks. Knowing their notebooks will be collected and reviewed at some point in time helps hold them accountable and could help them make honest assessments of their own work. When we ask them to assess their notebooks, it shows we take their work seriously and that we are interested enough in their writing to take their books home and read their writing.

You may or may not choose to create an assessment check-off sheet that you complete and return to the children after you have read their notebooks. (See Notebook Checklist, Appendix E.) Your decision to do this may be influenced by the class or particular students' and their need for that type of feedback. Leaving a sticky note with comments on particular entries is usually enough feedback for the students. Your regular conference notes combined with the quick notes you've taken from reviewing the notebooks at home are helpful resources when doing formal assessments and meeting with parents during parent/teacher conferences.

Keeping the Workshop Running Smoothly

You will likely be faced with predictable problems in classroom management. Here are some issues that may arise, and if they do, they must be addressed in minilessons or quick "pep talks":

Students talking during writing time

• It is very difficult for most students to concentrate on writing if there is background noise from conversations in the room. Additionally, if they are engaged in talk, there is very little chance for writing to accumulate on paper. While many teachers suggest that children be allowed to talk because that is the time for them to share ideas, we have found that often the talk is social and unproductive. Students must clearly understand that their talk must be related to their writing. To help you monitor this kind of work, here are some suggestions:

  ◆ When you send students off to write, designate a period of time during which there is no talking—only writing. After that time if there is still a need to get feedback from a peer, then a few students may use a designated area to do that oral work. Make sure the designated area is open and visible so you can monitor student interactions.

Transitions from the meeting area to writing spaces

• When launching the Writing Workshop, time must be spent providing supports that help children move quickly and quietly from the meeting area to their work spots so they begin their writing immediately without meandering, chit-chatting, or searching for tools. In Chapter 2 we talked about the importance of making sure tools are readily available and that children know the routines of the classroom. We must be consistent about holding them to these earlier established procedures until smooth transitions are as natural as picking up a pen to write. Here are some steps we can take at the beginning of the year:

  ◆ When sending children off from the meeting area, send them off in staggered small groups while having the students who are still seated in the meeting area observe how quietly and orderly the first group settles down. Send off other groups to do likewise. Gradually increase the numbers of students who leave the meeting area until the entire class is able to go off quietly and orderly.

  ◆ Avoid having a cluster of students who always seem to remain behind on the rug to ask you a question here and a question there. Before you know it, you have spent 15 minutes answering individual questions. As we mentioned before, at the end of your minilessons, always ask a student to repeat for the entire class what it is that you are asking them to do. Use this as an opportunity to clarify any confusions about the expected work to be done for Writing Workshop that day.

  ◆ Let students know they are responsible for their learning and they therefore have the responsibility to pay attention and to get further clarification if needed (from peers, from the teacher) to do the work they have been asked to do.

Interruptions during conferences

- Build structures for helping students find independence in writing so they do not interrupt you during the time you are conferring with other students with issues such as:
  - Students who proclaim "I'm finished" before the writing time is up: They need to know they are *never* finished. The end of an entry means the beginning of another. They need to get in the habit of rereading what they have written when they are done writing. The bottom line is: there is always work to be done.
  - Bathroom and water procedures must be addressed. Want to know our answer to this? "Don't Even Go There!!!" Take care of these needs during transitions except in cases of dire emergencies.

Students who "desperately" need to have a conference with you

- Establish procedures to take care of these pressing needs.
  - Some teachers have a "sign-up" sheet for this purpose and try to get to these students in addition to the ones they have designated to meet with. If you have spent time creating writing partnerships, there will always be someone beside yourself to confer with about writing.
  - Some share sessions may be used for students to talk about challenges they faced during writing that day, and to get possible solutions/feedback from peers and the teacher.

Supporting the Workshop Through Ongoing Rituals

In addition to the rituals of time and organization that structure our workshop in predictable and reassuring ways, the following "content rituals" bond us as a community of working writers, while providing additional support for quality writing.

Homework

During this and every cycle, students have writing work to do at home. We expect that they will write every night for about 30 minutes. Of course, it's only a dream that every student would follow through religiously. We must keep in mind that their lives, like ours, are busy and complicated and that even the best student with the best of intentions might not get to writing every night. So, if we build in the expectation of every night, we can realistically accept it when our students don't always comply.

Our homework assignments must be specific and clear and support the work we are doing in class. Students might:

- Continue an entry they wrote in class.
- Use the strategies we taught in our minilessons to help them get new ideas from existing ones (to be discussed later).
- Write a new entry from the expert inventory they developed.

- Write an entry about another idea they have not yet written about but that was inspired from a piece of literature we read aloud.
- Make a personal connection to something they were reminded about from their independent reading lives.
- Continue the work done in class as it relates to gathering around a topic, drafting, revising, and editing.
- Reread to edit for common errors as indicated on editing checklist.

Just as we know we are only going to confer with a limited number of students on any given day, we also know we cannot check every student's writing homework every day. Early in the year, we must build in rituals to insure that the students see writing at home as important work and that they receive the frequent response they need to support them as writers.

Each morning when the students arrive, they get themselves settled and move to the meeting area. This is the time for informal groups to share the entries they wrote the night before. The first person to arrive that day talks to the second. Soon, groups are sharing notebook entries and giving and receiving responses. When students know they need to share their work with classmates, they are more likely to take on the responsibility of getting it done. This sharing not only supports those who have done their work, but also opens up a world of possible writing ideas for those students who are finding it difficult to get ideas.

Weekend Assessment

We want our students to be reflective about the quality of the work they are doing. We have already said that the Weekend Writing Assessment is one of the tools we use to help students become better writers by scaffolding their thinking about their work. The weekend is a great time for them to do this. To accomplish this important work, we ask students to set up appointments during the weekend to share their work from the previous week with parents or older siblings, to celebrate accomplishments, to get feedback, and to set goals. They have their at-home readers sign and return their entries and come in on Monday morning ready to go through the same process with their writing partners. At the beginning of the year, the Assessment addresses some qualities of good writing not yet addressed in the Writing Workshop. However, it is important to get the ritual going. We do not want to keep updating the Assessment every time we introduce a new strategy, so we make it all-inclusive from the start and instruct children to put N/A next to the strategy we haven't gotten to yet. (See Figure 2–6 and Appendix B.)

The Class Journal

Each morning, our day begins with the reading of the Class Journal. This is a beautiful book in which the students record the happenings of each day. We begin with the very first day of school. One child keeps it for the week. It moves around the room until everyone has had a turn for a week. Then, we begin again with the first person. During the day, they take notes on what's going on. They might write about anything from strategies we tried in the Writing Workshop to hot books circulating around the room to recess gossip. At the end of the week, that student writes a letter home to families informing them of the highlights of the week. We copy the letter and send it home on Monday afternoon. It is amazing to watch the voices of the students change over time as they apply the qualities of good writing they are learning to this journal that then reaches an audience of their peers the next day with the read aloud. It is also a treat for students who are absent to hear about what they missed. Families love to receive these each week. They feel like they are eavesdropping on our days without having to question their own children. (See Figure 4–2.)

Our Manhattan New School colleagues have found other ways to use a Class Journal: Pat Werner invites a different student to take it each night. Joanne Hindley used to have a student or students take a photograph or a series of photographs each day. They'd paste them in a scrapbook, writing captions for each. The book

---

March 13, 2002

Dear Families,

I urge you to read this message because last week was a week of beginnings and endings. We began the week with the first meeting of book groups. In these groups, we discussed the big questions and predictions we had about our books. Judy said we did a great job, and we thought so too. We finished our read aloud book, *Tunes For Bears To Dance* by Robert Cormier, and we found out that Mr. Hairston was just trying to make Henry imperfect because he wasn't perfect.

We were lucky that Mr. Hairston wasn't in our math class because when it came to probability, we were perfect. We played "rock, paper, scissors" using math rules. We had to find what the chances were of landing on a certain symbol. We also used spinners to record the probability of landing on certain symbols.

Then, we spun ourselves to social studies. We continued learning about Lewis and Clark's journey west - why they went, what their accomplishments were, and what the effects of their journey were. One reason why they went was because President Thomas Jefferson wanted them to find out if there was a direct route to the Pacific Ocean, to make peace with the Indian tribes, and to learn about any new plants and animals that could be found on the Louisiana Territory. Later in the week, we started to learn about mountain men. We learned how and why these men trapped animals for their fur, and how these men affected the westward movement.

We also began a journey of our own. We started writing our own picture books. Judy helped us by reading picture books that are mentor texts, like *Mel's Diner,* by Marisa Moss, and discussing the author's use of structure, craft, and repetition. We read many pictures books to help us choose our own mentor texts as models for writing our own picture books.

Test prep was another concern of the week. Judy and Jill both gave us math and English practice questions and tests. Speaking of tests, we had a tough one in spelling, even though Colleen prepared us well. It was a test on using suffixes correctly. We had to write the base word, attach the suffix ending, and then explain what we changed to achieve the correct spelling.

Though there were no tests in gym, it was tough, too, because Mike made us do 5-second push-ups. Every so often you'd hear some kind of sickly groan from one of the students. I must say, it was very disturbing.

The week was hard, but like Lewis and Clark, we found the most direct route to the weekend. We did our best work all week, but we were glad when Friday rolled around.

Sincerely,

Sam Levy

Sam Levy

FIGURE 4–2. *Sam Levy's letter to families.*

would be displayed in the hallway outside her room and then taken home by the students to share with their families. Beri Daar has her students pick one moment that happened during the day and write about it on the left side of the book. On the other side, they write about one event that happened in the world that day. Beri says, "It's one way of making sure they keep on top of events happening in the world." The discussion that follows often becomes inspiration for writing notebook entries that day.

The Personal Thesaurus

In her wonderfully helpful new book *The Revision Toolbox*, Georgia Heard reminds us that the word *thesaurus* is a Latin word meaning "treasure." Since our hope is that all writing our students do become treasures, we encourage them to be on the look-out for words they love, words that can make their writing come alive. Georgia says that one way we can do this is by helping our students create their own personal thesaurus. We jumped on her wise and practical suggestion. Each student keeps a small, soft-covered notebook. To begin our study, we read through our notebooks to find words all of us seemed to be overusing, words that didn't seem to be specific enough to express what we heard or saw or felt. We decided they fell into the verb and adjective category. They included words like *move, say, happy, sad, beautiful,* and *ugly.* We noticed our transitions were weak as well. We seemed to be relying on *"and then"* to indicate time passing. We began by finding places in our notebooks where we used these words and tried to find more specific examples. We thought about the different ways that time moves and categorized them and began to look for more interesting and descriptive ways to show how time passes. We began a class bulletin board to chart our discoveries. (See Figure 4–3 below and on the website, <www.heinemann.com/davis-hill>.) Students continued to investigate their notebooks to find overused words and began their own personal investigations. These included words like *fun, nice, good, hungry, hot,* and *cold.* They began charts of colors

FIGURE 4–3. *Personal thesaurus/class bulletin board.*

and began to collect different adjectives that were more expressive of the different variations of colors. Each week, we shared our findings, adding to our class list and students' own personal collections. This book became a companion to their notebooks. We'd often find them open next to the students as they were writing. It became an invaluable tool when students were revising their drafts toward publication and revising their poems during our poetry study (see Chapter 10).

The Poetry Anthology

A poetry anthology is a book each student creates. It begins in September with a blank book. By June, it is filled with poems of published poets, their own poetry, and artwork. It is a great long-term project because it involves reading lots of poems, making choices about favorites, seeing connections between those published poems and the writing done in the notebook, rereading the notebook with the intention of revising those entries as poems, and imagining how the images created with words can also be created with art. What's so great about these anthologies is that they are an opportunity for every child to explore the possibilities. It is a golden opportunity for these writers, fluent and struggling, to begin to see themselves as poets, and for the artists, talented and reluctant, to experiment with a variety of media and to connect writing with artistic expression. Reading poems and listening to them read aloud in class strongly influences the quality of the entries in their notebooks. Poetry has a way of helping us create images in ways no other writing does. As the anthology grows with each passing month, students see the change in their writing and their art, and their enthusiasm for the project grows. For us as teachers, it is another assessment tool that can show us the footprints of our teaching in the work of our students. Above all else, the children love this project.

Judy began keeping poetry anthologies with her classes many years ago when she first began using poems as writing mentors in the classroom. So much of what the students wrote in their notebooks—their memories, family stories, and observations—were filled with powerful images. It was clear they were being influenced by the language and voice of the poets they were studying. They were becoming so familiar with poets like Nan Fry, Marianne Moore, and William Carlos Williams that it was not uncommon for them to find similarities in their own work.

ESTABLISHING A LOVE FOR POETRY

When she first imagined the way these collections would be developed, Judy hoped that the students would spend time every day reading selections from published anthologies they gathered and kept on their desks, bedside tables, and coffee tables. (See Figure 4–4.) Whenever they found one they loved, she imagined they'd mark it with a sticky note and continue on. She figured that after about a week of doing this, students would choose one of these favorites to copy into the blank book chosen for this project. Once the selection was made, she expected that the students would pour over their writer's notebooks and choose an entry to shape into a poem that could sit alongside the published selection. She hoped that if she spent enough time in Writer's Workshop talking about the qualities of good writing, they would begin to see that their writing had lots in common with published works. She expected they would see similarities in subject, in style, in shape, and in the mood of poems. Once this entry was identified, she imagined they would revise, edit, and copy it and the poem they had chosen from their reading on opposite pages in the anthology. She imagined beautiful illustrations to go along with the writing. This assignment would be due on the last day of each month.

BEGINNING WORK

Judy orders blank books, referred to as *Bare Books* from a company called Treetop Publishing. They are inexpensive, have unlined pages, and come in a variety of sizes. Since the covers are white, it is a perfect opportunity for students to begin this creative endeavor by designing a cover.

To launch the poetry anthologies, the first experience of the year is aimed at building community. Children pore through poetry books, trying to find a poem that connects in some way to who they are as a person, somewhat like a poetry self portrait. Once they find a poem, they begin to write a poem, allowing themselves

Dear Students,

This year, you will be keeping a poetry anthology. In it, you will be collecting published poetry you love and be writing many of your own. The following is an explanation of what I will expect you to do.

- Gather a few poetry books at the beginning of each month. You can borrow some from the class library or take some out of your local branch library. Spend some time each day reading and enjoying poems. Identify those you love by placing a sticky note on the pages.

- By the beginning of the next week, you should have found at least one poem you especially love. Copy or photocopy it. It will eventually get pasted onto the left side of your book. The right side will be for your own writing. If you hand copy the poem, be sure you copy it exactly as the poet wrote it. Do not change any spelling, punctuation or line breaks.

- Now you are ready to search through your writer's notebook for entries that you think could easily sit beside the published poem. You will see that your writing has a lot in common with published poetry; perhaps the subject is the same, the style, the mood or the feeling.

- Once you have identified the entry you will use, you have some choices to make. You can use everything you know about writing poetry and rework the entry so that it becomes a poem. You may, however, decide to use the entry as it is. If so, you need to revise, edit and enter it onto the right side of the page opposite the published poem.

- We will set aside a time somewhere around the middle of the month for you to share your work. At that time, you can schedule a conference with me or a classmate. During that time, we can give feedback and help you revise your work.

- Illustrate the poems, choosing the medium and style that best suits the subject and mood of each poem. Plan your illustration before you paste the poems in. This way, you can be sure you've used all the space wisely. You may do one illustration across both pages or you may choose to illustrate each one separately.

- Try to vary the medium you use each month. Remember to think about how the images created in the writing will influence the images you create with your art.

- Your anthology is due the last school day of every month. On this day, you will have an opportunity to share your work with your classmates and get their feedback. At the beginning of each month, you will receive a blank calendar to help you schedule time to work on this project. You will be expected to turn the calendar, signed by a parent, in with the finished anthology.

By the end of the school year, each of you will have a collection you will be very proud of and will cherish. You will be amazed at how your work changes over the course of the year.

I can't wait to see the remarkable work you will do this year.

Judy

FIGURE 4-4. *Judy's letter about the poetry anthologies.*

to be influenced by the content or form of the published one. For some students, writing a poem so early in the year might be a challenge, so some teachers ask the students to write about why they chose the poem instead. The students copy both poems, the published one on the left side, theirs on the right, on a large piece of white construction paper and illustrate it. Judy sets out a variety of materials for these illustrations. Some students use colored pencils, some use markers, some use water color, some use collage, some use tissue paper and glue water, some use a combination of these.

When they are done, students share what they learned from their experience with searching for a poem they loved, writing their own, and what they learned about creating art. Judy hangs these up around the room. When she is ready to begin the work on the actual anthology, the students reproduce this work on the first two pages of their blank books.

At this time, the students wonder about and Judy offers minilessons to address the following areas:

- layout on the page
- whether to copy the poem in their own handwriting or photocopy and paste
- whether to illustrate each poem separately or across the page with one illustration that would fit both their poem and the published work
- whether to try to revise their entries in the form of poems or leave them as entries
- which medium or combination of media would work best for their choices

WORKING INDEPENDENTLY

If your students are anything like Judy's, here is what you can expect to happen when your students begin to work independently each month.

- About one-third of the class will search for a published poem they love and then search through their notebook to match an existing entry to that poem.
- About one-third of the class will find their favorite and then write their own poem to match the one they admired. It's only natural when you love a particular piece of writing to be inspired by it.
- About one-third will find an entry in their writer's notebooks that they love and are particularly proud of and search for a poem that matches their writing.

This pattern continues to happen in approximately the same fashion each year. We should love the fact that kids are influenced and challenged by this project in many different ways. Although the project evolved differently than she first envisioned it, Judy believes the wisdom of the kids and inspiration they receive from the poems are evident in the poems they write. It proves, once again, that if we plant the seeds, the ideas will grow.

Remember, this project is started in September, long before any specific genre study on poetry is conducted. After the poetry genre study is completed, many of the children publish the poems they write in the anthology, adding them to the others from the months before. After the genre study, with more strategies for revision under their belts, the children can return to the work they did at the beginning of the year and revise. Judy reminds them of all they have learned about poetry.

They choose a poem from their anthologies that they feel they can rework. The students share them in class and discuss what it is about the poem they like that makes it worthy of revision. At this point, the children have the option of choosing another published poem to sit beside the new versions of their earlier work or to leave the original poem. We discuss the revision of the artwork as well. Does the revised work need a different vision? Should the choice of medium be different based on the changes made?

PLANNING AND IMPLEMENTING POETRY ANTHOLOGIES

• Spend a great deal of time, especially at the beginning of the school year, sharing poems.

• Continue to use poems as mentor texts in your Writing Workshop. Many students will ask for copies to include in their anthologies as the writing they do after you've introduced the poem is usually ready to be shaped into a poem.

• Build in time in your classroom to allow the students to share their favorites and talk about how they go about finding entries in their notebooks that belong with the selected poems. This is crucial. Students need to see how others see their connection so they can apply that thinking to their choices.

• If you choose to have your students purchase their own books for this project, or decide to make books, be sure to talk about the format of the blank book. Encourage larger, unlined notebooks as they work better for those who are ambitious about art and won't discourage children from choosing poems that are longer. If the book is too small, it is very difficult to fit poems and illustrations on the page and is very confining to writers and artists, especially younger ones who tend to write and draw big.

• Be sure you're clear about how you want the children to enter the poems into their anthologies. For instance, perhaps you prefer that they hand copy the poems as opposed to a photocopy to be pasted in.

• On the day the project is due, devote class time to sharing and enjoying each other's work. Judy finds that many of the students ask their classmates for copies of their original poems to use the next month in their books. We must remember that after our students produce, it is important to get their work into the community to be read and enjoyed by others. If we tuck the books away until next month, we're missing golden opportunities to allow their voices to be heard.

MANAGING TIME

Students work on one poem in September and complete all the related work in school. Judy doesn't give out any of the other due dates until this initial work is completed.

Many students have no idea about how long it takes and are grateful for the supports she gives in the classroom. Beginning in October, she carves out time on Friday afternoons for art. Many children do a more thorough job in class because they see what other classmates are doing. The enthusiasm of the artists in the room rubs off on those who feel less able.

At this time, Judy begins to encourage children to carve out big blocks of time at home for reading poems and rereading through their notebooks to discover connections in the writing. To support this planning, Judy gives each student a blank calendar at the beginning of each month. Their homework for that night is to schedule time throughout the month to work on this project. They are responsible for sticking to the time they set aside.

Parents are grateful for the support the calendar page gives the children and see it as a way to support the youngsters' time management skills at home. Even though many are still scrambling to finish the work at the end of October, by December, most of the students have the work done well in advance of the due date.

Of course, any long-term project and ritual you create in your classroom must be suited to the abilities and ages of your classroom. Younger children obviously need more support with this assignment. Older ones will probably be able to do more than one poem each month. You might choose to:

• use anthologies to simply collect published poetry and illustrations

• have the children write why they like the poems instead of crafting poems

• do the anthologies exclusively in class and support the students in class

• limit the medium so the project is more manageable for younger children

WEBSITE

See Figure 4–5 and additional samples on our website, <www.heinemann.com/davis-hill>.

FIGURE 4-5. *Sample of a poetry anthology layout.*

Helping Your Students Become Writers

"Our girls were taught to love words and to collect interesting and unusual ones. Like squirrels, they stored them away for future use in their writer's notebook and learned to fine-tune simple family stories or observations into true gems."

—FRED AND JEAN HERSCHKOWITZ,
PARENTS OF SUZANNAH, MNS GRADUATING CLASS, 2001
AND ELIZA, MNS GRADUATING CLASS, 1999

First Cycle : From Writing Idea to Notebook Entry

5

When we are faced with blank notebooks and children who need to understand how to live like writers and see the possibilities for topics in their everyday life experiences, we start the year by focusing on teaching children how to find ideas for writing and how to get those ideas down on the pages of their notebooks.

Cycle One is devoted to helping children learn how to use their writer's notebook as a tool for generating and collecting ideas.

During Cycle One our goal is to:

- Help children recognize they have stories to tell and to tell them well
- Teach children to pay attention to the world and to recognize it as a place full of ideas for writing
- Help students develop a repertoire of strategies for finding ideas
- Help students build stamina for writing
- Help children learn how to give and receive constructive feedback
- Help children learn to honor each other by listening to each other's stories and entries

Getting Started with Thoughtful Planning

The following are sample planning sheets for initiating a writing workshop in a fifth-grade classroom. (See Figures 5–1, 5–2.) We share them to illustrate how you might fill out planning sheets on your own. The jottings on these sheets are reminders for us as we sit down to conduct our lesson, but do not represent all the thinking that goes into planning a cycle. You will, however, find more detailed thinking as you read on in this chapter. Keep in mind that the hallmark of reflective teaching is flexibility and although we create plans, we need to know when we must pull back, give in to the day-to-day interruptions that occur in every school, or alter our agenda based on the cues we receive from our students. Although we realize that this planning may not be compatible with a school calendar, it does represent the order in which you might present minilessons during these first weeks of school to students who are unfamiliar with keeping a writer's notebook. Our choices of mentor texts

MINILESSON PLANNING SHEET FOR CYCLE ON: From Writing Idea to Notebook Entry

FOCUS FOR THE WEEK	DAY 1	DAY 2	DAY 3	DAY 4	DAY 5
WEEK: 1 Building Community Storytelling Read picture books all week: Camping (Hundal) Someplace Else (Saul) Hey World . . . (Little) Wilfred . . . (Fox)	Read picture book—Camping (Hundal). Make personal connection—tell stories Discuss: Purpose for a notebook Type of notebook Use of flip pads Distribute flip pads for jotting ideas *(Have kids bring in treasures for Storytelling)	Read Someplace Else (Saul)— Make personal connections leading to possible entries for notebook More storytelling in large and small groups Reinforce use of flip pads Share ideas being jotted in flip pads	Read "My Journals" from Hey World, Here I Am (Little) Storytelling from life experiences—Teacher modeling Adding ideas to flip books	Writing timelines—model by sharing teacher's timeline Talk about: Change over time . . . growing as a writer Experiences that supported growth and love for writing Goals for this year	Read Wilfrid Gordon McDonald Partridge (Fox)— Things they treasure stories Storytelling in small groups around treasures Add ideas to flip pads
WEEK: 2 Getting ideas down in the notebooks Continue reading picture books at other times during the day Mentor text: Family Pictures (Garza)	Big talk about care of notebooks Use of left side/right side First entry—return to jottings in flip pads to choose idea to write about in notebook *(Need to bring in photographs)	Begin "Expert Inventory" as the beginning of "Things I Can Write About" list— Teacher models her own—emphasize variety Transfer flip pad ideas to notebook list. Discuss future use of flip pads.	Family stories as possible ideas Read Family Pictures (Carmen Lomas Garza)	Photographs—emphasis is on the story behind the picture Teacher models with own photo	Observations—write about what see, hear, etc. Take kids outdoors to make observations Extend workshop to explain weekend assessments—begin in school, finish up at home
WEEK: 3 Getting variety in the notebook Mentor text: Someplace Else (Saul) Time For Kids	Meet in partnerships to review and discuss weekend assessments. Talk about goals —plans to achieve them Introduce notebook editing checklist and purpose	Diary vs. notebook entry Model how to take a bed-to-bed entry and write one that is more focused	Use article from Time for Kids —What are different ways one could write in connection to topics/issues without retelling?	Return to Someplace Else to chart a list of the possible ways to connect to a text. Help students see the different ways for connecting to a text are also ways to connect to their experiences and observations	Free-writing to get ideas . . . writing to discover Model how it's done Support weekend assessment work
WEEK: 4 Publishing Supports: Teacher writing Student writing Mentor texts: House on Mango Street (Cisneros) Childtimes (Greenfield)	Meet in partnerships to review and discuss weekend assessments—share goals. Rereading entries to choose an idea. Support strategies for choosing an idea Read mentor texts to support publishing	Gathering around a topic Webbing to focus topic and support gathering more ideas Genre considerations (What kind of info is included in mentor texts?)	Writing entries using web Becoming clearer about: What is the piece going to be about? What do I know about the genre? (How is the info organized in the mentor text?)	Drafting strategies Rereading entries. . . Getting started . . . Good beginnings—mentor texts	Rereading draft: Is it organized in a sensible way? Does it make sense? Does it say what I want it to say? Focus—does it stay on topic?
WEEK: 5 Publishing continued	Revision Rereading draft—finding parts to revise: Say it better Add details Use craft techniques they already know	Editing/rewriting Rereading to check for spelling and punctuation (connect with word study—words they should know how to spell) Peer editing/teacher edit overnight	Rewrite final pieces in class Teacher provides support in small groups Practice reading to an audience if necessary	Celebrate!!!!	Reflecting on the process (writer's reflection) (Can they articulate what they have done during this cycle?) Setting goals

FIGURE 5-1. *Minilesson planning sheet for a cycle.*

DAY-TO-DAY MINILESSON PLANNING SHEET

Cycle: *1*
Week: *3*

Focus: *Getting Variety in the Notebook*

DATE: *9/23*
Editing checklist in class/h.w.

MINILESSON FOCUS: *Supporting the Use of the Editing Checklist*

TEXT/MATERIALS: *Laminated editing checklists Student notebook entry*

Teaching Points
- *Reflect on weekend assessment in partnerships Highlight expectations for these new rituals*
- *Model w/ student entry—how to reread using the checklist for support*
- *Setting up margin numbers on multiple pages in notebook to coincide with items on checklist*
- *Using margins to try out spelling*

Practice
- *Rereading entries and using editing checklist*

Homework
- *Use expert inventory— Things to Write About List to write an entry*
- *Reread—use editing checklist*

Share *Strategies for use of the editing checklist*

DATE: *9/24*

MINILESSON FOCUS: *Diary vs. Notebook Entries*

TEXT/MATERIALS: *Teacher Writing*

Teaching Points
- *Show writing that lists events in chronological order*
- *Demonstrate through shared writing how to zoom in on an important event and write more about it*

Practice
- *Reread notebook to find an entry where they need to focus on one important event.*
- *Use right side of notebook to write a more focused entry.*

Homework
- *Find another entry—zoom in on a part using right side of notebook*
- *Use editing checklist*

Share *What did you do to make it more focused?*

DATE: *9/25*

MINILESSON FOCUS: *Making Connections to Issues in the World*

TEXT/MATERIALS: Time For Kids

Teaching Points
- *Help kids to see that there are big world issues we can write about in personal ways*
- *Model w/ article from TFK*

Practice
- *Retelling an event highlighted in TFK by responding with personal opinions, feelings, or concerns*
- *Editing checklist*

Homework
- *Respond to another article from TFK, the newspaper, or something you are concerned about that's happening locally or in the world*
- *Editing checklist*

Share *Identify issue—name how you wrote about it*

DATE: *9/26*

MINILESSON FOCUS: *Using Literature to Support Writing Connections*

TEXT/MATERIALS: *Someplace Else/Carol P. Saul*

Teaching Points
- *Using Someplace Else*
- *Push kids to make connections beyond the content*
- *Chart responses*
- *Stress big ideas/themes different perspectives*

Practice
- *Kids think of 2–3 different ways to connect to the text*
- *Write about one*
- *Add the others to "Things to Write About List"*
- *Editing checklist*

Homework
- *Write another entry*
- *Editing checklist*

Share *Discussion about the different ways we can respond to things*

DATE: *9/27*

MINILESSON FOCUS: *Learning to Freewrite*

TEXT/MATERIALS: *Teacher Demonstration*

Teaching Points
- *Freewriting is writing to discover*
- *Begin with what's on your mind at that particular moment—allow it to take you anywhere*
- *Demonstration—not censuring writing—allow it to take you anywhere—keep going until you get to a big idea*

Practice
- *Practice freewriting*

Homework
- *Weekly Writing Assessment*
- *Read entries—Place sticky notes on possible ideas for publishing*

Share *How freewriting helped them as writers*

THINGS TO THINK ABOUT FOR NEXT WEEK *Gather teacher writing, student writing, and short mentor texts to support the publishing process— Make sure to highlight connections between mentor texts and their drafts.*

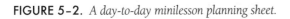

FIGURE 5–2. *A day-to-day minilesson planning sheet.*

and sample lessons are just that, samples. Your libraries are full of possibilities and you should make choices based on what you have available, from those texts you love and have used with success in the past. (Also see Appendices F and G for blank planning sheets for your use.)

Introducing the Notebook

Although the writer's notebooks are not in the students' hands yet, we begin to put in place the structures we know they will need for the year's work ahead. We establish the rituals and routines that will support our work. From the very first day of school, we make sure the structure of the Writing Workshop is what it will be for the rest of the year—time together in a meeting that establishes what we are working on for that day, time for the students to practice, and time for them to share the work they have done.

For some of our students, this may be the first time they are keeping a writer's notebook. They will need to learn how to use it as a tool for writing. They need to become aware of the expectations and rituals they will be engaged in as they write every day in their notebooks. Others, however, have had previous experience keeping a notebook, so we invite them to bring the notebooks and published work in to share some of the writing they have done. There are different ways in which this sharing may occur. A student may:

- read favorite entries from the notebook
- talk about how they have used the notebook in the past
- talk about where they find ideas for writing
- share a published piece and talk about their process from the notebook entry to the published piece
- reflect on the writing they have done and talk about goals for this year

We take this as an opportunity to share entries from our notebooks as well. Sharing our experiences around the use of the writer's notebook becomes an invitation to the children to begin to see themselves as writers and to imagine possibilities for their own notebooks. It also sets expectations for what we are going to ask them to do when they begin to use their notebook as a tool for generating and collecting ideas.

Building Inspiration

During the first days of school, we read aloud several of our favorite poems and picture books to awaken our students' stories, stir their thoughts, and to allow the sound of good writing to fill the room. We use read-alouds to spark memories so that every child will come to realize they have stories to tell and important ideas to write about. This early work builds inspiration for writing by cultivating an environment in which the students learn to value their own stories, memories, and experiences as sources for writing. It is no wonder that during the first days of school much of the time spent in the Writing Workshop is around reading, listening, storytelling, and sharing our experiences as we rehearse for the writing we will soon be doing.

Using "Flip Pads" (Temporary Notebooks)

Students enthusiastically share stories during those first few days of school and need handy reminders. We provide them with small "flip pads" to be used for jotting down these early ideas. This tool is an ideal way of recording ideas until the time comes when the students can expand on them in their notebooks. The flip pad can also be conveniently carried around in their pockets and used to jot down writing ideas both in school and while at home. When they begin to use their notebooks, the students are reminded to refer to the ideas they collected on the flip pad and to transfer them to the back of the notebook as the beginning of an ongoing list of "Ideas for Writing." Because of its convenience, many students continue to keep their flip pads in their pockets on weekends and short excursions. (See Figure 5–3.)

Drawing Stories from Our Memory Banks

In the book *Wilfrid Gordon McDonald Partridge* by Mem Fox, we are reminded that our memories can sometimes evoke different feelings. Some make us laugh or cry, feel happy, ashamed, sad, satisfied, disappointed, or proud. It is not easy when we just tell our students to write about their "memories." It seems to make it easier when they know they can think back to specific times when perhaps they felt proud and write about the experience they remember. With practice, this reflection makes it easier for them to tap into their reservoirs of memories and write about them.

We help our students write about their memories by also sharing our memories. There are few things that spark greater curiosity in students than when teachers tell their *own* stories, so we take the opportunity to model good storytelling. We don't tell the most earth-shaking events in our lives. We are also careful to stay away from the "time I got stitches or broke my leg story" because our experience tells us the room will soon fill with those tales. When we share our stories, we make sure we tell why they are important to us. When Judy told of the time she came face to face with

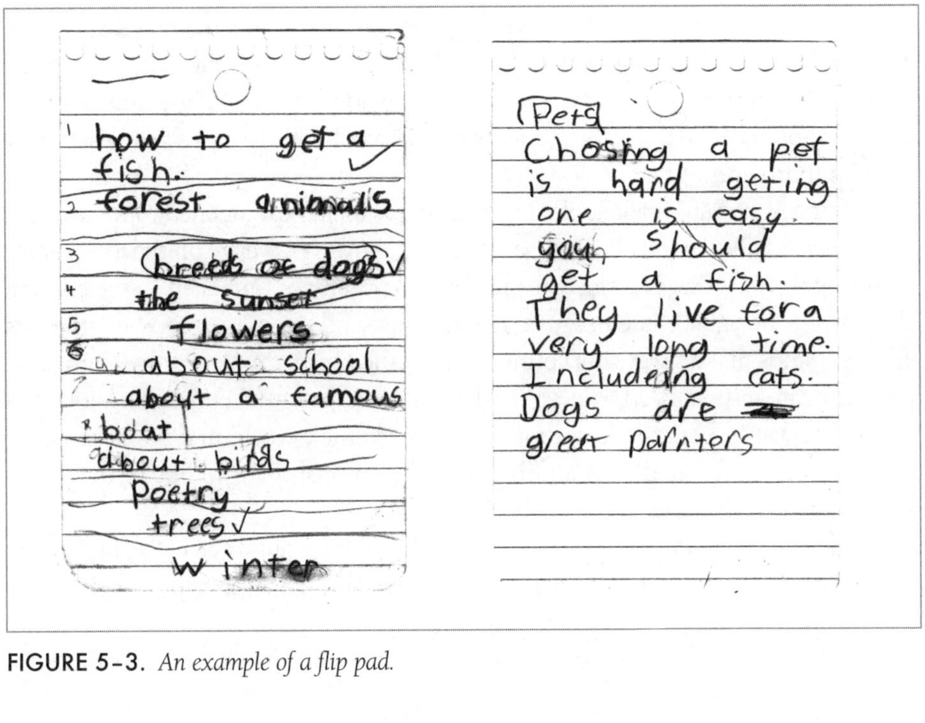

FIGURE 5-3. *An example of a flip pad.*

a deer in Yosemite National Park, she let the children know that this was more about her longing to connect with nature than about the actual spotting of the deer.

We encourage the children to begin to tell their stories to the entire class and help them tell them in ways that focus on the bigger meaning. When a few have been told, we send the kids off in small groups to tell their stories to each other. We move from group to group, conferring with those students. Our intention throughout this entire process is to get children to see what is important about the topics so they understand it as a verbal rehearsal for writing. Children need to understand that the way they begin the story, the way they capture an audience, the way they sequence the events of the story, will be just as important in the writing as it is in the telling. We provide time at the end of the workshop for them to jot down key ideas about the stories on the flip pads so they won't forget to write them in their notebooks.

Drawing Stories from Literature

Picture books, poems, and short texts are the major well we draw from to help our students begin to tell their stories. We rely on these to get our students to talk away the shyness that often clouds the atmosphere those first few days of school. When chosen carefully, literature always seems to magically awaken the stories that lay waiting to be told. We choose to read from books we love, trusting that because we love them, our students will love them, too, and become inspired by the characters, the language, and journeys of thought the writers take them on. We make sure we choose books that are close to their experiences so they can imagine their lives in new ways. When we share these treasured books, we are not only building community and breaking the ice, but we are also using these opportunities to help our students practice becoming good storytellers.

When we read *Family Pictures* by Carmen Lomas Garza or *Camping* by Nancy Hundal, we are reminded of our experiences, and we know the children will relate to them as well. Predictably, we expect that children will tell stories about their own camping experiences or family tales that closely mimic the ones we've read. We value the experiences and memories the children share by encouraging them to tell their stories well to their captive audience. We also encourage the class to be good listeners . . . to be a good audience, asking questions and making comments that help the storyteller. We ask the students to try to tell their stories so we know *why* it is of importance to them.

Granted, it is quite predictable that students will be most inclined to write about experiences similar to the books we have shared; however, we are on the lookout for those connections that are most surprising and may seem unrelated to the content of the story. We value these because they help us send the message to our students that our minds make surprising connections all the time to books, events, things we see and hear, and we need to grab hold of those as potential entries for our notebooks. We want to get them ready to not just see their world in a literal sense by retelling what they experience and observe, but to push their minds to think and grow new ideas about what they live and see each day.

While we use literature to inspire our students, we want to be clear that we are not advocating an exclusive reliance on literature to provide prompts for students. The last message we would want you to take away from this is that we would read *The Chalk Doll* by Charlotte Pomerantz, for example, then expect that all or most of our students would then go off to write about an experience they had with a doll. That would be no better than providing a story starter or topic for our students. Instead, if we were to use a story such as *The Chalk Doll*, we would want them to understand that the importance of the chalk doll in the writer's life was the driving force for the writing. As writers, they also need to find the stories that are important in *their* lives. Sometimes the literature we read can help take us in that direction.

Having said this, we use literature because it has the power of putting us all on the same page at the same time and allows us to share in that common experience. Yet, because we are individuals who bring different experiences and ways of thinking, we can benefit from the different ways in which we all may be thinking or connecting to

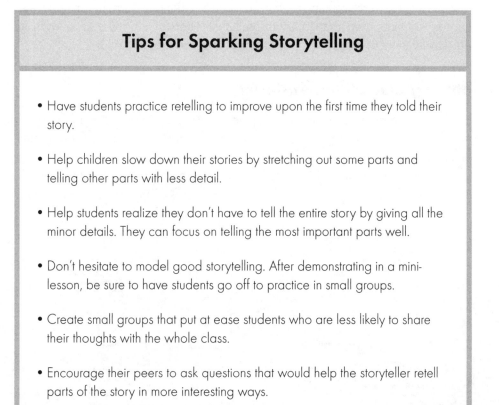

Tips for Sparking Storytelling

- Have students practice retelling to improve upon the first time they told their story.

- Help children slow down their stories by stretching out some parts and telling other parts with less detail.

- Help students realize they don't have to tell the entire story by giving all the minor details. They can focus on telling the most important parts well.

- Don't hesitate to model good storytelling. After demonstrating in a mini-lesson, be sure to have students go off to practice in small groups.

- Create small groups that put at ease students who are less likely to share their thoughts with the whole class.

- Encourage their peers to ask questions that would help the storyteller retell parts of the story in more interesting ways.

- Share your own well-told story or memory with students. Have students help you make a list of the things you did in order to do a good job. Have them go off in small groups to practice.

- Encourage students to keep track of the different inspirations that come to them as you read a story out loud. At the end of the reading, have students share their thoughts. Help them to begin to see those thoughts as possible notebook entries. Although we love the stories, be sure to honor wonderings and opinions.

These tips are the foundations for minilessons.

that common text. How amazing it is to see the many different ways in which our students connected to a text. We celebrate all of the ways in which they connect, but we are especially ecstatic when students can make meaningful connections that go beyond the literal content-related connections, express their opinions and go as far as making connections to issues in the world. Just as they are able to make different kinds of connections with literature, they can do the same with the memories, thoughts, experiences, everyday events they notice as they go about living their lives.

As time moves on and the students begin to write in their notebooks, reading texts in their entirety during the Writing Workshop gives them less and less time to write. Though we enjoy and take advantage of the opportunities to read an abundance of picture books during the workshop for the first several days of the school year, we make some adjustments to maximize the amount of time students spend writing. We try to read them at other times during the day. As the year progresses and the students have a repertoire of books they know well, we are able to make quick references to them in our minilessons, craft and genre studies.

Sharing Our Writing Histories

By the time most children reach the upper grades, they have had writing experiences they can reflect on and share. As we work on building a sense of community, reflecting on and sharing past experiences in writing is a good place to begin.

Conversations about their writing lives become easier and easier as students talk about how they feel about their writing experiences. Some teachers have gone

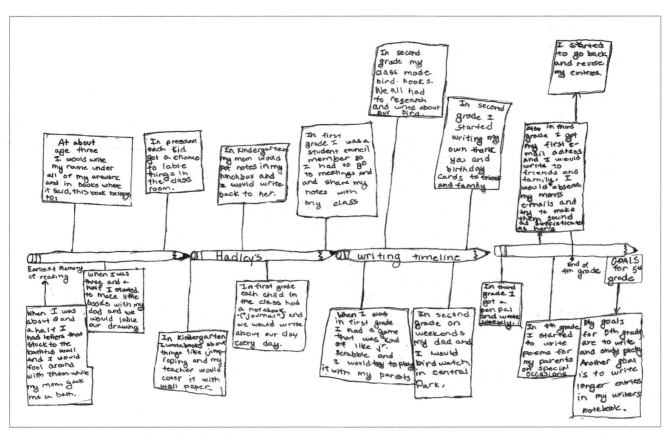

FIGURE 5–4. *Hadley's timeline of her life as a writer.*

beyond conversations and have encouraged children to construct timelines of themselves as writers. Children are asked to think back to their earliest memories of writing and to explain what they remember about them. (See Figure 5–4.) Sharing their histories at this early stage of the year helps children recognize who they are as writers, who the other writers are, and to set goals as to the kind of writers they might like to become.

When Haden brought letters that her aunt had written to her and talked about their ongoing correspondence, we knew Haden was a true writer. Oh, what an insight it was into a child's writing life when we discovered that Zack had pages and pages of a book he had been writing for years. We invite children to bring in books they wrote in kindergarten, writer's notebooks from previous grades, collections of original poems and illustrations, and cherished letters parents have kept and are willing to share. It is important to build in time in these early workshops to allow kids to boast about the work they've already done. Above all, we want our children to see themselves as writers and to build on their experiences.

M i n i l e s s o n s

Writing Histories

- Teacher talks about her writing life. Then, have students talk in groups about their writing lives. The following questions help support the talk:

  What kind of writing do you like to do?

  When have you felt most successful as a writer?

  When have you felt most frustrated or disappointed?

  What pieces are you most proud of?

  Who/where do you turn to for help?

  What do you remember about your past writing experiences?

- What seems to stand out along the way in your history as a writer?

- Have children do timelines or make a list, then get together in small groups and talk about similarities and differences.

- Invite children to bring in books, writer's notebooks from the past, collections of original poems, and cherished letters and notes parents may have saved over the years. Have children gather in small groups and talk about these artifacts for the purpose of revealing who they are as writers.

Personalizing the Writer's Notebooks

On the appointed day when children bring their notebooks to school, if they are regular composition notebooks, the only feature that distinguishes one from the other is the name on the cover. Inviting children to personalize the covers so that it tells something about who they are is one way of asking them to share important parts of their lives. This becomes a metaphor for what they will be doing within the pages of the notebook as they write their thoughts, feelings, opinions, memories, and wonderings about their world.

Children often decorate the covers with photos of themselves and family members, magazine pictures of favorite rock or sport stars, artwork done specifically for the notebook, or collages that combine many aspects of their lives. They may be covered with clear contact paper for long-term preservation.

Minilessons

Making the Notebook Your Own

Show samples of your notebook or notebooks that have been decorated by students from previous years. Talk about why you or why the former student placed those artifacts on the cover. Elicit from your students some of the kinds of artifacts they might choose to put on their covers and why. Discuss their appropriateness.

Introducing Writing in the Notebooks

If we were to begin simply by having our students open up the pages of their notebooks and begin to write, we can guarantee there would be those who would have no problem getting started and those students who might still struggle with how to begin. There are many ways to launch our students into writing in their notebooks. We want to share with you some of those we have successfully used.

Once again we turn to the literature we read those first few days of school and the family stories and experiences the students have already shared in the classroom. We will also talk about the use of artifacts the students bring in from home such as photographs and other objects that hold importance, as well as taking "expert" inventories, recording observations, rereading entries in the notebook, and learning from how others have chosen to write in their notebooks.

From year to year we have chosen to "launch" in different ways. The choice should be based on what has been happening in your classroom during those early experiences and interactions with your students. At any rate, this is the time for them to look back on their notes in the flip books and choose ideas they would like to write about in their notebooks.

Stirring Up Stories Through Literature

The memories awakened by the stories we have read together and listened to each other tell need to find their place in the students' notebooks. We provide direct instruction for this work. Let's look at four of our favorite books and see the ways in which children have responded in writing to them.

The Sunsets of Miss Olivia Wiggins by Lester L. Laminack, Illustrated by Constance R. Bergum

This is a charming story that showcases one Miss Olivia, who seems not to be aware of the events happening around her; nevertheless, when her daughter and her great-grandson come to the nursing home to visit, they are able to stir up some pleasant memories of her past. Our students were touched by this story and shared the following responses:

- The way the world appears to someone who might not be able to hear well
- A lot of people have memories of holding babies
- How I had to get used to holding my baby brother when he was younger
- Watching the sun set
- I wonder if I am too old to be playing with dolls and stuffed animals
- How I loved to listen to the song my mother made up and sang to me at bedtime
- When I am older, will I remember the things I do now?
- What makes a person forget when they get older?

Daddy Played Music for the Cows by Maryann Weidt and Henri Sorensen

This is the story of a young girl growing up on a farm and the impact of the music she heard from her father's radio that constantly played while he worked in the barn. In response to this book, our students said:

- Each year your body gets taller, but growing up is about growing smarter
- Morris, my grandpa's cat
- When I went to a farm and watched how they milked cows
- My baby story and how I got my name
- Pretending I am a famous singer in my bedroom
- Listening to the same song every night when I go to sleep
- I love when my family and I look at my baby pictures and they tell me stories
- First day of kindergarten
- The sounds of the city
- My mother always tries to get me to listen to music with her and not watch so much T.V.

Camping by Nancy Hundal, Illustrated by Brian Deines

The story unfolds when a family packs up and heads for a campground. From the moment their camp fire is established, the family slowly begins to discover the wonders of life in the wild—quiet nights, star gazing, cooking over a fire, swimming in the lake, climbing trees, and just lolling in the sun. Students ponder:

- How I am an expert at toasting marshmallows
- How much fun it is to sleep in a tent
- When things that you might not want to do turn out to be fun
- Swimming in the cold lake
- Not always getting your way
- Things don't have to cost a lot of money to be fun

• The sounds I hear at night when I am trying to go to sleep

• I never get a chance to just do nothing because my mom thinks it's not a good thing

• Making tents in my bedroom

Someplace Else by Carol P. Saul

Mrs. Tillby is tired of living in the white house by the apple orchard so she sets out to find a new and more exciting place to live. Students said they might write about:

• Wondering what school is like in other countries

• How I love to identify the constellations in the sky

• I still can't get over the loss of the twin towers

• Being afraid to try new things

• When I read about exotic places I wonder what it would be like to visit

• How easily I get bored of things

• The things that remind me of the smell of the beach

• How I hate the new skyscrapers that block the view from my apartment

• Diversity in New York City

• Living for the day and not thinking about the future

• Feeling like I don't belong

• Being homesick

• You never know until you try

• I have such a hard time making up my mind

Minilessons

Literature Links

• Read a notebook entry that you wrote in response to a picture book or poem you read. Talk about how you came to make the decision to write about that idea and its importance to you. Listen to the student's ideas for writing. Send them off to write.

• Remind the students of a story you read and the thinking it inspired in you. Demonstrate for the students by doing a shared writing. The advantages to doing this are: it gives the children the opportunity to watch you quickly compose an entry right before their eyes. It provides a point of reference for us as we confer with students, allowing us to remind them of what we did while we were writing in front of them.

• Choose a powerful picture book and chart the possible different ways to connect to the story. For instance, one writer might relate to a similar experience and tell that story. Another might relate to the topic. Still another might relate to the feelings evoked by the book. Others might connect to the bigger issues underlying the story. Some might connect to a word or phrase that triggers a response. One might relate to a particular character that reminds them of someone they know. One could relate to the place. Encourage students to try to envision different ways in which they may relate to texts they have read, things they have seen or heard, entries they have previously written. The picture books featured previously and the students' responses highlight the possibilities of responses.

Reliving Family Stories

One type of entry that often appears in writer's notebooks is the family story. The students may or may not have lived it, but might have heard the stories told so many times they can easily retell them with the kind of detail we know will transfer easily to their writing. Sometimes we model storytelling for them by telling our family stories. Judy shares the time when her grandmother finished sewing the hem of her mother's wedding dress just as the wedding march began to play and the doors opened for the bride. Sharon shares this story that her mother enjoys retelling: Prior to reciting her first poem at the annual Christmas program, her mother told her, "remember to look up." She meant, of course, at the audience. Well, at four years old, Sharon proudly recited her poem while looking up at the ceiling. It was funny to all who watched. She still does things that make people laugh. Before we know it, we're reading entries of immigrant grandparents' journeys to America, parents' adventures and misadventures, as well as holiday rituals passed down from generation to generation.

Minilessons

Family Stories

- Briefly remind students of the family stories they told during the previous days. Engage a student in telling his/her story, but this time, to also tell of the significance of the story in his/her life. Send the children off to write in their notebooks. Remind them to make sure that they are not just telling the story, but to ensure their writing is influenced by what makes that story important.

- Do a shared writing experience in which you write down one of your family stories. Share your thinking with them as you make decisions about what to write on the chart or overhead transparency.

- Encourage the students to ask you questions to help you get at the significance of your story.

- Share (using an overhead transparency) a family story you have already written in your notebook. Read it out loud to the students and share with them your reasons for writing that entry and how that directly influenced the content you actually included or didn't include in the entry you wrote.

- Read aloud a picture book in which the author relates family stories as a way of inspiring students to tell their own.

Drawing Inspiration from Photographs

Another way to unearth stories is to ask the children to bring in photographs. Photographs hold important memories and stories that need to be told. The trick here, however, is not to ask them to tell about what the photo shows, which often produces the predictable retelling of events. We ask them to tell the story behind the picture—the story that cannot be told from simply looking at the picture.

So, when Eric brought in a picture of his brother and him in front of Space Mountain in Disney World, he told about how it was the third year he and his family had vacationed in Florida, but the first time he was able to join his brother on the ride because he was finally tall enough to "measure up." It would have been easy for Eric to tell the story of his trip to Florida, complete from packing to watching the clouds out of the airplane window—a story many of us could tell with the same detail. Our minilessons are geared toward helping writers see the importance of not simply retelling events, but focusing on telling stories in ways that show the importance.

Minilessons

Photographs

- Demonstrate by sharing one of your photographs. Tell the children the obvious story that anyone could tell from looking at the picture. Then tell them what is *really* important about the picture, demonstrating how that information could not be extracted just by looking at it. The picture, just like a simple retelling of any story, only holds part of the story. You, the writer, hold the other part, and that's what is important for you to uncover in your writing.

- Allow the students some time in the meeting area to try to find the deeper meaning using their picture with a partner. Circulate from partner to partner, assisting the students to do the work of finding the story behind the picture. After several minutes, get the attention of the whole group and have a few students share their picture, telling what the picture shows, then more significantly, what is the story "hiding" behind the picture that needs to be written about. Send them off to write.

- In days to come, further support this work by asking students who have successfully completed this work to share their photograph and their entry of the story behind the picture.

Taking an "Expert" Inventory

When the children actually have their notebooks, we encourage them to begin a list of possible ideas for writing at the back of their notebooks. We call this list "Things I Can Write About." (See Figure 5–5.) It is important to frequently incorporate the jottings in the temporary flip pads into this list of possible ideas for writing. We want the children to be aware that ideas for writing are endless, and they need to be on the lookout for them, and grab hold of them so they are never at a loss for what to write about. To help our students cultivate the habit of building this idea list, one of the early goals we establish for them is the requirement to add at least two new ideas for writing to the list each week. This is usually easy for the students because quite often, the ideas they write about each day spark new ideas. If they fail to record these newly sparked ideas on the list, they'll quite likely forget them, decreasing the likelihood that they would ever be written as entries in the notebooks.

The list begins with an "expert" inventory—a list of things they feel they know a lot about and could easily write about. We model our own list in early minilessons, trying hard to include surprising things that the children might not consider one could be an expert at. Judy's list includes things like:

Being a good mother
Taking care of a cat
Baking poppy seed cake
Making chicken soup
Being a good friend
Skiing
Making up excuses for not working out at the gym
The downside of being the oldest child in the family
Building snow angels
Planning parties

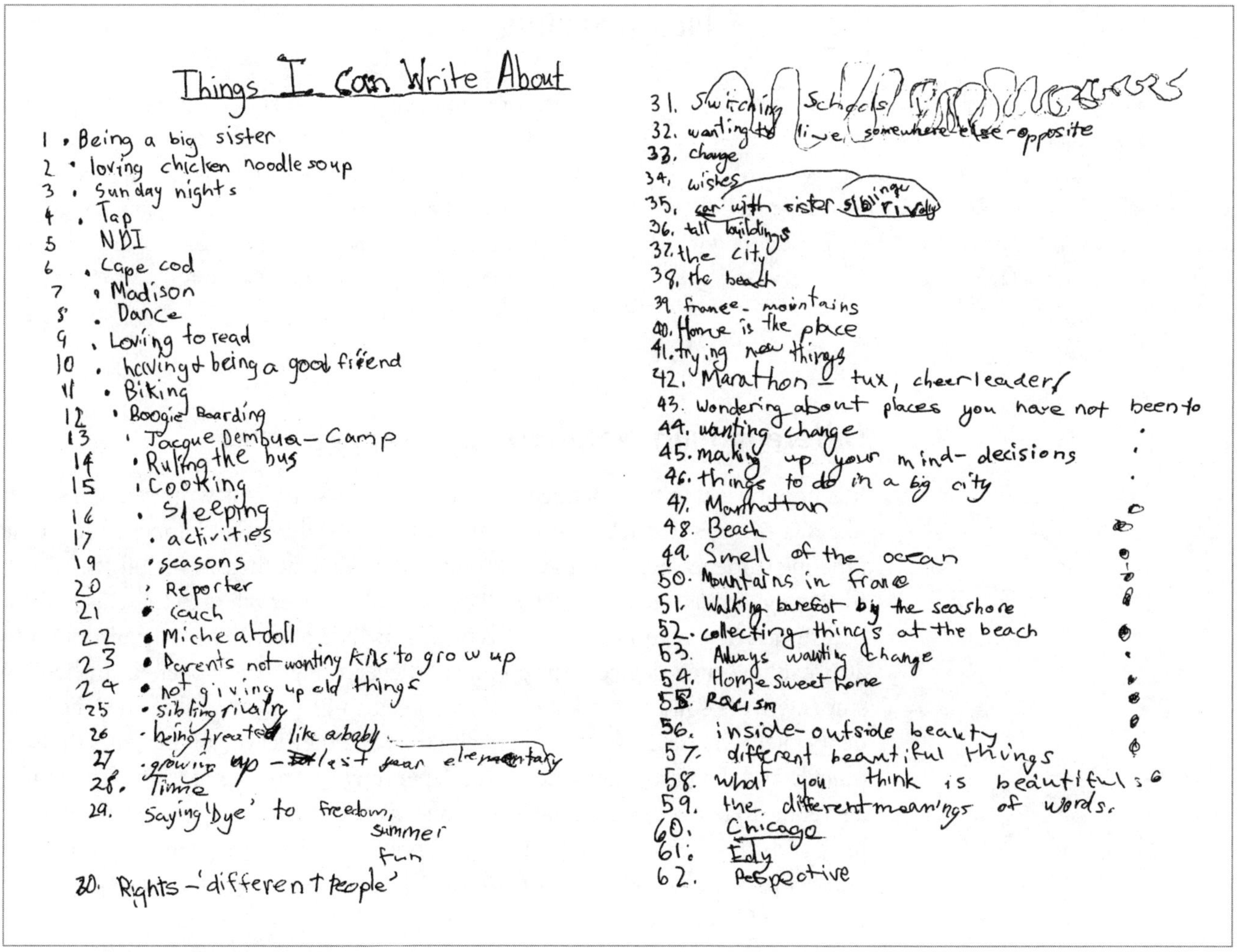
Things I Can Write About

1 • Being a big sister
2 • loving chicken noodle soup
3 • Sunday nights
4 • Tap
5 NDI
6 • Cape cod
7 • Madison
8 • Dance
9 • Loving to read
10 • having & being a good friend
11 • Biking
12 • Boogie Boarding
13 • Jacque Dembua-Camp
14 • Riding the bus
15 • Cooking
16 • Sleeping
17 • activities
19 • seasons
20 • Reporter
21 • Couch
22 • Micheal doll
23 • Parents not wanting kids to grow up
24 • not giving up old things
25 • sibling rivalry
26 • being treated like a baby
27 • growing up — last year elementary
28. Time
29. Saying 'bye' to freedom, summer fun
30. Rights — 'different people'
31. Switching Schools
32. wanting to live somewhere else - opposite
33. change
34. wishes
35. car with sister sibling rivalry
36. tall buildings
37. the city
38. the beach
39. france - mountains
40. Home is the place
41. trying new things
42. Marathon — tux, cheerleaders
43. Wondering about places you have not been to
44. wanting change
45. making up your mind - decisions
46. things to do in a big city
47. Manhattan
48. Beach
49. Smell of the ocean
50. Mountains in France
51. Walking barefoot by the seashore
52. collecting things at the beach
53. Always wanting change
54. Home Sweet home
55. Racism
56. inside-outside beauty
57. different beautiful things
58. what you think is beautiful
59. the different meanings of words.
60. Chicago
61. Edy
62. Perspective

FIGURE 5–5. *Maxine's "Things I Can Write About" list.*

Modeling this list for the children helps them to see that they, too, can write about a lot of ordinary, everyday things. The items on their "expert list" are usually the first items they choose to write about. We are sure to help the children understand that the writing from their "expert list" is not about writing a "how to" entry, although some of our younger writers might be inspired to do so. Instead we demonstrate how in thinking back to these experiences they might think about: some of the reasons why they are so good at doing these things; why they enjoy doing them; the people who are usually involved with them when they are doing them, and the significance of those relationships.

We build in rituals for ensuring that they keep up with this list. During our minilessons, a good suggestion if the kids have more than one idea they're thinking about for writing that day is to pick one and enter the other on the list for another time. At times when writing eludes them, whether during workshop time in school or during writing time at home, the list is a reliable source for ideas.

Minilessons

Expert Inventory

- Share with the students your "expert inventory." Share an entry you wrote and demonstrate how you wrote about it meaningfully instead of just telling how to do it. Send students off to create their expert inventory and then choose one topic to write about that day.

- Ask willing students to share entries they have written from items on their "expert inventory." Help students demonstrate how they wrote meaningfully by making the entry more than just a documentation of something they are good at. Send them off to write about other topics on their lists.

Differentiating Notebook and Diary Entries

It is not unusual to find that many of the first entries students write seem to sound like diary entries that retell events, chronicling everything that happened from the time the students awake in the morning to the moment their heads hit the pillow. In *Writing: Teachers and Children at Work,* Donald Graves refers to these as bed-to-bed stories. These entries not only typically include all the minor details, but also attribute the same degree of importance to everything that happened. In helping students write solid notebook entries we need to help them realize that they can deliberately choose the parts they tell and the parts they leave out, the parts they tell quickly and the parts they stretch out, depending on what's important. They must also come to know that retelling is only one way of writing about the events in their lives and that they can choose to write about their feelings, their opinions, take another perspective, or write entries in which they wonder about the events in their lives. (See Figure 5–6.)

FIGURE 5-6. *Students working in their notebooks.*

Minilessons

Diary Versus Notebook

• Use an entry where a child has listed, as they would in a diary, the things they have done on any given day. Ask the writer to look over the list, pick one event, and decide what is really important about that event. Have the student tell it orally as you write it down on a chart tablet. Clarify for the class the difference between the previous writing and the new entry.

• Model for students a retelling of events from a typical day, indicating that this type of retelling is not what makes good notebook entries. Point out that if you were to choose to tell about a particu-

lar aspect of the day, highlighting its significance, that could become an entry suitable for the notebook. Help students understand that notebook entries do not necessarily have to start from the beginning of an event to the end. The writer could choose to write about a small part of an event in a "big" way.

• Using a typical diary entry chronicling the events of the day, model different ways in which you could choose to write about that topic or event. You could choose to express your feelings, opinions, wonderings, or explore another perspective.

Freewriting

Freewriting is an opportunity to write as much as possible in a very short amount of time without pausing to dwell on what is to be written or to censure your thoughts. Instead, you simply keep the pen going while allowing your mind to take you wherever it will. Oftentimes what starts out to be lighthearted thinking can lead to something quite surprising and meaningful. That is the time when the real writing focus begins and the heart of idea can be developed.

Minilessons

Freewriting

• Using a chart tablet or transparency, write quickly without pausing to think or contemplate on what you should write on the page. Keep your pen going as you allow your thoughts to flood the page. When your thoughts get to something you think you would like to focus on, begin to write your thoughts on that idea.

Recording Observations

In our attempts to help our students learn to see the world as writers, we want to help them pay special attention to the everyday things that they have grown accustomed to seeing and seem to take for granted, like the people they pass by on the streets, overheard conversations, and the flock of pigeons that seem to play "follow the leader" in the early evening hours. When they do pay attention, they'll begin to observe things in ways they never have before. We want them to realize that the way they describe the things they see and the significance they attach to those things, will go a long way in helping them bring new thinking and meaning to their writing.

As we help students practice making observations, it is important to use excerpts from familiar texts to highlight how other writers do this well. They describe, they write their impressions or opinions, and they draw conclusions.

Helping children to understand the importance of making good observations is laying the foundation for future writing. From the very beginning of the year we must help our students understand that making observations is more than just getting details down.

• We practice creating images by using our senses to describe our observations.
• We show how observations can help enlighten or clarify our thinking.

- We practice looking closely by zooming in and writing the details or writing about the big picture.
- When we make observations, we try to make meaning of what we see, so we push ourselves to see with our eyes as well as with our minds.

Through practiced observations, students can learn to take time to notice the unnoticed, become more critical about what they see, and interpret and express those ideas on paper.

Minilessons

Paying Attention to What We Observe

- Invite the students to bring in objects (or provide the students with a variety of objects they could choose from) to write about. Direct the children to observe and write about what they notice. We talk to them about using their senses to help them first notice carefully and then to write down their observations. We also invite them to not just write about the obvious—what everyone else might see—but to try to experience the object in surprising ways and write about that. (We get a lot of mileage out of using poetry written by authors such as Valerie Worth and Ralph Fletcher who describe simple objects in surprising ways.)

- Direct the children to observe a person doing something and to record what they notice about their actions, their appearance, their movement, or some other aspect they've chosen.

- Direct the students to write well about a place and to record the details specific to that place—the sounds, the smells, the sights, the atmosphere, etc.

- Direct students to not only make observations, but to write also about what they think.

Learning from the Work of Others

We read from our notebook and from the notebooks of former students during our minilessons at the beginning of the year. As teachers of writing, we feel it is important for us to keep a writer's notebook. We have found that being writers ourselves helps sharpen our practice as writing teachers. Our mentor, Donald Graves, has said, "If writing is not for us, why should it be for our students?" We choose some of our entries to help clarify for our students our expectations for the quality and variety of entries we expect from them. We also share some examples of entries our former students have written. We make it a point to notice not only the variety of topics but the craft as well. We hope the children will recognize not only great topics and ideas, but also strong leads, surprising language, use of metaphor, comparisons, strong verbs—those craft strategies that leap off the page of good writing. Of course, we will study these craft strategies in depth in future cycles.

Minilessons

Drawing from Others' Work

• Select entries from your writer's notebook with specific qualities you would like to highlight. Read the entries and teach the specific qualities of good writing. Have students go off to try writing to achieve that specific quality in their writing.

• Begin partnerships within the class and possibly across the grade. At the start of the year, it is about helping each other generate ideas for their writing. Later, as these partnerships continue, the support extends to all aspects of the writing process. During your minilesson, talk to the students about the kinds of questions they might ask of each other. They might include:

  • How do you get ideas for writing?

  • How do you decide what's important about your topic?

  • What do you do when you don't have an idea to write about?

  • What suggestions could you give me about my writing?

Highlighting Student Work

The following Figures 5–7 to 5–11 are a series of notebook entries from students that we use to model the kinds of writing we hope to see in the notebooks. You can also find additional samples on our website, <www.heinemann.com/davis-hill>.

WEBSITE

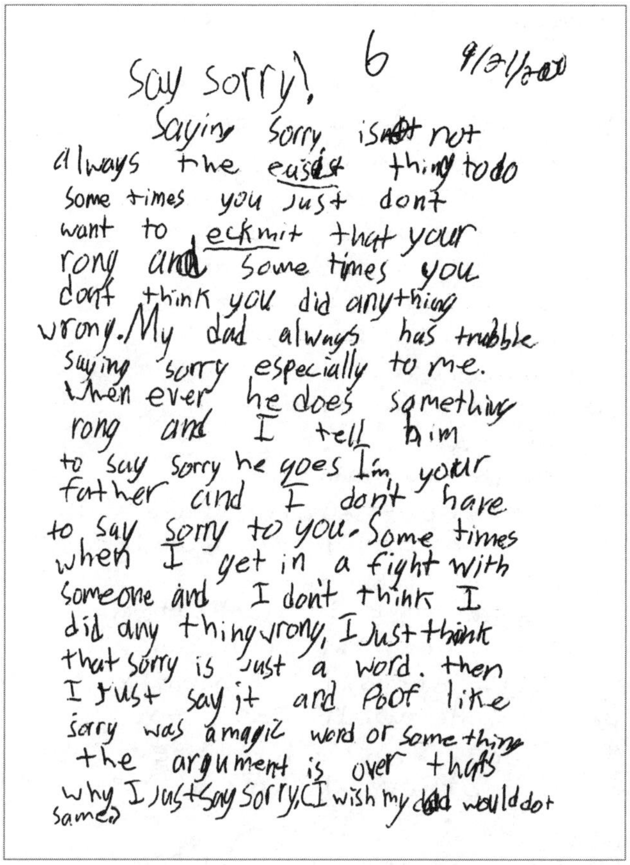

Say Sorry!   6   9/21/200

Saying Sorry isnt not always the easest thing todo some times you just dont want to eckmit that your rong and some times you dont think you did anything vrong. My dad always has trubble saying sorry especially to me. When ever he does something rong and I tell him to say sorry he goes I'm your father and I don't have to say sorry to you. Some times when I get in a fight with someone and I don't think I did any thing vrony, I Just think that sorry is just a word. then I Just say it and Poof like sorry was a magic word or some thing the argument is over thats why I Just say Sorry, I wish my dad would do the same.

FIGURE 5–7. *Todd's notebook entry, "Say Sorry."*

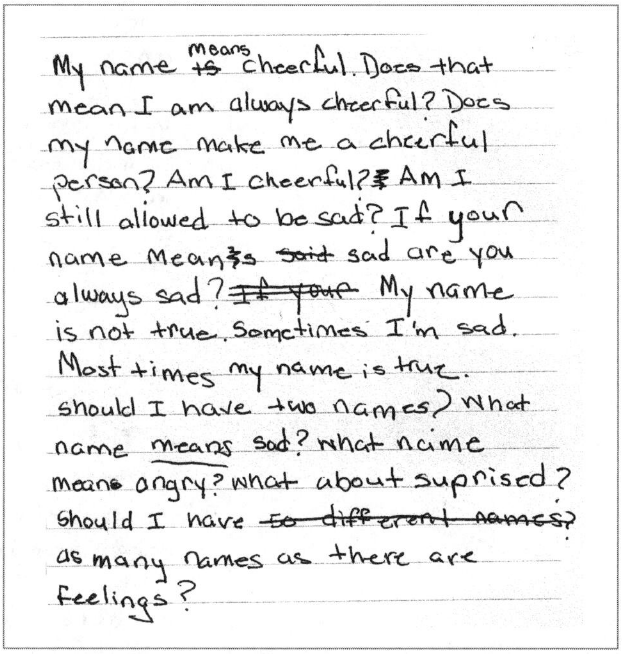

My name means cheerful. Does that mean I am always cheerful? Does my name make me a cheerful person? Am I cheerful? Am I still allowed to be sad? If your name means sad are you always sad? My name is not true. Sometimes I'm sad. Most times my name is true. should I have two names? What name means sad? what name means angry? what about suprised? Should I have so different names? as many names as there are feelings?

FIGURE 5–8. *Sarah J's notebook entry, "My Name Means."*

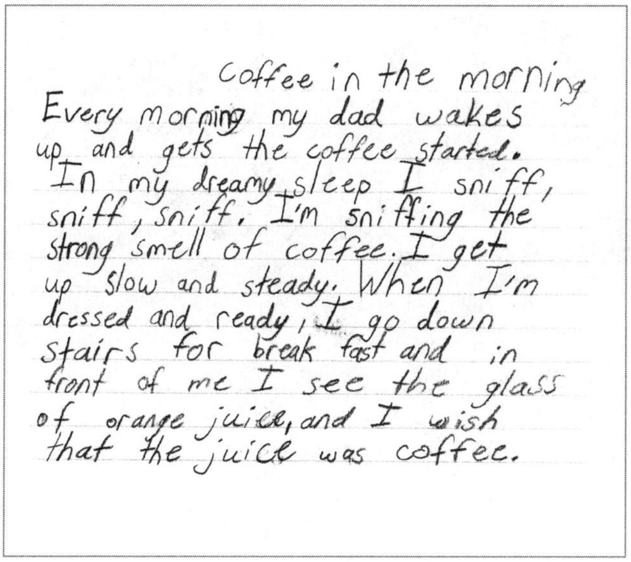

Coffee in the morning

Every morning my dad wakes up and gets the coffee started. In my dreamy sleep I sniff, sniff, sniff. I'm sniffing the strong smell of coffee. I get up slow and steady. When I'm dressed and ready, I go down stairs for break fast and in front of me I see the glass of orange juice, and I wish that the juice was coffee.

FIGURE 5–9. *Julia's notebook entry, "Coffee."*

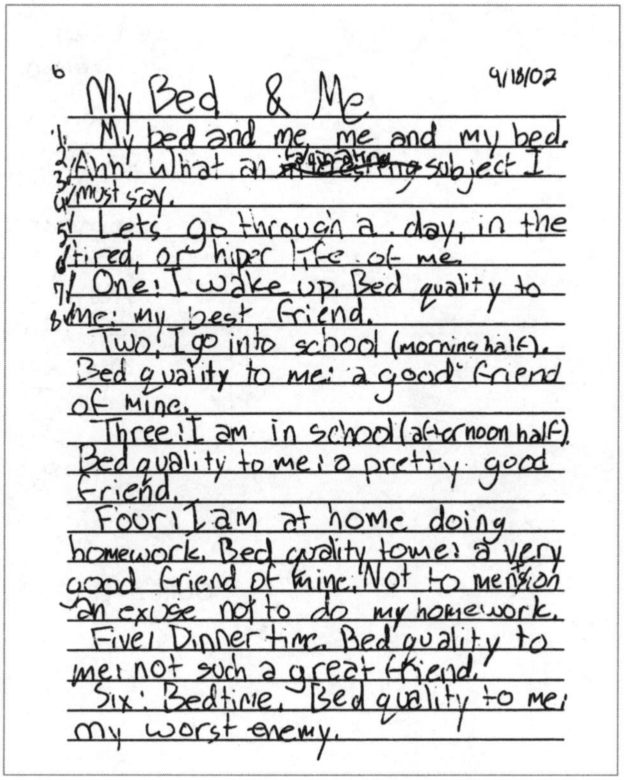

6   9/18/02

My Bed & Me

My bed and me, me and my bed. Ahh! what an amazing subject I must say. Lets go through a day, in the tired, or hiper life of me. One: I wake up. Bed quality to me: my best friend. Two: I go into school (morning half). Bed quality to me: a good friend of mine. Three: I am in school (afternoon half) Bed quality to me: a pretty good friend. Four: I am at home doing homework. Bed quality to me: a very good friend of mine. Not to mention an excuse not to do my homework. Five: Dinner time. Bed quality to me: not such a great friend. Six: Bedtime. Bed quality to me: my worst enemy.

FIGURE 5–10. *Toby's notebook entry, "My Bed & Me."*

On Saturday afternoons, I'm sitting at my desk, starring off into space. My sister lies on her bed, combing her thick blond hair. My mother takes a shower, humming along with the Irish ~~movie~~ CD she always listens to. My dad goes off to the post office.
BORING.
Why can't life be as interesting as our minds ~~cut~~ are? In my head, I'm having arguments with at least 12 different people. I'm telling my mom I _can_ go to school alone, I'm not a baby. I'm saying to my dad that I am _not_ wasting my time on junky books. I'm saying to my sister how ugly that shirt is.
 I always win all 12 arguments.
 I am also dreaming.
There are 5 rivers in my mind. But I can step over them as though they are puddles. The mountains, to me, (which there are 4 of) are like pebbles.
 There are no mountains in Manhattan. Rain beats restlesly on the windows, decorating them with drops, like small beads of sweat. People walk fast to get out of it. There feat hit the ground like a mothers hand on her
nauthy childs behind. Time goes as fast as Christmas comes. Minutes feel like hours. My lips are nearly completely chewed up, from all the thoughts going on in my head. I want to say them, but I can't, so I bite my lips. I have a strand of brown hair that ~~cur~~ curves and bends around my ear from me twirling it. It never looks like that, only on a Saturday afternoon, where every-thing takes too long to finish.

FIGURE 5–11. _Sarah's notebook entry, "On Saturday Afternoons."_

6

Teaching What Your Students Need

One of the challenges of teaching writing is learning to look at student work with an eye toward instruction, not only for the child with whom you are working directly, but for others who may struggle with the same needs. Predictably, this is a continuous challenge. We frequently hear teachers say, "So, my kids are writing, what happens next? How do I know what to say to them when I sit down to confer?"

The students will have their challenges as well. After many years of teaching writing, we can safely predict the problems you will encounter as well as the troubleshooting that's needed. It is easy to look at student writing and pull apart the mechanics and teach toward that. However, that is not the goal of the Writing Workshop. Over the years, Shelley Harwayne has reminded us to look first at a student's writing for what they do well. Then, and only then, should we attempt to help the student identify what they need to learn.

In order to help you look at student writing with an eye toward instruction, this chapter will first give you a quick glance at typical notebook entries of five students: Christine, Sam, Donna, Driton, and Julianna. For each entry, we have highlighted what we believe each writer does well and what we might like to teach in a follow-up conference. These examples represent predictable problems that are most likely to occur at the beginning of the year in the initial writing cycles, but may need to be addressed with some students throughout the year.

Next, you will meet Max and Scott. We have chosen to be more specific with these two students by including a sample of each of their notebook entries, the transcript of a conference with them aimed at teaching a particular strategy, the writing that resulted from the conference, and some follow-up minilessons to support the work of students in the class with similar writing issues.

The chapter concludes with early-in-the-year troubleshooting and teaching suggestions for a conference with a student who faces a particular writing need.

Highlighting Student Work

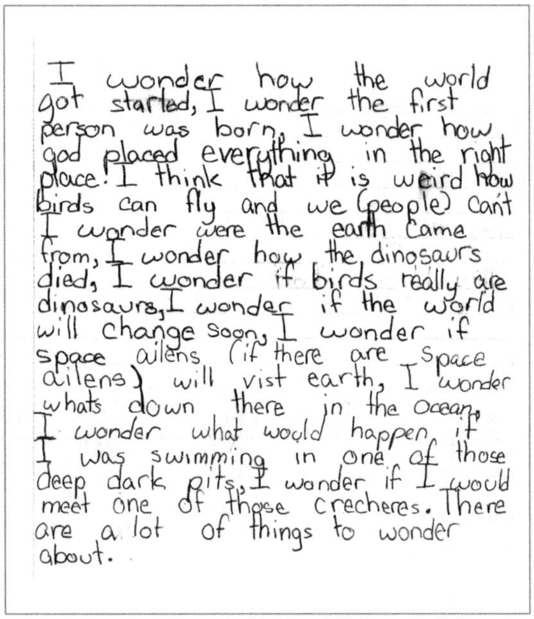

I wonder how the world got started, I wonder the first person was born, I wonder how god placed everything in the right place. I think that it is weird how birds can fly and we (people) can't I wonder were the earth came from, I wonder how the dinosaurs died, I wonder if birds really are dinosaurs, I wonder if the world will change soon, I wonder if space ailens (if there are space ailens) will vist earth, I wonder whats down there in the Ocean, I wonder what would happen, if I was swimming in one of those deep dark pits, I wonder if I would meet one of those crecheres. There are a lot of things to wonder about.

FIGURE 6-1. *Christine's writing.*

Meet Christine, a third grader who comes to Writing Workshop with:

- a curiosity that inspires her to wonder about big ideas in the world. This is the kind of thinking we hope our students will do.
- an understanding of voice, which she demonstrates by the use of parentheses to suggest her thinking.
- the power of repeated lines.

Although these qualities make this a very good notebook entry (see Figure 6-1), we want her to begin to slow down this thinking and begin to explore each of the wonderings further. During a conference, we might discover that she has a particular curiosity or knowledge and might choose to explore only one wondering.

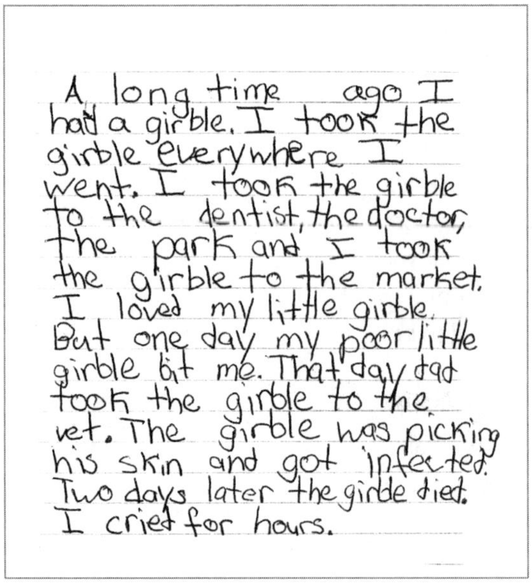

A long time ago I had a girble. I took the girble everywhere I went. I took the girble to the dentist, the doctor, the park and I took the girble to the market. I loved my little girble. But one day my poor little girble bit me. That day dad took the girble to the vet. The girble was picking his skin and got infected. Two days later the girble died. I cried for hours.

FIGURE 6-2. *Sam's writing.*

Meet Sam, a fourth grader who understands how to:

- tell a story, "a long time ago . . ."
- move stories along in time
- give specific examples using a list
- save the punch line for the end

While the entry shown in Figure 6-2 certainly holds our attention, we talk to Sam about building his stamina, particularly with a topic that he clearly cares so much about. We might talk to him about not getting to the end too fast, by slowing down the second part of his entry in much the same way as he did in the beginning.

Meet Donna, a fifth grader who knows how to:

- show the importance of the memory by repeating, "I remember . . ."
- pay attention to detail
- use language to create images
- sustain her writing by thinking through her memories
- bring closure to a piece of writing by using a "play" on words, "the *first sight* . . . " "I wish it lasted longer."

Donna is doing so many important things as a writer, as shown in Figure 6-3. We want to make sure she is aware of them, so we are sure to point them out to her and encourage her to keep doing them. We point out to Donna that sometimes her images are clear and breathtaking and other times unclear, as in, "I remember swimming in the lake." We give her books like *When I Was Young in the Mountains* by Cynthia Rylant, to show her how writers sustain the images they create over a body of work.

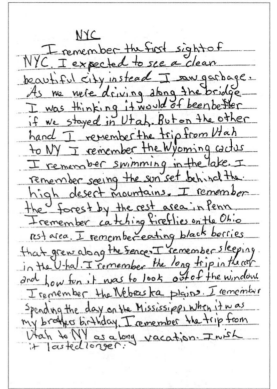

FIGURE 6-3. *Donna's writing.*

Meet Driton, a writer who:

- embraces clear opinions and knows the power of expressing them in his writing
- understands the power of using a voice in his writing that speaks to the reader
- takes a personal topic and writes about it in a way that many can relate to

Driton will benefit tremendously from learning how to develop his ideas and organize his thinking (see Figure 6-4). We help Driton create a list of the rules he hates and the reasons why he hates them.

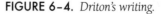

FIGURE 6-4. *Driton's writing.*

Grandpa's hands
My grandpa Geza's
hands are smooth
as a flower petal
and warm like
a towel fresh out
of the drier. His
right and left hands
work back and
forth working
night and day
building what ever
comes to his mind.
my grandpa's left
hand is rough and
week from doing
all the work. his
right hand while
reachs for a tool.
one of his idea's
was building a swing
out of hard and
rusty pipes. Grandpa
also built a flower
pot out of
an old washing machine.
Every year the
flowers blossum
and bloom with
their blue and
red colors. He
also built a 5
pound white
and blue water
gun that shoots
12 feet in the
air. His hands
help his wonderful
idea's come to
life.

FIGURE 6-5. *Julianna's writing.*

1 ✓
2 ✓ I like boxing because you don't have
3 ✓ to be big or whigh a lot, all you need
4 ✓ is strong arms, that I've got. When I
5 ✓ grow up I am going to be a pro
6 ✓ boxer, I can hold a good stance for
7 ✓ balance and I have strong fists.
8 ✓ I like money, an Think of all the
wigh money I would get in boxing.
whigh
(weigh)

FIGURE 6-6. *Max's notebook entry.*

Max	Minilessons
Has "trouble writing large amount."	—Rereading to find loaded parts, circle & write new entry.
Writes lots of ideas into 1 small entry. . . .	
Boxing—being small, size affects everything.	
Brother/fighting money/grandpa	
*Reread then circle parts that are "loaded." Write about each one in n.b. Write to end of page. Gradually push to write more.	

FIGURE 6-7. *Teacher's conference notes.*

Meet Julianna, a writer who:

- knows how to use comparisons that work
- creates images by giving details and description
- takes something seemingly small, "grandpa's hands" and makes it big, "his hands help his wonderful ideas come to life."

Although it is tempting to look at this piece of writing in Figure 6-5 and do nothing but pat Julianna on the back for a job well done, we must remember we have a responsibility to take writers from where they are to the next step. In spite of Julianna's effective use of imagery, we are wondering, what's the importance of this entry to Julianna? What is the significance to Julianna of her Grandpa using his hands to make the things he does? We encourage her to use her wonderful writing ability to explore for this deeper meaning.

Meet Max, a very bright, articulate fifth grader who:

- has a lot to say but writes very briefly about potentially big ideas, combining them into one short notebook entry as shown in Figure 6-6. Basically, Max doesn't see the payoff in writing and chooses the easy way out.

Conference with Max and Conference Notes (See Figure 6-7)

Teacher: How is your writing going?

Max: Fine.

Teacher: As I look over these entries in your notebook, I notice they are very short. What do you think about that?

Max: I have a problem writing a large amount. I just cram all my writing into a small space. I say everything I need to say real fast and then I feel like I have said it all.

Teacher: I think that's true too because when I read them, I think they are short, but they seem so powerful, because in those short entries you have said so much, they're like little gems about a number of different things. Let's look at this entry about boxing. It seems to me that this is a short entry about a lot of different things and that you could probably write more about each thing you mention. As you read over this, what are some of the different ideas that seem to jump out at you?

(The teacher jots Max's ideas down on a sticky note as he is suggesting possible ideas for writing. Later, she will give Max the note to put in his notebook to remind him of the things he spoke about in the conference.)

Max: Well, the part about boxing and about me being small.

Teacher: Is this really about boxing, or is it really about you being small for your age and the way that affects your life?

Max: That and about how someone's size affects everything they do.

Teacher: One potential thing you could be writing about is you being small and how that affects you, or a bigger issue beyond just you, how size affects people in general. Those are two big things that you could write about. Anything else jump out at you?

Max: My brother and me fighting. Just play-fighting I mean.

Teacher: Okay, but what about this? "I like money"—"think about all the money I could get from boxing." I thought that was interesting.

(Conference continues . . .)

Minilessons

Helping Writers Who Have Multiple Ideas in One Notebook Entry

• Find a notebook entry, such as Max's, that is full of short but loaded lines. Using this writing as a model, you would say, "Boys and girls, yesterday I had a conference with Max. Like many of you, Max's notebook was full of very short but loaded entries. Take a look at the overhead as Max reads the entry to you. (Max reads) Max, could you tell the class what we talked about . . . what I mean when I say your entry is loaded." Max proceeds to explain that it was about three important things rolled up in one, short entry. Max tells the class how he realized he had more to say about how he likes money, about being short, and about he and his brother fighting. "Boys and girls, what I'd like you to do is reread your notebook to see if you have any entries like Max did where you think you wrote about more than one idea in one entry. Put a sticky note on them. Choose one and use the right side of the notebook to begin writing about one idea. Could someone repeat what your work is for today?" Once the students are sure they know what to do,

they go off to write and we begin moving around the room to conference with students during that time.

• Find a published piece of writing where the writer has focused on one topic. Have the students identify the strategies they notice the writer uses for staying focused. Encourage students to either find an old entry that could be developed by using the strategies of the mentor piece or write a new entry trying to stay focused on the topic.

• Show the children a piece of writing you have done and talk through your thinking as you develop the entry in front of them.

• Have a student ask for help in developing an entry that needs to be focused. This means the class participates by asking questions and offering suggestions. The student develops his entry along with the class using a blank overhead or chart tablet.

1√ 2√ 3√ 4√ 5√ 6√ 7√ 8√ When ever someone passes me they call out "history" "hi shorty." I have been teased all my about being short all my life. I am shorter than most of the kids I know. Some kids take advantage of that and call me "shorty" or midget. They expect nothing negative to them when they call me midget instead of my real name.

When other kids are jumping to hit the rim of the basketball hoop I try to do the same but only getting half way up. When I land back on the ground I am hit with volley after volley of laughter for many people take pleasure in me failing to do something because I'm short.

FIGURE 6–8A.
Max's writing as a result of the conference.

1√ 2√ 3√ 4√ 5√ 6√ 7√ 8√ For some people being short is a disability for me it is passed on from my ancestors. When I hear the song, Short People, I am not offended because I know that there are people older than me who are shorter.

I sometimes put short people in two catagories, one midgets and two people with short ancesters.

Short people are viewed as weak, while taller bigger people are known to gang up on them.

Sometimes you are shorter than everyone else when you are a kid but when you are an adult you pop up and you are taller than the kids who had been taller than you when you were a kid.

FIGURE 6–8B.

Max: When I was a kid I always wanted more money. Instead of toys I asked for money. My father and my grandfather always talked about worrying about money. I wanted to make sure I never had to worry about not having money.

Teacher: Max, what you tend to be doing as a writer is cramming many big topics into one, short, underdeveloped entry. In this entry, there's a line about being short, a line about fighting with Sam, a line about money. I think a good thing for you to do is when you think you have finished an entry, you need to reread and look for places where you seem to jump from one idea to another. Circle or underline those ideas and see each one as a potential entry for your notebook.

Max: I see what you mean. Circle the part about money, being short.

Teacher: That's exactly what I mean. And although you will only choose to write about one today, you should add the others to your list of "Things to Write About" for another time. Which one do you think you'll write about today?

Max: About being short. I think I have a lot to say about that.

Teacher: Good. Don't forget to add the others to your list.

Max's Writing as a Result of This Conference

You can see how Max's subsequent three entries (Figures 6-8a-c) showed greater focus and attention to the subject matter. Max needed to have someone with whom he could talk out his ideas. As he discussed his ideas, Max was able to see that these topics were important to him and that he did have more to say about them. Moreover, Max needed a monitor who would not allow him to slip by with being lazy about his writing. Student partnerships and writing groups will also support writers like Max as the students learn to confer with each other.

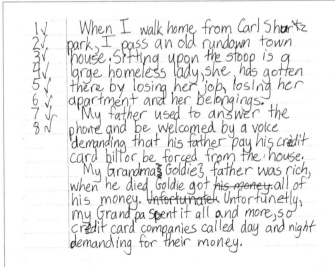

1√ 2√ 3√ 4√ 5√ 6√ 7√ 8√ When I walk home from Carl Shurtz park, I pass an old rundown town house. Sitting upon the stoop is a large homeless lady, she has gotten there by losing her job, losing her apartment and her belongings.

My father used to answer the phone and be welcomed by a voice demanding that his father pay his credit card bill or be forced from the house.

My Grandma's Goldie's father was rich, when he died Goldie got his money. all of his money. Unfortunate Unfortunetly, my Grandpa spent it all and more, so credit card companies called day and night demanding for their money.

Goldie was scared, scared of those men on the phone, scared that her children would be, kicked out on the street.

My father has always been careful with the money earned for the family. All bills are payed on time and taxes, got that covered. When I was ten I came up with a financail plan, I would save money so when I am older I can spend freely and have a job so I can keep and hopefully grow my income. To help me I set goals for myself, I started with $500 and when I got to that I tried for a thousand.

I hope to reach a thousand soon and I am almost there.

FIGURE 6–8C.

Meet Scott, a fifth grader who:

• enjoys participating in writing conversations. When it comes to putting words down on the page, he is capable of writing a fair amount, but he delivers just the bare facts (see Figure 6-9). Indeed, most of his writing tends to be list-like.

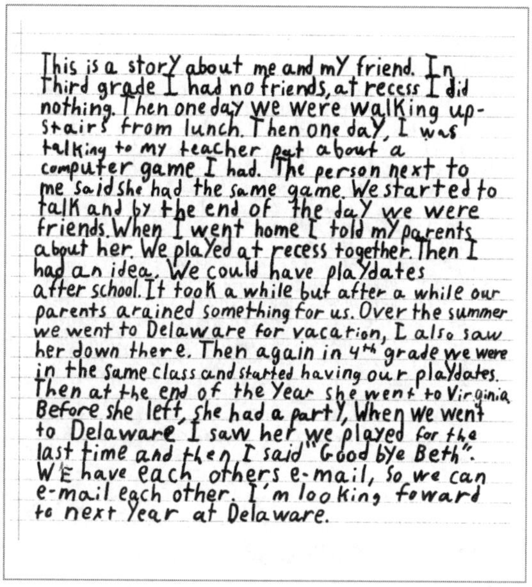

Conference with Scott and Conference Notes (See Figure 6-10)

Teacher: Your notebook tells so much about you as a writer. I am reading your entries about your friend Bethany moving, about going to Delaware in the summer, and about your father barbecuing. You fill up the entries with so much of what happened or what you saw. That's something that writers do. And you do that so well.

Scott: It's easy for me to write things that happened in the past. I remember them and it's just easy to write what I remember.

Teacher: Scott, it's my job to help you grow as a writer. And since I know that writers not only write about what's happening on the outside, I want to help you think about what's happening on the inside. Do you know what I mean?

Scott: Yes, I think so, but I'm not so sure.

Teacher: Let me see if I can help you understand what I mean. Let's take a look at this entry about Bethany. I remember Bethany and I know her moving affected a lot of your classmates. And probably many of them who knew Bethany well could have told the same story about her leaving. But what's important about Bethany leaving for you? What parts of that story could no one else tell?

Scott: Like what's inside of me that's not on the page?

Teacher: Exactly. The inside story.

Scott: Well I think I haven't put that down yet . . . I kind of told the story of what happened but not what I am feeling or what might happen later or anything that could have happened.

Teacher: You just said three things, Scott. You could tell about what you are feeling, what might happen later, or what might happen in the future. What do you think would be the most important thing to write about?

Scott: My feelings.

Teacher: You probably had a lot of feelings about Bethany moving. What seems to stand out the most for you?

Scott: Ummm. . . . Well at first I got teased a lot because my best friend was a girl. So at first I wasn't sure if I should be friends with her or not.

FIGURE 6-9. *Scott's writing.*

FIGURE 6-10. *Teacher's conference notes.*

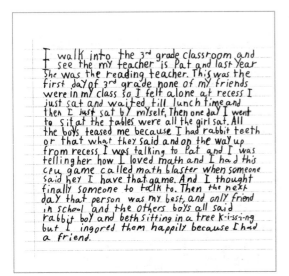

I walk into the 3rd grade classroom and I see the my teacher is Pat and last year she was the reading teacher. This was the first day of 3rd grade none of my friends were in my class so I felt alone at recess I just sat and waited till lunch time and then I just sat by myself. Then one day I went to sit at the tables were all the girl sat. All the boys teased me because I had rabbit teeth or that what they said and on the way up from recess I was talking to Pat and I was telling her how I loved math and I had this cpu game called math blaster when someone said hey I have that game. And I thought finally someone to talk to. Then the next day that person was my best and only friend in school and the others boys all said rabbit boy and beth sitting in a tree k-i-s-s-i-ng but I ingored them happily because I had a friend.

FIGURE 6–11. *Scott's writing as a result of the conference.*

Then I thought, well why should I listen to them, I have my own ideas? I am going to be friends with her.

Teacher: Do you see the difference between writing about what you are feeling and just telling the facts of what happened? Telling your feelings is important because that's what helps you tell **your** story. So that's an important thing to learn as a writer. It's okay to tell the facts. That's part of what writers do. But then you also need to go back and think about, "what's at the heart of this story for me?" And that's what you are not doing yet in your entries. So what I want you to do is to get to the heart of the matter. On the blank page opposite this entry, tell the feelings you just told me. Okay, Scott?

Scott: Yep.

Scott's Writing as a Result of This Conference

You can see how Scott's follow-up entry (Figure 6–11) shows a deeper understanding of the importance of the experience in his life. With future focused minilessons and references to this and other conferences, we can help Scott and other students write more thoughtfully.

Minilessons

Helping Writers Who Tell Their Stories Without Explaining (or Recognizing) Their Importance

- Using a writing sample like Scott's, demonstrate for the students how one writer can tell a story and then personalize it by telling what is really important about the story. Very often, you will hear us repeat in conference after conference, "How can you tell this story in a way that no one else could? How is your experience different from anyone else's? What is the inside story?" These words become familiar to the children and become the classroom vernacular in Writing Workshop.

- Choose a short text or a picture book that the students are familiar with. Have students identify the telling of events and the parts where the writing clearly demonstrates the importance of the events.

- Help students understand that writers can tell the external story (what they saw, heard, or what happened), but they can tell the internal story as well (how they feel or think about events). You may show before and after samples of student writing in which this strategy is demonstrated or you may model for them how you would go about doing this with your own writing.

Troubleshooting

Here are some other predictable problems you will most likely encounter at the beginning of the year. We have provided some suggestions for addressing them in conferences. Remember always to allow your conferences to inform your mini-lessons, especially if you know other students can learn from what you have taught.

The student is facing the blank page with nothing to say

1. Remind the student to use their "expert" inventory as a resource.

2. Tell them to think about what's going on in their lives right now that makes them happy, sad, excited, anxious, worried, anticipating, etc.

3. Remind the students of the stories they have told or to think about how other students' stories may relate to their lives.

4. Reread with the student an entry he/she has already written to see if he/she can say more about it, or if there are other possibilities or ideas he/she might see that are connected.

The student lacks stamina and writes only a few lines then declares "I'm done!"

1. Get the student talking about the entry. This helps them see they have more to say about the topic.

2. Have them talk to a writing buddy who could help them focus.

3. Have them reread entries as part of the writing process to see them as jump-starts for new writing.

4. Remind the student about your expectation for them and insist they try a little harder.

The student is writing about the same topic every time they set out to write

1. Encourage the student to find different ways of writing about the topic.

2. Encourage the student to find different things to say about the topic.

3. Encourage the student to add more to their expert inventory.

4. Talk to students about some of the ideas others are exploring in their notebooks.

The student repeatedly writes diary-like entries, recording events chronologically

1. Talk to the student about what is really important about the list of events then help him choose one to write about.

2. Have the student work with a buddy and compare his "diary-like" entry with ones that are not diary-like.

3. Share with students other notebook entries that sound more like the kind you'd like them to do.

4. Use sticky notes to help them plan out ideas that are important to include in the entry.

Students don't understand the way to use a notebook (they title every entry, write "The End" when they are done, draw lines between entries, draw pictures instead of writing, skip too many pages, etc.)

1. Tell them what you expect, no *ifs, ands,* or *buts* about it.

The student writes about having nothing to write about, or chooses topics that are not important and therefore finds it hard to be thoughtful

1. Get the student talking about some of the items on his/her "Things I Can Write About" list in an effort to identify some of the ones that might be more important.

2. In an attempt to spark his/her own ideas or interests, have the student talk to other students to find out the kinds of things they are writing about.

Inevitably, when we closely examine our students' writing, we discover the wide range of unique personal needs and individual developmental challenges that are present in every classroom. But what a gift! This concrete proof of our students' needs is our launch toward smart, sensitive instruction that we can tailor, to some extent, for each student. The more you talk with your students, the more comfortable you become with naming what they do well and helping move them forward. And this, of course, is the joy of teaching.

Moving from Notebook Entry to Finished Piece

Too often with so much focus on gathering writing in the notebook, the notebook can take on a life of its own. We can lose track of the purpose of collecting in the notebook—the goal of publishing. If we truly believe in process instruction, then we must also believe that process without product is a futile effort. Children must publish frequently in order to practice the drafting, revision, and editing skills we are teaching throughout the year. In addition, if we truly believe that the power in learning writing conventions lies in correcting one's own work and not in the skill and drill work we find in spelling and grammar workbooks, then we must provide opportunities for our writers to correct their own work by preparing it for an audience. The nightly ritual of going through a notebook entry using the editing checklist (see Chapter 2) helps students realize that editing is a separate process from getting their thoughts down; but, nonetheless, it is their important responsibility as writers. As our students ready their writing for an audience, they learn to be more critical about their own writing.

Published writing may range from very simple pieces that don't stray too far from the original notebook entry (as is often the case in the first cycle when you are just getting started with collecting in the notebook) to more complex pieces that are quite different from the original notebook entry. How this process unfolds relates directly to the experiences the writers bring with them and your own expectations for their work. Earlier in the year you may be satisfied with simple publishing, as your goal is to complete a cycle and to make sure your students have published. As the year progresses and the children learn more about good writing, you can expect to see the evidence of good writing in their published pieces.

In this chapter we describe the stages of the publishing process for Cycle One and all future cycles. You need to know that the strategies for choosing an idea to publish and developing an idea basically remain the same throughout the year. What changes as a result of our teaching are the students' abilities to organize information into drafts, their abilities to apply revision strategies and crafting techniques, as well as their abilities to edit their own writing. In this chapter, we present some of our thoughts and ideas for the different levels of drafting and for helping students learn editing strategies. There is, however, a wider and more complex repertoire of revision strategies that we need to build on as our writers develop and grow. For this reason, we address revision and craft instruction in Chapter 9.

Choosing Ideas from the Notebook

It is important to demonstrate for students how to closely reread their notebooks for entries that seem to "jump out" at them and how to identify the ones they might possibly work on for publication As students spend some time making this decision, they may use sticky notes to tab the pages that hold the possible ideas they'd like to work with. They are then encouraged to narrow their choices down to one. Of course, as students reread their notebooks in order to make the decision, we are having individual conferences that help to support them in using the criteria for making good choices that we've demonstrated in the minilesson.

During the share session at the end of the Writing Workshop we ask students to tell very briefly about some of the ideas they are considering and to say why they are leaning toward those choices. This is one way of making public what others are planning on doing, and can help more reticent students make their decisions. The students are encouraged to continue to work on narrowing down their choices to one by the next day, so we can begin to use strategies to collect more about the topic.

M i n i l e s s o n s

Reasons for Choosing Something to Publish

In a minilesson, develop criteria that students might use as they review their notebooks to choose an idea to publish.

• You think an entry is important and you have already written a lot.

• You realize an entry is not your best writing, but you know you have more to say and would like to pursue it.

• An entry sounds like a genre or form you are familiar with (a poem, a letter), and you know you can develop and revise it easily for publication.

• You have a series of entries about a topic or idea that is important to you and you can envision combining the entries, or parts of the entries, into one piece.

• An entry is written well, you like it a lot, and you think you can work on it to make it even better.

• You think readers will find an idea interesting because it addresses a universal issue; for example, concerns about the environment.

• There is an ongoing theme threaded through your entries, and you recognize the potential for developing that idea, for example, feeling out of place.

Predictable Problems

The student can't find an idea

Daily ongoing support should ensure that every student, even struggling writers, will have entries to choose from. Some students, however, may need extra support in making choices. So, during your conferences, support those students in selecting from among those entries that hold the most potential.

The student keeps picking the same idea

During your conferences with this student, point out other ideas in the notebook that have potential to be developed into a published piece of writing. This student needs support in moving beyond a topic he/she is already very comfortable with. In future cycles, set goals for this student to develop a wider variety of ideas to write about.

The student has chosen an idea that may not be fruitful or may be too difficult to develop at this time

Redirect the student. It is important that students choose work that they will be able to successfully bring to final publication.

Developing Material Around an Idea

At this point, students focus only on the idea they have chosen to write about. Their purpose is to gather more entries in the notebook around that idea.

Minilessons

Strategies Students Might Use to Help Them Do This Work

We develop a list such as the one below that highlights the strategies students might try as they begin to develop one idea.

- Write more.

- Interview and do research to find out more about the topic.

- Think about other examples that support your thinking on that topic.

- Do some wondering about the topic. Ask yourself why you are writing about this particular topic at this time.

- Create a web with the topic in the center and then try to brainstorm ideas that are connected with the topic.

- Write from a different perspective. How might someone else view this idea or experience?

- Take some time to make observations that might inform you about your topic.

- Think about how your topic relates to issues happening in the world.

- Try to find other memories or stories connected with your topic.

- Try to see a connection between entries and think about the main point.

- Reread and find your big point—to do this, ask yourself questions about the topic, then try to answer them. Sometimes the main point of a piece is found in the concluding lines of an entry, and that becomes the point of focus for the student to begin developing ideas.

Drafting

Now that students are ready to work on a piece for an audience, it is time for them to get out of their notebooks and on to composition paper. This is an important transition for two reasons:

1. It clearly supports making the distinction that writing in the notebook is for the writer. Once the writer begins a draft s/he has clearly begun to consider an audience and is writing toward publication.

2. Composition paper allows the flexibility for cutting, pasting, and getting messy in a way that the notebook does not support.

At this point in the process, the children use their dual-pocket folders to hold their drafts as well as their mentor pieces. They are told to save all drafts in the folder and to never discard writing they "don't like." We explain to them that their "mistakes" or "changes" are important pieces in their growth as writers and help us understand their process, to see their thinking, and show their growth as they progress through a piece. These "pieces" all add up, giving us a bigger picture of who they are as writers. Ultimately, these insights enable us to support them in the best ways we can. In this age of technology, students are often drafting on the computer. We teach them to copy and paste each draft so we can track the changes. We also teach them to use the tool bar to engage the track changes option so we see the revision changes that occur.

Minilessons

Drafting Strategies

The following are strategies we demonstrate in our minilessons as students begin to draft their writing.

- Underlining a strong line and using that to begin the draft.

- Return to a mentor text and ask the students to outline the ideas. Then discuss why they were sequenced in that order. This way, when they need to think about the organization of their ideas, they can refer to this experience.

- Underlining or circling parts of the entries they want to use and organizing them into their draft.

- Rereading all they have gathered in the notebook about the topic, then closing the notebook and beginning a draft with the thoughts that are swimming around in their heads.

- Photocoping all entries related to the topic, cutting and pasting them on to another sheet of paper in the order they belong, being sure to leave spaces for revision

- Making a list, a simple web, or a flowchart to help identify and organize the information that needs to be included.

- Trying out the draft in different ways, then deciding on which one works best for the piece. For example:

  ◆ Try out the draft first in present tense then in the past tense.

  ◆ Try writing the draft as if you were talking directly to someone.

  ◆ Try writing as though it were a flashback.

Although students are working on composition paper, the writer's notebook is still an important part of their writing. It is open right next to them as they draft so that they can access the many ideas they may have collected around their topic.

While the students have spent one or two Writing Workshops as well as time at home gathering around the topic, drafting occurs very quickly—during one Writing Workshop session. Once this is done, you will slow down the process again as you move through the revision stage.

Before we begin to talk about revision, it important to note that as the year moves on and the students have more and more revision strategies under their belts, the line between revision and drafting may become blurred. This is a natural thing to happen for writers who understand that writing toward publication means revision. As they draft, they are already thinking, "How can I make this better?"

As we mentioned earlier, the drafting techniques may change as the needs of our writers change. As students broaden their strategies for finding and developing ideas they become better at gathering information. We have found that they need a tool to help them organize this information. The flowchart (Figure 7–1 and in

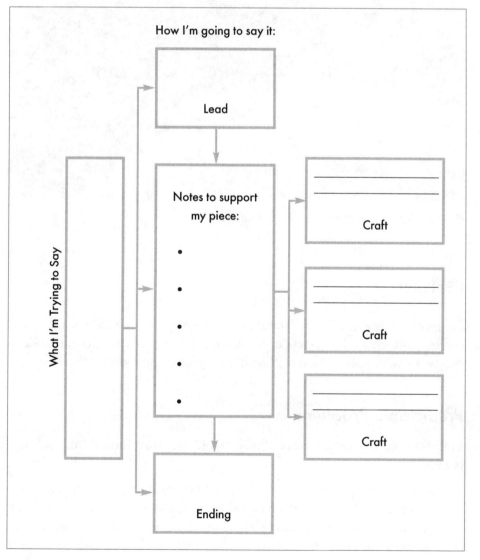

FIGURE 7–1. *Flowchart.*

Appendix H) helps them organize their ideas in a more thoughtful way. It asks them to think about what they really are trying to say before they organize ideas that will become drafts. Some ambitious students may experiment with different ways of organizing the information and complete more than one flowchart, later choosing to develop the one that makes the most sense. Sometimes while in the process of developing the flowcharts, students get ideas for possible ways of crafting the writing. They may use the crafting boxes next to the flowchart to jot down those ideas and use it as a reference during the revision stage. (See Figure 9–5B.) Many students, however, are not able to think of crafting strategies until they have composed the draft. (See Figure 7–2 below and on the website, <www.heinemann.com/davis-hill>.)

FIGURE 7-2. *A student working on a draft using a flowchart.*

Revision

Chapter 9 deals with revision strategies to support your work in later publishing cycles. However, for this first cycle we teach the revision strategies that our students can most easily apply to the typical writing they are doing earlier in the year.

Predictable Problems

The child has copied the entry almost "word for word" and thinks he/she is done

One of the criteria the children may have used in this first publishing cycle is to choose something they think they have written well. If this is the case, then help the student identify places he thinks he could make it even better. You might make some suggestions and push the student toward making other changes on his own. Then pair him up with another student who will make other suggestions.

The student over-revises, changing lines that were good to begin with

Get the student to think about the purpose of revision and to compare what he had before with what he currently has. Help the student understand that his job is to make revisions that enhance his writing.

The student's piece lacks focus

Help the student to determine what the piece is really about. Have the student list the information that needs to be included so she can write with that focus in mind. Look back at the draft to eliminate parts that do not belong or add information to help focus the piece. Return to the notebook if necessary to find or to further explore and develop parts that need to be added to the draft to make the focus clear.

Minilessons

Revision Through Reseeing

- Use a piece of student or teacher writing to demonstrate how to use asterisks or numbers to identify places in the draft where some revision might occur. Model for the students how to make those revisions on a separate piece of paper or on the right side of a notebook page, which will then be inserted into the draft.

- Brainstorm with students what they already know about making a piece of writing better. Make a list then send them off to try those strategies in their writing.

- Choose a draft and go through it with the students to make it better. List the ways in which we have done that. For instance, if we add more description about a person, we would add that to the list we have begun to create. The students then go back to their drafts to find a part they would like to work on to make their writing better. Again, remember we keep crafting/revision as simple as possible during this first publishing cycle, knowing there will

- be many opportunities to do in-depth work during future cycles.

- Teach students how to work on a better beginning or a stronger ending. For this you may refer to a picture book or two you have used during this cycle to discuss the purpose of beginnings and endings and what the writers have done to make them effective.

- Teach them to expand on simple statements that simply tell. For example, using a piece of writing, pointing out lines that tell and do not show: "I had fun," "he was nice," or "I had a good time." Help the students understand how they can improve the writing by showing *how* they had "fun." Use mentor texts to help them see how authors "show and not tell."

- Have the writer look at the draft, choose a part that needs to be revised, draw what the words say, then try to add detail to the drawing as a way to inform the writing.

Editing

Everyone asks about editing, and for good reason. It is one of the most frustrating things we need to do in the Writing Workshop, and the least fun to teach. We know the old red pen is not the answer. What teacher hasn't had experiences when we've corrected student writing, only to have it returned with the same errors. The more we understand about editing and conventions, the more we must realize that it is the writer's intentions that drive punctuation. So, clearly, the students must learn to edit in more meaningful ways.

Young writers should learn to edit their own work, for who knows better what the intention for the reader is than the writer? We've come far enough to know that grammar textbooks containing workbook pages meant to teach conventions are not the answer to our editing woes. Our writers have become more attentive to spelling and punctuation because we've held them accountable to do it every night with the addition of the editing checklist to their nightly writing work. We see a marked difference in the overall correctness of the grammar in our students' published work when checking their work for spelling and punctuation, verb agreement, proper use of homophones, etc. become nightly rituals.

Conventions of print need to be taught outside of the Writing Workshop and applied to work in the Writing Workshop. This means that ongoing investigations meant to teach spelling patterns and generalizations and investigations aimed at teaching proper usage and punctuation should be an ongoing part of our Literacy Workshop. For instance, when children are investigating the way writers use commas, categorizing their findings and writing their own generalizations, then they see the impact of this work on the writing they do in their notebooks. This translates to greater ease in editing their published work. When students are engaged in regular word study investigations, by that we mean regular time set aside outside of the Writing Workshop when we investigate spelling patterns and generalizations, then the overall quality of the spelling in their writing gradually improves.

Demonstration, as in all areas of learning, is crucial to the learning of any skill. So, too, is it for the acquisition of editing strategies. So, if we engage in shared and interactive writing experiences, we are providing many opportunities for our students to watch us compose writing in front of them, share our decisions about proper spelling, use punctuation and paragraphs appropriately, and make decisions about organization. During interactive writing, we are providing opportunities for

FIGURE 7-3. *Editing Nina's writing.*

them to try out these conventions with the support of the community and then for them to take it back to their own work. When we are conferring about editing, we can refer to the work we did publicly and draw on that common experience.

We're often asked whether a piece has to be perfect when it is published. We believe a piece should be "perfect" for an audience with regard to spelling, grammar, and punctuation. While we expect children to edit their pieces, we are mindful that their editing skills at a particular point in time will allow them to go only so far. As the final editors, if a piece that is prepared for an audience comes to us with errors, we do correct it for the student. We do this knowing that students may not learn from the final editing we have done. Our final editing is strictly for the audience reading the piece. We know that the minilessons, investigations, and conferences we do around editing are where we best provide the real learning experiences for our students.

Some books to reference for ideas on the teaching of spelling and punctuation are *Spelling K–8* by Diane Snowball and Faye Bolton and *A Fresh Approach to Teaching Punctuation* by Janet Angelillo. These and other books on the subject can help you plan and implement a course of study in your classroom that enables the editing of writing to come from acquired knowledge rather than guesswork. It also takes the responsibility of editing out of your hands and puts it into the hands of the writers in your class. Eventually we hope they come to see editing as an important stage of the writing process.

Minilessons

Editing Skills

- Help students understand they need to reread with a particular focus on one editing issue at a time. For instance, read through the piece once checking for punctuation errors, then reread again with a focus on spelling errors, etc.

- When reading writer's notebooks, take note of run-on sentences or thoughts that don't make sense and copy them down. Periodically, present this work to the students and ask them what they think the writer is trying to say. Ask them to write, either on a dry erase board or on a post-it note, a possible correct way to express the idea. Share the possibilities with the class.

- During the editing stage of the writing cycle, put a student's work on an overhead, with his permission of course, and have him edit his work in front of the class. With the help of others, have the student make decisions about punctuation, grammar, and spelling conventions. (See Figure 7-3.)

- Remove the punctuation from a short, published piece of writing and have the children insert punctuation where they think it is necessary. Then show them the original writing and discuss their decisions.

- Fishbowl a conversation between students who are engaged in editing each other's work, paying special attention to the ways in which they support each other and their conversations about the decisions they made and why.

Editing Outside the Writing Workshop

INTERACTIVE WRITING

At the end of each week of content-specific study, engage in an interactive writing experience where the children help you write a summary piece describing the learning that has taken place. As you work your way through the writing, stop to make decisions about organization, paragraphing, subject/verb agreement, punctuation, and spelling.

DICTATION

Engage in periodic dictation so that children have the opportunity to practice the editing strategies you teach. You can use dry erase boards for this. When the children have written what you dictate, they can share with partners and groups to discuss the decisions they have made.

WORD WALLS

Word Walls, large bulletin boards with words arranged alphabetically, are great ways to help children collect and pay attention to the words they use regularly in their writing lives.

INVESTIGATIONS

Engage children in investigations of published work to study how authors use particular punctuation conventions. They should gather sentences, categorize, and come up with generalizations about when to use the punctuation they are studying.

Predictable Problems

The student has read the piece and claimed it to be "ready" or "finished" yet you find glaring errors—obvious misspellings, omitted words, etc.
The student may be reading the piece too fast and needs help in slowing down and noticing errors. Establish partnerships for this work. Two students could read the piece together and check for errors.

Publishing

One of our goals is to get the students to publish *often*. It is very easy to fall into the habit of lingering in the notebook for too long. When this happens, we miss the opportunity for frequent drafting, revision, and editing from our writers. These are the places in the process where the concrete learning happens. Writers also need readers in the classroom, in the school community, and out in the world. The ultimate satisfaction a writer can derive from having written is the reader's response. What powerful affirmation it is when writers see readers being moved, entertained, or informed by their work.

One of the messages we send to our students early on in the year is that they are expected to revise and edit their work regularly and publish in a variety of ways over the course of the year. Publishing could mean neatly written, illustrated work. It could mean a piece that is typed and mounted on a colorful piece of backing paper.

It could mean the piece is framed with a colorful border. It could mean a piece that is submitted to the school paper or more elaborately published in a student-made or bound book purchased from any number of suppliers.

If we think about including structures for publishing when we make plans for the year, we will certainly be more likely to do it. Thinking ahead gives teachers the opportunity to order the appropriate tools such as a variety of types of paper, "blank" books, and other media that students can delve into over the course of the publishing year.

Writer's Reflection

We have spoken about the Writer's Reflection in Chapter 2. This reflective thinking not only gets students to think about the work they've done, but asks them to focus on what they have learned during this cycle that they'll apply to all future writing. It is a perfect opportunity to set goals for future publishing work and to bring closure to the cycle. (See Figure 7–7K and Appendix C.)

Celebrating the Work of Writers

We must also provide ways to celebrate the children's work. Celebrations are important because they provide opportunity for writers to receive recognition for their hard work. Writers not having the the opportunity for sharing their work with readers is like actors rehearsing for a show that never gets performed. On the other hand, every celebration need not be a grand performance. Some may be quiet and more private while others involve a larger audience. Baskets of published work arranged by genre is one way to make writing public. (See Figure 7–4 below and on the website, <www.heinemann.com/davis-hill>.) We must be sure to provide a variety of forums for celebrating the work of our young writers.

FIGURE 7–4. *Celebrating students' work.*

DISPLAY WORK ON BULLETIN BOARDS

Create a bulletin board either in your classroom or in the corridor that provides a space for each writer to display his/her work. The first could go up as early as the end of September. Subsequent pieces build on top of the first. This way, you collect one on top of the next, allowing the audience to read the work and see the writer's growth over time. Include a comment sheet next to each writer's space, encouraging the reader to make supportive comments about the work. At the end of the year, take down the cumulative work, paste comment sheets on the back, and bind them into a portfolio of the year's writing. (See Figure 7–5 below and on the website, <www.heinemann.com/davis-hill>.)

FEATURE WRITING ACROSS GRADES

Create a similar bulletin board for the entire school where each grade features certain published pieces. The remaining pieces go in a three-ring binder, one for each grade. These sit beside the display on a table or shelf below the bulletin board so readers may see all published work. This board should be updated regularly as teachers publish in their classrooms. When the display is removed and changed to make room for new ones, the pieces that are taken down go into the three-ring binder, which is obviously growing over the course of the year. It might be a good idea to give this responsibility over to your student council, upper graders, even parent volunteers.

CELEBRATE KEY FEATURES

Create a "Great Lines" bulletin board in your room or in the corridor. Later, this could become a Great Leads, Great Comparisons, Great List display as you study craft more closely. Leave blank paper and pens nearby to invite other students in the school to add their Great Lines. (See Figure 7–6 on the following page and on the website, <www.heinemann.com/davis-hill>.)

FRAME YOUR SUCCESS

Purchase or have donated inexpensive plastic frames in which you display published work. This is particularly good for poems. Find places in your building to

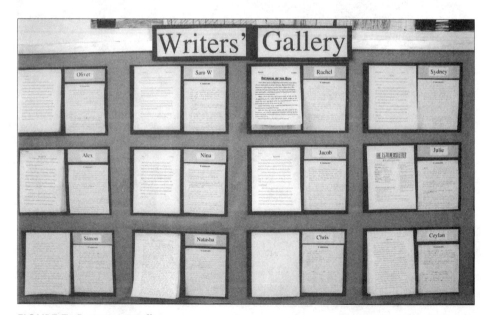

FIGURE 7–5. *Writers' Gallery.*

display published writing—teacher's room, corridors, above water fountains, in the main entrance, on the walls of the lavatories, in the lunchroom, or on the walls lining the stairways. If your school has a laminating machine, you can also simply laminate before displaying. Use Velcro so it becomes easy to substitute pieces.

PUBLISH A CLASS NEWSLETTER

Send home a newsletter featuring a few published pieces each month. Ask a parent volunteer to help with this. Over the course of the year, the entire class should have an opportunity to be featured.

CREATE NEIGHBORHOOD DISPLAYS

Call upon neighborhood merchants to display published work either in the windows of their stores or in three-ring binders and placed where patrons/clients can read the work. If the piece is about money, why not the window of the bank? If it's about pets, the vet's office; about being sick, the pediatrician—you get the point!

SPONSOR A HOME EXCHANGE

Invite children to swap pieces and send the writing samples home. Provide a comment sheet so the adults can write remarks back to the students.

HOST PUBLISHING PARTIES

Publish celebrations in the classroom where others are invited to join the students as they share their work. These visitors may include families, other classes within the school, classes from other schools, or other teachers and administrators who join the hosting class.

Creating Partnerships

Develop cross-grade relationships with lower-grade classrooms to share and teach strategies learned.

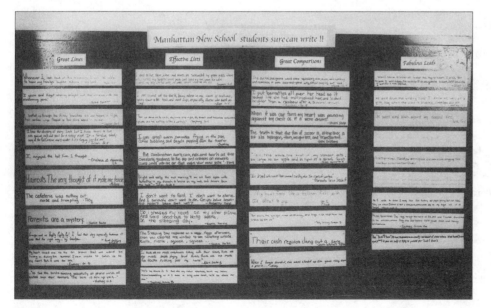

FIGURE 7–6. *Great Lines bulletin board.*

Highlighting Student Work

WEBSITE

In the following pages, we invite you to join Driton in the process of moving from notebook entry to his first published piece. See Figure 7–7A–K. Also see our website for additional samples of student work at <www.heinemann.com/davis-hill>.

---

                                    parents
          At My Grandparents house
        I got there and meet everybody
    except my grandfather because
    he went some where and as soon
    as I put my bags away I
    was out in the farm and
    working which I liked doing
            for   the
    except my brother because only
    thing
    ^liked to ^run around and make
    trouble. Later I heard a tractor
    coming in to our parking lot...
    It was my grand father coming
    from the mountains. We said hi
    and all that stuff and Our uncle
              And also
    came lets go in Fuzi and hang
    out and meet your friends. We got
    there which only toke five minutes
    to get there. We came back and
                aunt
    Said to our ^ let go up
    Lekaj and back down in Vronea
    to See people She said o.k.
    after my work is down.

FIGURE 7–7A. *Driton's notebook entry.*

              Yugoslavia
              Yougoslavia

    I feel like I belong there
    because I like working
    there, Seeing my uncle, anut,
    grandpa, and grandma. I fix
    things, Seeing people, and I also
                            ing
    take care of the farm just
    like my grandpa. In Manhattan
and there is no houses, no farms,
    no work for kids. (except chores)
    I also like growing stuff
    for my grand pa like figs,
    straw berries, peachs and wheat
    we have a lot of grapes (which
    I still have that bee sting
    on my finger) Every year after
    we grow them and pick them
    we mush the grapes (which
                          you mushit
    I got to) to make wine. you
    boil it and we got it. Thats
         would
    why I ^ like to live there.

FIGURE 7–7B. *Driton developing his topic.*

    The village is related Some
    way excepet 2 people Serbias serbs
    and a new person
    from another village that
    move to ours. I like people
    that I know and know me
                the
    and See us every day
    and I like my uncles friends
    too.

    I love staying with my Uncle
    Gjeka we go to the lake to
    ride the boat or go hunting
    for crocidiles. We buy tods
                            we fix
    and parts for motors

    I like feeding the animals
    and looking for eggs. I also
    like walking my grandpas
    dogs. When I walk the dogs
    I run them around our village.

FIGURE 7–7C. *Driton developing his topic further.*

         My Draft
    1 My family is in Yugoslavia
    and I belong there
                and animals
    2. Farming with my uncle Grandpa

    3. Working with my Uncle Gjeka

    4. All the things I get to do

FIGURE 7–7D. *Driton organizing his ideas before drafting.*

Driton

Yugoslavia   Draft 1

Most of my family still lives in Yugoslavia. I go there and I love it because I feel like I belong there and I think its my real home.

Over there I love farming with my grandpa. we grow things like grapes, peppers, straw berries, corn, tomatoes, and salad. [We also feed the animals like the cows, the chickens, and two dogs. After they eat, I go looking for eggs if I could find them.]

I love staying with my Uncle and his name is Gj'eka. We both go to places like the lake to ride the boat or go hunting for crocodiles. and We even, buying things like tools or parts for motors. My uncle work for those stuff which also lets me work with him.

Thats why I like going there cause I do those things every day there.

**

FIGURE 7–7E. Driton's first draft.

My uncle is a Mechanic so he teaches me how to start a motor. Fix broken things.

* How to start a motor where I should not touch and to fix things when broken

We grow things like grapes, peppers, straw berries, corn, toematoe and lettuce

We
feed the animals like the cows, the chickens and two dogs

We gride the grapes in stone pool until it becomes wine There is so many bees around I usually get stung (I still have the mark on my finger)

FIGURE 7–7F. Driton's revision work.

Ending

In Manhattan I never get to do good things like farm and fix motors

* In Manhattan there is no grandpa Uncle Gjeka, no small family house and only chores for Kids. Thats why I belong in Monetenegro, my real home

FIGURE 7–7G. Driton's revision work.

Draft 2

Most of my family still lives in Yugoslavia. I go there and I love it because I feel like I belong there and I think its my real home

Over there I love farming with my Grandpa Lucaj. We grow things like peppers, straw berries, corn, and tomatoes, We also feed the animals like the cows, the chickens, and the two dogs. After they eat I go looking for eggs if I could find any. We gride the grapes in stone pools until it becomes wine. There are so many bees around I usually get stung (I still have a mark on my finger)

I love staying with my Unde Gjeka. We go places like the lake to ride the boat or go hunting for crocodiles. We even go shopping for things like tools or parts for motor. My Uncle is a Mechanic so he teaches me how to start a motor, where I shouldn't touch, and how to fix things when they are broken.

In Manhattan there is no Grandpa Lucaj, no Uncle Gjeka, no small family house and only chores for Kids. Thats why I belong in Monateneyro my real home.

FIGURE 7–7H. Driton's second draft.

Driton N   September 28, 2001

Yugoslavia

Most of my family still lives in Yugoslavia. I go there and I love it because I feel like I belong there and I think its my real home.

Over there, I love farming with my Grandpa Lucaj. We grow things like peppers, strawberries, corn and tomatoes. We also feed the animals like the cows, the chickens, and the two dogs. After they eat, I go looking for eggs if I could find any. We grind the grapes in stone pools until they become wine. There are so many bees around I usually get stung. (I still have a mark on my finger.

I love staying with my Uncle Gjeka. We go places like the lake to ride the boat or go hunting for crocodiles. We even go shopping for things like tools or parts for motors. My uncle is a mechanic so he teaches me how to start a motor, where I shouldn't touch, and how to fix things when they are broken.

In Manhattan, there is no Grandpa Lucaj, no Uncle Gjeka, no small family house, only chores for kids. That's why I belong in Montenegro, my real home.

FIGURE 7–7I. *Driton's published writing.*

Driton

Home

I love Yugoslavia
Uncle Gjeka
and the tools and the motors.

I love farming,
Grandpa Lucaj
and the chickens and the dogs.

I love Yugoslavia,
planting and growing
till kingdom come.

FIGURE 7–7J. *Driton trying the published piece as a poem.*

Name Driton N

Writer's Reflection

The notebook entry I chose to publish was about The things I like about Yugoslavia

As I drafted and developed the idea, I realized that what I was really trying to say was I feel like I really belong there and not in Manhattan

The craft strategy I used to lift the quality of my writing was explaining more about the things I like and the things I do there

My favorite part of this piece is "My Uncle Gjeka is a mechanic so he teaches me how to start a motor, where I shouldn't touch and how to fix things when they are broken."

It is my favorite part because I like the list of things

One thing I have learned about good writing that I will apply to all my future writing is That it is important to not be lazy (which I could be) and always give more examples for the reader

FIGURE 7–7K. *Driton's Writer's Reflection.*

8

Future Cycles

Lifting the Quality of the Writing Notebook

By the time you are ready to undertake the work of the next cycles, the children should understand the purpose of keeping a writer's notebook and appreciate the freedom that comes with writing about the ideas that are important to them. In our classrooms, the mornings are alive with excited voices productively sharing entries from the night before. Partners are beginning to get to know each other, validating each other's efforts and helping each other flesh out new ideas by asking the types of questions they have become accustomed to hearing us ask during writing conferences. Everyone is becoming a writing teacher. Earlier we stated our deep belief about the importance of cultivating good writing in the notebook so that when the students are ready to publish, they have something worth building on. By doing this kind of deeper thinking about the work in the notebook, the children can begin to come to some bigger understanding of their purposes in writing, clarifying and organizing their thinking in ways they tend not to focus on when getting down those initial entries.

Goals for future Cycles

To accomplish this work, we spend the next few cycles lifting the quality of the writing in the notebook. Our goals for future cycles are:

• To continue to build on the work from the first cycle by introducing new strategies for gathering a wide variety of entries in the notebook

• To support the rereading of the notebook as a ritual toward helping writers find ideas for new topics from old ones

• To begin working on lifting the quality of notebook entries

• To build stamina for writing longer entries and staying with an idea for a longer period of time

• To study mentor texts to understand that writers have a purpose for writing

- To study mentor texts as models for revision strategies

- To stay with a topic longer to discover big ideas and to clarify thinking

- To move from the "me"–centeredness of the earlier writing to exploring connections to issues in the world

- To reinforce rereading the notebook to build on the variety of entries and to support writing opinion pieces and commentaries

- To develop strategies for organizing writing

Broadening the Strategies for Gathering Ideas

Studying Mentor Texts

Our grandparents and our parents have said to us in a variety of ways, "It's the company you keep that rubs off and influences your life and how you live it." The same holds true for our writers. To be great writers, they must be in the company of great writers. When opportunities present themselves, we invite writers to our classrooms. Since that cannot happen on a regular basis, we keep company with them through their writing.

After reading "My Grandmother's Hair" by Cynthia Rylant (see Figure 8–1) for the first time and asking our students "So, what does this piece leave you thinking about?" we can easily predict that many of our students will write entries that are very closely connected to the content of that piece. It was not surprising when Rachel wrote an entry about playing with her mother's hair (see Figure 8–2). When we reread this mentor text to push our students to see beyond the obvious, beyond the story of Rylant playing with her grandmother's hair, we asked, "What do you think this piece is really about? What are the bigger ideas?" Michelle, a third grader, writes about what she wants to be when she grows up, connecting to a bigger idea in the writing in Figure 8–3. Suzannah, a fifth grader, picked up on the idea that spending quiet moments with someone you love is so important and wrote about her quiet moments with her sister as shown in Figure 8–4. For more responses by Ellen and Josh see our website, <www.heinemann.com/davis-hill>.

My Grandmother's Hair

When I was living in my grandparents' small white house in Cool Ridge, West Virginia, I loved to comb my grandmother's hair. I was a thin, blond-headed little girl, and I would climb up on the back of the couch where my grandmother was sitting, straddle her shoulders with my skinny six-year-old legs, and I would gently, most carefully, lift a lock of her soft gray hair and make my little pink comb slide through it. This always quieted us both, slowed down our heartbeats, and we would sigh together and then I would lift up another lock.

We talked of many things as I combed her fine hair. Our talk was quiet, and it had to do with those things we both knew about: cats, baking-powder biscuits, Sunday school class. Mrs. Epperly's big bull. Cherry picking. The striped red dress Aunt Violet sent me.

But we didn't always talk. Sometimes we were quiet. We would just think, and my small hands would move in my grandmother's hair, twirling, curling, rolling that soft grayness around. We thought about good things, the big clock in the living room ticking, and sometimes my grandmother would shiver and we laughed.

I often put bobby pins in her hair, made pin curls with them, and the rest of the morning or afternoon my grandmother would wear these pin curls I had made. Later, I'd watch as she stood before her mirror, taking them out one by one, and her gray locks would be tight as bedsprings and would dance if you pulled on them. But when she brushed through these tight little wads of curl, her hair became magic and grew and covered her face like a lion's mane.

I thought many times that I might grow up to be a hairdresser, twirling ladies' gray locks into magic curls and watching their faces light up as they saw themselves change.

But I became a writer instead. And used my pen like a little pink comb, and got quiet, and thought good thoughts, and twirled and curled and rolled words into good stories. The stories became books, and with the same hands I had once combed her hair with, I handed these books to my grandmother and watched as she turned the pages one by one, the big clock in the living room ticking.

Sometimes she shivered and we laughed.

There are many ways to learn to be a writer.

FIGURE 8-1. *"My Grandmother's Hair" by Cynthia Rylant from* To Ride a Butterfly. *Reprinted with permission.*

When I was young, I would put barrettes all over my mother's short, brown hair. I would wet her hair and comb it until it was straight.

With so many colorful barrettes in her hair, it seemed like her hair was multi-colored.

I always wished she would grow out her short hair so I could put it into little messy ponytails and funky twists instead of braids, which I couldn't do yet.

We used to laugh, and then we would fall silent. She would make me shriek with laughter again by tickling my toes, while I sat on the back of the couch, with my back on the wall, and my legs draped over her shoulders.

My mother and I spent lots of time sitting their, laughing and braiding.

FIGURE 8-2. *Rachel's entry.*

I think about what I want to be when I grow up. I read about fun jObs in booKs. I am only 8 but it sounds fun. I think about being a ariplane pilot, Because when I was on a plane, the pilot asked me if I wanted to sit in his seat I said yes. It was fun, Thats why I want to be an ariplane pilot. I also think about being a vetinaren, Because you get help animals, thats why I want to be a vetinaren. I also want to be a hair dresser, Because you get to play with hair, thats why I want to be a hair dresser. I also want to be a teacher, Because you help children learn, Thats why I want to be a teacher. I want to wait a few years to make my final decision.

FIGURE 8-3. *Michelle's entry.*

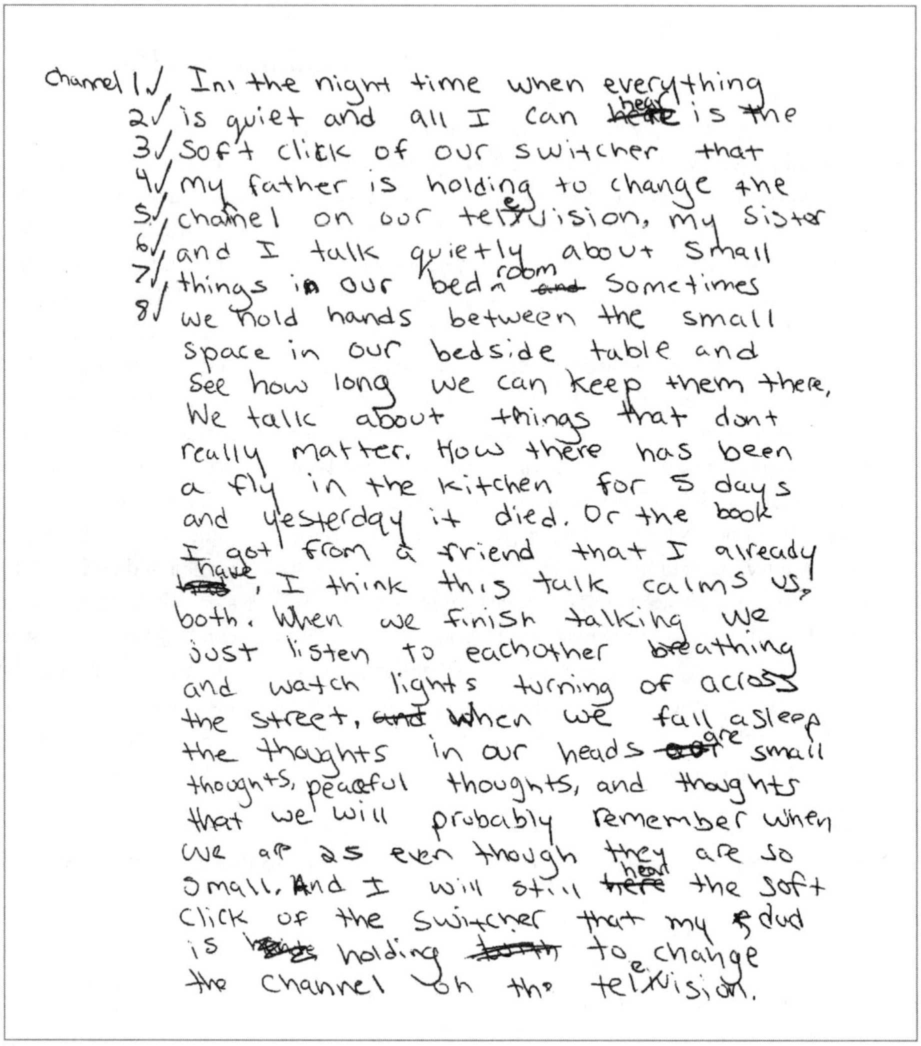

Channel 1√ In the night time when everything
2√ is quiet and all I can hear is the
3√ soft click of our switcher that
4√ my father is holding to change the
5√ chanel on our television, my sister
6√ and I talk quietly about small
7√ things in our bed room Sometimes
8√ we hold hands between the small
space in our bedside table and
see how long we can keep them there,
We talk about things that dont
really matter. How there has been
a fly in the kitchen for 5 days
and yesterday it died. Or the book
I got from a friend that I already
have, I think this talk calms us,
both. When we finish talking we
just listen to eachother breathing
and watch lights turning of across
the street, when we fall asleep
the thoughts in our heads are small
thoughts, peaceful thoughts, and thoughts
that we will probably remember when
we are as even though they are so
small. And I will still hear the soft
click of the switcher that my dad
is holding to change
the channel on the television.

FIGURE 8–4. *Suzannah's entry.*

Drawing Help from Powerful Poetry

After reading "Plenty," a poem by Jean Little shown in Figure 8–5, students were able to come up with the following list of possible ways to connect to the ideas in this poem. Notice how the wise choice of this mentor text easily inspired thinking beyond the memories and family stories they would have typically written about.

Big Ideas Inspired from "Plenty"

- Things you want
- Homelessness—how the homeless are treated
- Being a charitable person
- Appreciating what you have
- The things we take for granted
- How lucky we are when we have a lot of things

Plenty

I have plenty of everything
   but want.
I try to imagine hunger,
Try to imagine that I have not eaten today,
That I must stand in line for a bowl of soup,
That my cheekbones angle out of my hollowed face;
But I smell the roast in the oven.
I hear the laden refrigerator hum.

I think of people whose walls are made of wind.
I stand outside in the cold.
I tell myself I am homeless and dressed in rags;
But my shiver lacks conviction.
I stand in fleece-lined boots and winter coat.
Home is a block away.

I leave my wallet at home.
Pretending I have no money,
I walk past stores and wish.
"I have no money, no money at all, no money—"
I turn my head in shame as I pass the bank.

I pay for a parcel of food. I gather clothes.
I adopt a child under a foster parent plan.
I do what I can. I am generous. I am kind—

I still have plenty of everything
   but want.

Jean Little

FIGURE 8-5. *"Plenty" by Jean Little from* A Round Slice of Moon.

- Having your own money so you can do what you want with it
- Being spoiled
- Thinking about children in poor countries
- Learning to be a good person from the people you admire
- The difference between need and want
- The different kinds of wants
- If we could make the laws
- When parents say you can't have the things you want
- Wondering how people become homeless

Figure 8–6 is Noah's response to "Plenty." For more responses by Justin and Emma, see our website, <www.heinemann.com/davis-hill>.

Using Magazines and Newspaper Articles

We use *Time for Kids, Junior Scholastic,* or any other newspaper/magazine articles of interest as mentor pieces to help our students connect to current trends and issues that affect them, their friends, and their families. Although we have used magazines in the classroom, we have never before systematically woven them into the work of our Writing Workshop. Our expectation was that students would see the articles and topics discussed in these magazines as possible sources for writing about their opinions or for questioning their world. In order to hold our students accountable for using the magazines, their weekly assessment shown in Chapter 2 requires them to reflect on their use of the magazine articles as inspiration for writing. Ronnie's reaction to an article written about how scientists are beginning to understand the human genome is shown in Figure 8–7.

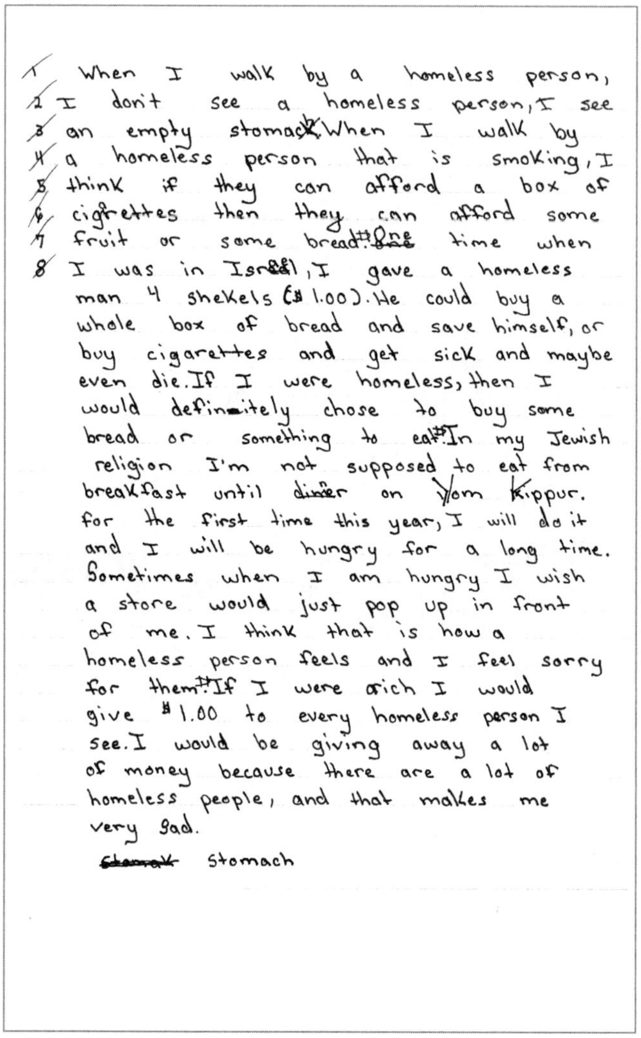

When I walk by a homeless person, I don't see a homeless person, I see an empty stomach. When I walk by a homeless person that is smoking, I think if they can afford a box of cigrettes then they can afford some fruit or some bread. One time when I was in Isreal, I gave a homeless man 4 shekels ($1.00). He could buy a whole box of bread and save himself, or buy cigarettes and get sick and maybe even die. If I were homeless, then I would definitely chose to buy some bread or something to eat. In my Jewish religion I'm not supposed to eat from breakfast until diner on Yom Kippur. For the first time this year, I will do it and I will be hungry for a long time. Sometimes when I am hungry I wish a store would just pop up in front of me. I think that is how a homeless person feels and I feel sorry for them. If I were rich I would give $1.00 to every homeless person I see. I would be giving away a lot of money because there are a lot of homeless people, and that makes me very sad.

~~stomack~~ stomach

FIGURE 8-6. *Noah's response to the poem "Plenty."*

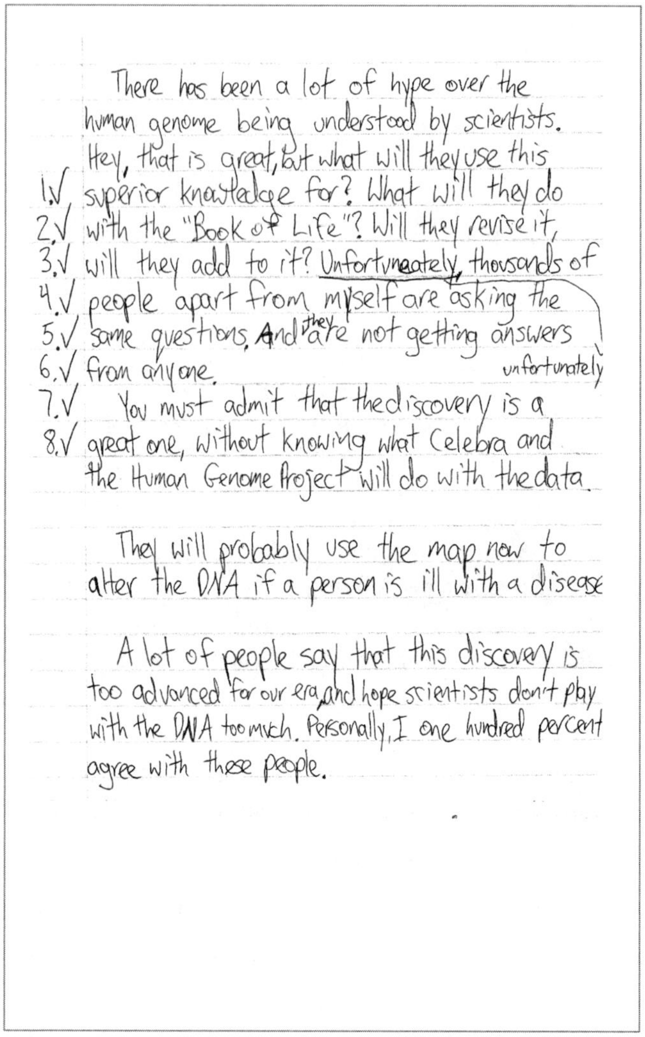

There has been a lot of hype over the human genome being understood by scientists. Hey, that is great, but what will they use this superior knowledge for? What will they do with the "Book of Life"? Will they revise it, will they add to it? Unfortunately, thousands of people apart from myself are asking the same questions, And they're not getting answers from anyone. unfortunately

You must admit that the discovery is a great one, without knowing what Celebra and the Human Genome Project will do with the data.

They will probably use the map now to alter the DNA if a person is ill with a disease

A lot of people say that this discovery is too advanced for our era, and hope scientists don't play with the DNA too much. Personally, I one hundred percent agree with these people.

FIGURE 8-7. *Ronnie's entry, "Hype over Human Genome."*

The Notebook as a Tool for Gathering New Entries

For many students, especially our more reluctant writers, once they'd written about a topic they considered their writing "done" and that there was nothing else to say. It was as if they could write the words "The End," and often, some of them actually did! The most powerful practice for generating new ideas while at the same time deepening the students' thinking is rereading the notebook. We knew the structure of the blank right-hand page (Chapter 2) of the notebook would support these discoveries after repeated readings. Joanne Hindley, a founding member of the Manhattan New School and author of *In the Company of Children,* reminds us that "writing does not always need to begin with the blank page." The following is a list of strategies we teach our students.

Strategies That Inspire Minilessons

Think More Deeply About What Is Already in the Notebook

Lifting a word or a line: After rereading a notebook entry, a student might lift a powerful word or line by placing it at the top of the right side of the notebook opposite the entry and begin a new entry from there. This strategy might lead to an entry about a totally different topic, or might take the same topic in a different direction. For an example of this, see Sam's entries on our website, <www.heinemann.com/davis-hill>.

Getting a new idea from an old one: After rereading a notebook entry, the student might realize that there are lots of other ideas that can come from this one. For instance, a student wrote about ice skating in the park with his brother. After rereading the entry, he might be inspired to write about other things related to ice skating like how easy or hard it was to learn; or he might decide to write about his relationship with his brother. The important work the teacher must do here is to help the students stretch their thinking so they are always looking for possibilities.

Wondering about the topic: When children read the notebook to find entries they can wonder about, this usually leads to some sort of discovery. This means encouraging them to read their notebooks and allowing questions to meander through their heads until they come to some conclusions. Take Luke for instance, who after reading "My Grandmother's Hair," wrote an entry about time he spends with his father and how precious that is because his father is in school and has very little spare time. Luke began to wonder about the kind of father he'll be and wrote about how he is going to spend lots of time with his kids. For Luke's work, see the website, <www.heinemann.com/davis-hill>.

Taking a new perspective: After rereading the notebook, students select an entry that allows them to see the situation differently. For example, Lia wrote an entry about being in the library and being annoyed by a group of boys who were being very noisy. She thought they were inconsiderate and selfish. When she tried to see the situation from another perspective, she wrote about the fact that the boys seemed so engaged in the research they were doing and had found what they were looking for and were just excited. They didn't mean to be noisy or disrespectful of others. It was through her writing that she realized she might have been a little too hard on them, and wanted to take back the dirty looks and the complaints she made to the librarian.

Combining entries that are seemingly unconnected: This is not easy for many students to do but forces them to reread with this focus in mind. Kyla had an entry about rain and how sometimes it is calming and other times it is frightening. Another entry was about giving money to the homeless and how badly she feels when she sees someone living on the street. By teaching her this strategy, Kyla pushed herself to write about what it must be like for homeless people in the rain. For Kyla's work, see the website, <www.heinemann.com/davis-hill>.

Deciding on the "so what" of the idea: Many children write about their personal experiences without thinking about *why* they are doing this. For example, Anna, a student who had recently moved from Bulgaria to New York, described one of her favorite places in Bulgaria. When she was pushed to discover the "so what" of it, she wrote about finding a bit of Bulgaria in her new home, and by doing so, lifted the quality of the writing. See Figure 8–8a–b. Remember Rachel and

Continued on page 106

Strategies, continued

Suzannah (see Figures 8-2 and 8-4 on pages 101 and 102). To see how they came to the "so what" of their topic, see the website, <www.heinemann.com/davis-hill>.

Making a class list of "Where We Get Ideas for Writing": We ask the students to look over the entries in their notebooks and think back to where they get ideas for writing. Figure 8-9 is the list generated by fifth graders at the Manhattan New School. Once the list is compiled, it is typed and copied for each student and placed either in the back of their notebooks or in their writing folders for future writing support.

Rereading the notebook routinely to check on the variety of entries: For this we often ask the children to read through their notebooks, labeling the types of entries with sticky notes. This helps them take stock of the kinds of things they tend to write about and make plans for broadening the variety of their entries. If a student tends to write mostly about memories or things they do on weekends or after school, we push her to check the "Things They Can Write About" list or the class list of "Where We Get Ideas for Writing" or to form a study group in which students confer with each other to share notebook entries and the origin of their thinking.

A special Place in Bulgaria were me and my friends
like to go. It's beautiful there. The small town
river is just landed at the bottom of the hill and at our
Place there is a waterfall. The hill rises from the
river, so around the bank there is only grass. Grass
with a carpet of glowing purple flowers. Rock almost in
the river standout like mountins. We like to sit there.
On the rocks. Sparkles of water touch our faces
and the sun spreads it's fingers to us. It penetrates
the shadow of the maple tree that branches over us. I
dont know why but me and my friends just like sitting there
and smelling the fresh flowers, feeling the cool broez
and touching the sunshine.

FIGURE 8-8A. *Anna's first entry.*

A Special Place
by Anna S.

My friends and I like to go to a special place in Bulgaria. It's beautiful there. The small town river lands at the bottom of the hill. At our place, there is a small waterfall. The hill rises from the river so around the bank there is only grass covered with a carpet of bright, beautiful flowers. Rocks, almost in the river, stand out like mountains.

We like to sit on the rocks and feel the sparkles of water touch our faces. Sunshine spreads its fingers on us and penetrates the shadow of the maple tree that branches over us. My friends and I just like sitting there smelling the flowers, feeling the cool breeze and touching the sunshine.

Ever since I moved to New York I have made wonderful new friends and I have tried to find a special place like the one back home. I have looked and looked but the only place I can find is the Bulgarian Mission. The water doesn't flow freely there and there is no grass growing. The sunshine never touches my face and there is only the smell of dusty books and documents. But the sound of my language still rings through the air, making me feel at home. This place, so different, feels right for now.

FIGURE 8–8B. *Anna's further attempt at lifting the quality of her writing.*

WHERE WE GET IDEAS FOR WRITING

- From something you're reading

- From listening to:
  - The news
  - Someone else having a conversation
  - Talk radio, or just the radio
  - To music
  - Things you hear in your environment

- From events you attend
  - Sports
  - Theater
  - After school activities

- From experiences you had when traveling

- From observations you make of people and things

- From issues in the world you have strong opinions about
  - Listening to the news and reading newspapers
  - Reading Time For Kids and Junior Scholastic

- Other magazines for children

- Conversations with adults and other kids

- Internet to research something you're interested in

- From other entries

- From paying attention to your emotions

- From looking at things that remind you of memories or family stories
  - Photo albums
  - Old games
  - Family traditions
  - Home movies
  - Your treasures

- Interviews
  - With parents
  - With grandparents
  - With your doctor or other professionals you find interesting

FIGURE 8–9. *The class-generated list of "Where We Get Ideas for Writing."*

Using Picture Books and Short Texts to Model Specific Writing Techniques

For this work, we are looking at the writing in our students' notebooks and thinking about how we can help them lift the quality of their writing without doing a focused craft study. The following are important minilessons that go a long way in helping students become better writers.

Minilessons

Using Literature to Inspire Writers

Show and Not Tell: We often refer to this strategy when we read students' writing and notice that they've told us that they've had a good time or that the ice cream was good, but don't show us by giving a specific example. To help students see how writers show and not tell, we choose parts of texts. For example, we might use this page from the picture book *Waiting to Sing* by Howard Kaplan.

> The piano lamp was shaped like a G-clef, and it poured a fountain of light over our hands. He'd play and then I'd play. Sometimes I'd place my hands on his as we traveled the path of the keyboard together. Our hands were like skimming stones, smoothing over the foamy white keys, navigating the black ones as if they were rocks.

Turning Small Things into Big Writing: Picture books like *How to Get Famous in Brooklyn* by Amy Hest model this well. In one part of this book Amy Hest shows us so well how she steps into Bibi's Old World Bakery and proceeds to paint a picture with her words of the best black-and-white cookies money can buy.

> Bibi's Old World Bakery is where you get the best black-and-white cookies money can buy. They are so big you have to eat them in stages, two bites, rest your stomach, two more, rest your jaw. Like that.

 For an example of this work, see Josh's entry on the website, <www.heinemann.com/davis-hill>.

Getting Right to the Story You Have to Tell: We often notice writing that is well intentioned but gets lost in the clutter. For instance, a student intends to tell about building a sand castle on the beach. Instead of starting directly with building the castle on the beach, the student spends a page writing about waking up, brushing their teeth, packing the pails and towels in the car, and driving to the beach. There is perhaps one line about the sand castle in the entry. Using a piece of literature, we demonstrate how writers don't tell unnecessary information. They get right to what they want to say. For example, when Donald Crews writes about his trip to see his grandmother in his book *Bigmama's*, he never tells about packing his bags, buying the tickets, how he got to the train. The book begins with him and his siblings on the train. He only includes the information that is important in telling his story.

Slowing Down a Moment: Young writers often don't realize the power of slowing down an important moment in order to capture a visual of the event as it actually happened or to explain the anticipation they felt. One way to help students develop this skill is to identify moments that actually happen very quickly but are important and need to be slowed down. To do this work, we use a poem called "Foul Shot" by Edwin A. Hoey from the anthology *Opening Days*. This poet skillfully stretches the final two seconds of a basketball game for an entire page-long poem building anticipation while giving vivid images of the events. Students practice this skill by trying to do the same with events such as the moments before reaching the peak on a roller coaster, jumping into an icy pool, waiting for a friend to come for a play date, the moment before the curtain comes up for a debut performance, saying goodbye to a loved one who you won't see for a while, or approaching the finish line at the end of a race.

Using Literature to Practice Particular Styles of Writing

Sometimes a good way to lift the quality of student writing is by deliberately having them practice writing in the style of a mentor they admire. The following excerpt from Karla Kuskin in *Jerusalem, Shining Still* is a wonderful example of powerful comparisons and scene setting.

> *The bread is baked before sunrise. I have seen a loaf that looks like a pair of eyeglasses. And another in the shape of a ladder. Every morning sixty-four kinds of bread are baked here. Every day in these narrow old streets seventy languages are spoken. This is not a very large city. It is far, far away from many that are much larger and newer. Then why should so many people come from everywhere to here? And why should they have been coming here for more than three thousand years?*
>
> *Sit beside me. The sky is getting lighter. The sun comes up behind that ridge. It puts gold on the crescents and stars of the mosques, gold on the crosses of the churches. It touches the Western Wall and turns the old, enormous stones pure white. This is a city made of stone sitting along the tops of stony hills.*

During our minilesson, the students named what this writer did well and proceeded to try to imitate her style of writing in an entry about a place they know very well. The following is our list of what this author does well:

- Writes about a place she knows very well
- Talks to readers as if they are there and makes them feel as if you are the only ones reading this ("Sit beside me.")
- Describes the bread by comparing it to everyday objects (a pair of eyeglasses)
- Uses numbers to be specific and show the contrast of the small city and the many breads and languages ("sixty-four kinds of bread" . . . "seventy languages")
- Asks questions and begins to answer them by describing the beauty of the city and giving information
- Stays with one thing for four to five sentences, using descriptive words to create a clear picture of what she is describing (the bread, the sun)
- Describes the city by taking the reader through the morning and into the night
- Repeats her description of the sun on the the final page the same way as she did on the first page

Figure 8–10 shows Zack's published piece after this study.

In *Nocturne* Jane Yolen uses repetition and word patterns in very surprising ways. Watch what happens when Jacob tries to mimic her style in Figure 8–11A–B. For another example, see Kathy's poem on the website, <www.heinemann.com/davis-hill>.

In her book *Writing Through Childhood*, Shelley Harwayne writes about using a body of work by one author, naming what he does well in each of his books, then sending students off to practice the same in their writing. Jonathan London is one author she likes to use for this work.

Many teachers of writing don't realize that sometimes it is important to do such focused work in the notebook. Many writers will use the right-hand side of the notebook to work in a particular style, as Jacob did with his entry. For others, new topics will emerge from these studies and they will begin new entries. Either way, students are flexing their writing muscles.

Zack S.

My World

My world is where buildings grow high, blocking the sun. My world is where, in the earliest hours of the day, pigeons with small beaks and broad wings peck around just to annoy you. My world is where fresh air is replaced by thick foul air, produced by loud peace-ruining machines. If this is true, why do floods of people come here every day? If you come over here, I'll tell you why people enjoy trips to Manhattan. We still have the rest of the day ahead of us.

When you look beyond the shortage of sun, you can turn to Central Park. All the trees and animals are surely as good as the sun. In Central Park the animals never go to sleep. You can walk around Central Park during the day and scout for squirrels and hawks and look for owls and rats at night. If you're a bird watcher, you'll never forget Central Park. There are actually over 175 species of birds in Manhattan! In fact, I can name a whole bunch of birds off the top of my head: pigeons, hawks, sparrows, cardinals, woodpeckers, and even mocking birds, if you can believe it.

If you're the kind of person who wants to go on a vacation to somewhere very busy, Manhattan's the place. Every day when you wake, the great smell of action is in the air. When you walk outside you quickly spring into action mode. People vigorously rush around you, searching for a taxi to take them to one of Manhattan's 157 fantastic museums. Or they might just be going to one of Manhattan's Chinese, Japanese, Italian, or Mexican restaurants. You can never tell. You fell like there's no beginning and no end.

It's getting late now. I can barely see you in this darkness, but don't worry, the lights of Manhattan are sure to light up sooner or later. Even at night you can have a fun-filled time. You can hop down to Times Square and see a Broadway show, or you can venture just about anywhere and have a peaceful, delightful meal. There are still many, many more positive things about Manhattan, but I'll never have time to name them all. Just come to Manhattan and see for yourself.

FIGURE 8–10. *Zack's published piece influenced by Karla Kuskin's writing.*

FIGURE 8–11A. *Jacob's original notebook entry.*

FIGURE 8–11B. *Jacob attempts to mimic Jane Yolen's style in "Nocturne."*

Highlighting Student Work

Though we have laid out some specific strategies and minilessons for gathering new entries and improving the quality of student writing, we realize that nothing beats looking directly at student work and having conversations with them about their intentions. For this reason, we invite you to meet three more students and look closely at the work of helping them lift the quality of their notebook entries.

Meet Maxine, a prolific writer who:

• knows what she wants to write about, but during her conference we realize she loses focus on many entries and strays from the subject.

Knowing this about herself, Maxine needs to reread her notebook with the intention of focusing her writing. We help this writer focus her writing by using a web.

Conference with Maxine

Teacher: Tell me about your writing, Maxine.

Maxine: It's about how much I love tap dancing.

Teacher: How are you doing that?

Maxine: By showing I love it—How I love the sound—How long I've been doing it.

Teacher: So, you were six when you started?

Maxine: Yes. And I was so short. I couldn't get into a class of kids of my own age, I had to be with much taller, older kids.

Teacher: Maxine, can you show me exactly where you talk about how much you love tap?

Maxine: I guess it's just the first line where I say I love tap.

Teacher: Maxine, it feels like you began to write a piece about how much you love tap but you actually told more about your first class than your love for the dancing. Can you tell me what you love about tap?

Maxine: Well, I love the shoes, the sound they make, performing anywhere I can, proving I can tap, things like that.

Teacher: Maxine, I think if you began a web and wrote "Loving tap" at the center, it would begin to help you focus on the things you like about it, which are the things you began to tell me just now. I think it would help focus your entry on what you said you were writing about in the first place. Do you think that would help?

Maxine: I guess so.

Teacher: So why don't you work on that now and then begin a new entry that focuses more on your love of tap. I'll check in with you later.

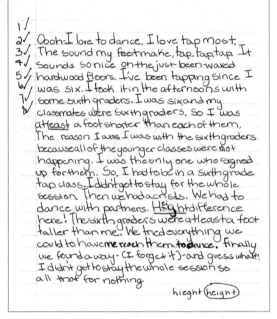

FIGURE 8–12. *Maxine's original notebook entry.*

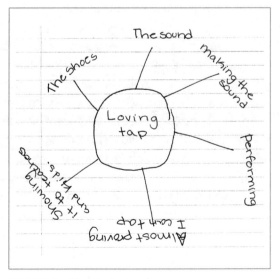

FIGURE 8–13. *Maxine's web.*

1/ "Stop! Stop Maxine, just stop." My mom
2/ angrily whispers into my ear at Liberty
3/ House, a store. I stop abruptly in the middle
4/ of a loud tap routine. I walk into another
5/ part of the store with my shoulders hunched.
6/ I look around. A lightbulb pops into my
7/ head. Dressing room! My shoulders slip up
8/ and I straighten my back. I look both
ways to make sure no one sees me,
then I slip quietly into-okay, I sprint
into the dressing room. I go over another
quieter, longer routine. I love to tap. I'm
also pretty good tapper. So what's so bad
about that?, you ask. Well, I have to
admit, I tap everywhere and get in trouble.
I tap in stores, on the sidewalk, in class
at lunch, at tap class, (at all the wrong
times, like when the teacher says, "quiet
please class") And no matter how much I
like doing it, the grown-ups say quiet! or
shhh or stop Maxine! Stop now. But I
can't stop, because I love it. I keep
tappin' and tappin'. I wanted to be perfect

to get into the more advanced class. —
Even this summer when the tap teacher
accidentally learned that I could tap as
well as some Celebration dance team kids,
and I got the solo, I knew that I wouldn't
be moved up, — But I kept trying. The solo
was a bit annoying when some celebration
boys started pestering me about it, and
when I had to curtsy but something went
wrong and I fell on top of the girl next
to me. (I had to curtsy after my solo -
not my idea, some other kids. But that's
another story. My first tap class when
I was six, I skipped 1 year but I take
one now.

FIGURE 8–14. *Maxine's writing as a result of the conference.*

Minilessons

Helping Writers Stay Focused on an Entry and Develop One Idea

• Use a notebook entry like Maxine's. Begin by saying, "When I read your writer's notebooks I notice that many of you begin to write about one subject and quickly lose your focus as you continue to write the entry. Today I want to talk to you about a writing strategy that might help you focus your work. . . . " We show Maxine's writing and her web, demonstrating for the students how they might try out this strategy in their own writing. "When you go off to write today, I would like you to reread your notebook to find an entry where you might have lost your focus. Once you have decided what it is you *really* want to stick with,

create a web on the right side of your notebook next to that entry. Use the web to help you write a more focused entry."

• Use another student's writing or your own writing. Find other pieces of writing where the writer seems to go back and forth inserting unnecessary information that causes the entry to become unfocused. Have the writer demonstrate for the class how he/she would circle or underline the parts of the entry he/she would include in a more focused piece and to brainstorm the kinds of information that should be included.

Minilessons like these not only help students refocus and lift the quality of the writing already in the notebook, but draw their attention to the need to work at developing a topic. It also helps students understand how to slow down their writing and not be in such a hurry to tell their stories.

You can see from Maxine's second try that the web did in fact help her stay focused on her love for tap dancing. She does veer off at the end and begins to talk about a specific tap dancing experience—indicating that Maxine does need more opportunities to practice staying focused. The more Maxine and other children practice webbing and other strategies to help focus their writing, the more the habit will be developed. Be careful that you help your students to see the web as a way to focus their writing, not broaden their focus.

We understand that the notebook is a place for children to explore topics. As they do so, their minds will take them to other places connected to that topic, as happened with Maxine. These minilessons are not aimed at stopping that, but rather at helping to focus the parts of the entry that deal with what the student really wanted to write about in the first place. It is therefore important that we encourage students to get in the habit of rereading their notebooks with an eye for focusing their ideas. We build into our homework assignments the opportunities for them to reinforce this work. Minilessons are reinforced by ongoing homework assignments that require students to reread old entries to determine what is important. They then write a new entry on the right-hand side using strategies that help them focus their writing.

Meet Alex, a student who:

• writes about important topics and issues, but as you read his notebook, you see the potential for further development of his ideas. We need to help this writer slow down his writing and develop his ideas.

At first glance, Alex's notebook entry seems quite good and in fact if all of our students wrote like this in their notebooks we would be happy campers. However, our job each time we sit down next to a student is to help that student become a better writer by building on what they already know. So we don't just pat them on the back and send them off, we also think about what would take them to their next level as writers.

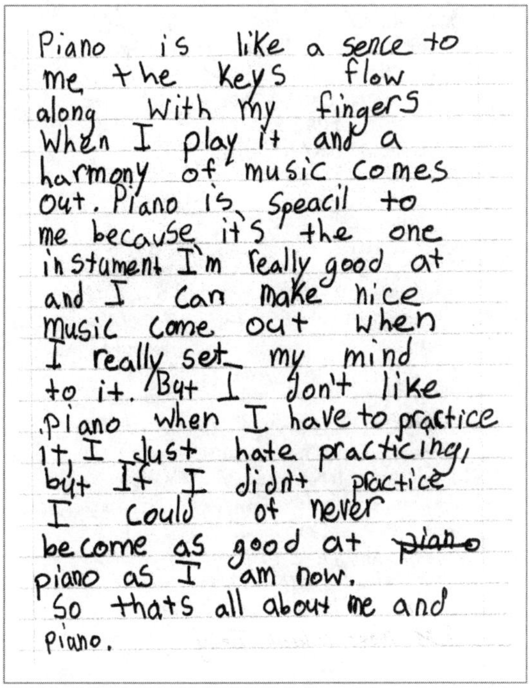

Conference with Alex

Teacher: Alex, I can't help but notice the first line of your entry. "Piano is like a sense to me." That's quite a powerful line. Can you explain what you mean by a sense?

Alex: When I play piano, it's so natural. I feel like I was born to play it.

FIGURE 8–15. *Alex's original notebook entry.*

I started piano when I was four. It was fun and I really liked it. But as I got older I I didn't like practing as much, But I still practiced as much as I ever did.

But I didn't always play the pieces I was suposed to play, I liked to 'mess around a lot making up my on songs, and the songs turned out good too. Now I started really advanced songs like sonatinas and rondos.

But I still complain about practicing as much as ever, ever if I still like to play.

The reason I like piano is, is because it just comes to me natruly which makes my fingers flow with the song most of the time.

In piano I absoulutly hate practicing. Whenever I'm called to practice I'm usually doing stuff like playing legos or watching T.v. finally when I'm sitting down to practice my twin brothers start killing each other (not literally) or watching T.v. When the start doing these things I have the urge to stop playing and join them. finally when I'm done practicing my brothers sudenly finish their games and I never join them. To me, it seems like a curse, that whenever I work they have all the fun, then when I finish the imediatly stop.

However, the case is at certain times I just agree to practice, Just to have the joy of music while playing it. During these rare moments when I do want to play, both of my hands melodies Join as one and the music comes like a whole orci'shtra playing perfectly together. I feel like I'm playing in a Solo Concert I play the best I possibly can and everything turns into one. These are the times when I love to practice

FIGURE 8-16. *Alex's writing after the conference.*

Teacher: I really get the feeling from that line that piano is a big part of your life. But when I look over the rest of the entry, you don't say that much about your piano life. As a matter of fact, before I know it, your piece ends with the line here that says, "that's all about me and piano." Can that really be all there is after such a powerful beginning?

Alex: I just love when I play and the music comes out just right.

Teacher: You talk about hating to practice. Can you say more about why?

Alex: Well, I'm so frustrated because when I have to practice, it seems my brothers are having the best time playing and all I can think about is playing with them. But, I have to practice and by the time I'm done, they're finished with the good game.

Teacher: Alex, I can hear that you have so much more to say about this. You told me so much more about yourself and the piano that if it were written in the entry, you'd be getting closer to figuring out what's really important to you about your music.

Alex: I guess I didn't write all the things I think about it.

Teacher: Are there other things you're thinking now besides what you said about the practicing?

Alex: I guess about how good I feel when I do decide to practice and everything comes out sounding so good.

Teacher: Writers need to find entries that are worthy of slowing down their thinking in order to come to some big understandings. So why don't you go off and try to slow down your thinking by going back to times when you hated practicing and times when you loved practicing. Write about your thoughts and feelings at those times.

Alex: O.K.

Although Alex begins his entry and others like it with big ideas, he fails to pursue his thinking. Writing is hard work, even for our more proficient writers. They tend to want to get their thinking down and be done with it. With this in mind, we need to have our "teacher radar" tuned to those places in their writing that hold potential for deeper thinking, flesh out those thoughts in our conferences, and send the students back to do some more work. Minilessons and conferences like these are our best shot at helping to support writers in acquiring the habit of slowing down their thinking, ultimately leading toward more developed, thoughtful writing.

Minilessons

Helping Writers Develop Their Ideas

- Use a mentor text that helps you point out to students the ways in which the writer has slowed down their writing by including specific details of the experience. In Naomi Shihab Nye's short nonfiction narrative entitled "Mint Snowball" from *In Short*, she slows down her writing by giving specific information about the people and the place.

  My great-grandfather on my mother's side ran a drugstore in a small town in central Illinois. He sold pills and rubbing alcohol from behind the big cash register and creamy ice cream from the soda fountain.

  Other techniques are:

  - telling lots of relevant facts

  - telling their feelings

  - talking about how others involved might have felt

  - describing the place or the people involved

  - describing exactly what they were doing and why

  Point out to the children how weak the piece would be without these specific details.

- Put student writing on the overhead, reading along with the children to see places where that writer could slow down their thinking. Actually create the opportunity for the writer to add the information into the piece.

- Show a piece of your own writing where you have left out lots of details. Talk to the children about the quality of the writing. Then, show them a more detailed piece about the same topic and discuss the difference and the power of the more developed writing. Share your thinking about why you chose to include those details and how they make for a more highly developed piece of writing. Instruct the students to go back and find a piece of writing in their notebooks where they can insert more information to develop their writing. Make sure you let them know that when you come around to confer, you'll be interested in hearing why they made their decisions. Clearly, lots of your conferences at this point will be about helping writers decide what details to include.

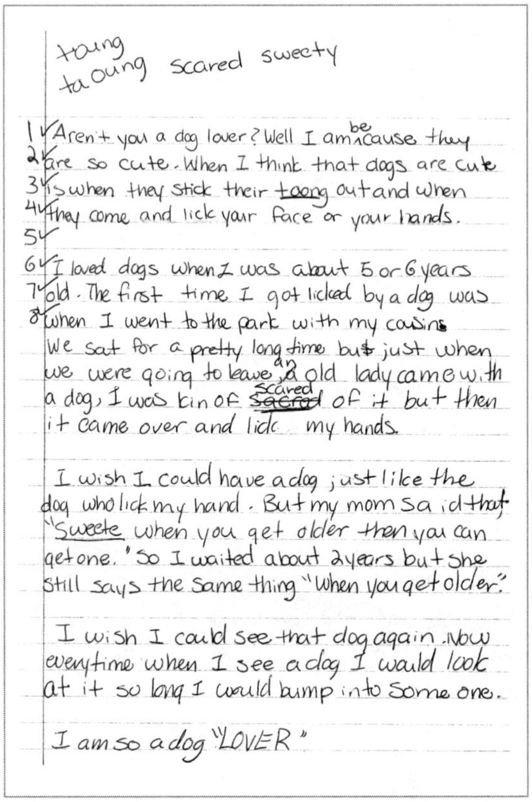

FIGURE 8–17. *You Xiao Dan's original notebook entry.*

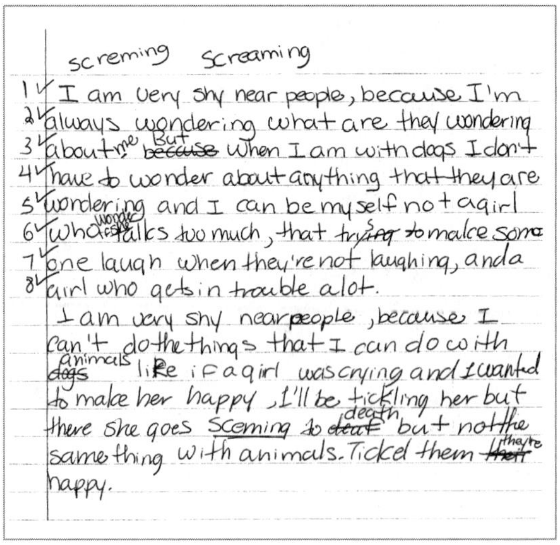

FIGURE 8–18. *You Xiao Dan's writing as a result of this conference.*

Meet You Xiao Dan, a second language learner who:

• loves to write, but does not realize that writers need to get to the importance of events in their lives. We help her ask questions to decide the importance of the events she writes about and get to the heart of her writing.

Conference with You Xiou Dan

Teacher: I see you're writing about being a dog lover.

You Xiao Dan: Yes, I really love dogs.

Teacher: What have you written about why you really love dogs?

You Xiao Dan: I've written how cute they are, how they lick you, how much I really want a dog and my mom says over and over again, when I'm older I can have a dog. I don't think she will ever get me one.

Teacher: You know, if I asked the other children in the class if they wanted a dog, they'd all say yes and tell me the same things you just told me. I am wondering what's so important for you about getting a dog that would be different from every other kid who writes about wanting a pet?

You Xiao Dan: Well, you can do anything you want with a dog.

Teacher: Say more about that.

You Xiao Dan: You can be silly, you can say anything you want, you never have to wonder about what they're thinking about you.

Teacher: What does that tell you about your relationship with dogs?

You Xiao Dan: I feel more comfortable with dogs. I'm kind of shy around people.

Teacher: You Xiou Dan, that feels very important. That's the story you should be writing about. What you need to know is, as a writer, you need to question why you write the things you do to get to the things that are really important. So, when you go back to write today, see if you can write to discover more about the really important reasons why you want a dog.

You Xiao Dan: O.K.

When the teacher asked You Xiao Dan the strategic question, "I am wondering what's so important for you about getting a dog that would be different from every other kid who writes about wanting a pet?" she was leading her to do the kind of thinking that would help her make her writing more specific. In addition, when the teacher helped the student clarify her thinking by saying, "What does that tell you about your relationship with dogs?" it was at that moment that the real discovery occurred. That questioning opened up a new window into her thinking and her own understanding of her topic.

Keep in mind that these minilessons and conferences come as a result of the work our students were doing during this cycle. Through our regular conferences and careful recordkeeping, we pay very close attention to the types of problems some children are having and assume that others are having the same issues. Remember that your students are evolving as writers in many different ways. Some will still need the types of basic conferences we modeled and discussed in Chapter 6.

Minilessons

Helping Writers Get to the Heart of Their Writing

• **Share Information by Creating a Chart:** Say to the children, "During this cycle we have been talking a lot about not just listing facts you already know, but rather writing to discover why the facts you have included are important. One way to write to discover is to ask yourself questions that help you think about what you have written. I have made a list of some of the questions that have helped many of you during our conferences. . . . "

Asking Questions to Find Out What You Really Want to Say

♦ Why am I writing about this now?

♦ Why is this important to me?

♦ What am I really trying to say?

♦ How is my experience with my topic different from someone else's?

♦ What details would help me tell my story?

♦ Which part of my writing stands out as a possible big idea?

♦ What have I discovered from this experience that feels bigger than just the story?

♦ What's behind the story?

"Boys and girls, when you go off to write today, I want you to make sure that whatever you choose to write about, you ask yourself these kinds of questions until you are satisfied that you have written what's really important."

• **Using Student Writing:** Prepare a transparency ahead of time and display the student's entry on the overhead. Ask the class to ask questions from the chart in order to help the writer discover what's really important about the topic he has chosen to write about. As the writer shares his/her thinking out loud, record the responses. Take some time to pause and reflect with the student on whether or not his/her responses are helping the writer to get to the importance of the topic.

Deepening the Thought

By the time you are ready to take on this work, you should be seeing the footprints of your teaching and beginning to notice that the intentions you had for your students are in fact becoming the intentions they have for their own writing. They are writing because they understand that the notebook is a place to capture what they want to say and for uncovering new thinking. So rereading the notebook as a source for new ideas has likely become second nature, and it is often the first thing the students do each day when they set out to write. They understand that when they linger with ideas they have already written, it brings them closer to discovering the importance of the piece and helps to clarify their thinking.

We are reminded of the year-long goals we set in Chapter 1, helping our writers have intentions for what they want to say, and how they want to say it. All the work we have done so far comes into play as we begin to ask students to question their ideas and to write to discover what is truly important. This work is at the heart of all good writing. Kids who have stories to tell will always be telling their stories—they will forever be describing and observing things and writing descriptively. But we cannot just settle for that. It's time to push them to think about how they fit into the bigger picture of the world. Just like we provided the practice for them to find ideas, we must provide the practice for them to do this deeper work. Again, we rely on literature to help our students see what good writers do and how to get to the heart of what they want to say. Good writing is not just about telling stories with lots of details or describing a person or a place with the use of beautiful language, but is also about discovering and writing about the importance of those stories so they matter to the reader. Shelley Harwayne says it so well in *Lifetime Guarantees* when she declares, ". . . we've come to realize the 'me, too' feeling we often get when we've read something powerful is no small thing." The following are some more ways in which we continue to support students in their effort to deepen their thinking, bring clarity to their ideas, and organize their writing.

Using Mentor Texts

We turn to slightly more sophisticated writing to hopefully push our students to think beyond the world of the story. While some of these pieces are clearly written with an adult audience in mind, they allow us to look for the bigger ideas and issues the writers want us to be left thinking about. We look to editorials in newspapers, letters to the editor, children's and adult magazines, the end-paper sections of newspapers, as well as picture books with bigger messages. We are forever grateful to Shelley Harwayne for her voracious appetite for reading the newspaper. We would often find a clipping in our mailboxes with her handwritten, "FYI. Thought your students could do some big thinking about this."

"The World of a Child in an Old Chair," by Hank Lubsen (see Figure 8–19) is a newspaper piece that our students immediately relate to. In this piece, the writer sets out to tell the story of an old chair the family had inherited. Their plan to reupholster the chair fizzled as their son took a liking to it and the chair became his source for many imaginary adventures. Years went by (the chair still not

The World of a Child in an Old Chair

By HANK LUBSEN

MY wife's great aunt passed away, and we were given a chance to look over her old furniture before it was sold. So off we went to Aunt Gertie's apartment way up in the Bronx where we chose a beautiful mahogany bedroom set from the 1920's. We were heading toward the door when Linda stopped before a big old comfortable chair. It had wooden legs and arm rests and was upholstered in a beige, green, peach and orange floral pattern.

"That," I said, "is one ugly chair."

"The chair itself is not really ugly," Linda countered. "It's the pattern. All we have to do is get it upholstered."

We rented a U-haul, filled it with our booty and brought it back to our apartment in Brooklyn. The bedroom set went into the master bedroom, and we put the chair in the living room, right next to the TV. We stood back, trying to visualize the chair upholstered in something new and tasteful.

Then our year-old son Nicholas threw his milk bottle on the seat cushion, hoisted himself up, grabbed the bottle, took a swig, leaned back, looked at us and smiled. In our turn, Linda and I laughed, suddenly recognizing the folly of putting new upholstery in a living room inhabited by a 1-year-old.

Nicholas quickly made the big ugly chair his own. Over the last few years be has slept, eaten and played on the chair. The grape juice and apple sauce stains bear witness.

The chair has served as his pirate ship, which he has navigated through a sea of carpeting. With a blanket draped over its back and attached to a nearby door knob, the chair has made an excellent tent, a base camp from which Nicholas has explored the jungles and deserts of our living room.

> Adults see furniture. A child sees a pirate ship to navigate a sea of carpeting.

There have even been times when Nicholas has come right out and said, "Daddy, I really love my chair."

One day I was sitting with him in the chair when, starting to get up, I leaned on the arm rest too hard and heard the wood crack.

Linda let out a yell, ran for the wood glue and frantically set about repairing the damage.

"Relax," I said. "It's just a chair." She looked up at me sadly, and I quickly realized my mistake. The chair had become so intertwined with our son's early years that it was clearly much more than "just a chair."

Nicholas is 4 now, and when he sits on the chair his feet already reach the edge of the cushion. I wonder how long it will be before his knees bend over the edge and his feet hit the floor.

There will come a day, I know, when he won't remember how he once felt about the chair. There will also come a day when we'll practically have to tie him down just to get him to sit with us for a while in the living room.

After that he will be off to live his own life.

And then one day Linda will walk in the front door with fabric swatches. She will spread out the swatches on the chair and we will stand back to examine the different colors and patterns. She will point to one and say, "How about that?" And I'll say, "Looks fine."

So we will finally get the chair upholstered. We will be careful to keep the wood polished. We'll even proclaim a new house rule: "Hey, we just spent all this money to redo the chair, so no eating or drinking on it."

But as I think of the years ahead of us, and imagine the new splendor of the chair, my heart sinks. Because what we would really like is to stop time and keep our little boy and his ugly chair in our living room forever.

FIGURE 8–19. *Reprint of a newspaper story used as a mentor text.*

reupholstered) and the little boy's legs gradually grew to reach the end of the cushion—a reality check for the parents that he would one day be off on his own. Many students wrote about things that are special to them—things they could never imagine getting rid of; imaginary games they've played; places in their homes that had special meaning. After our students had done their personal response to this piece, we reread "The World of a Child in an Old Chair" to begin our focused work of this cycle—to help students deepen the thinking behind their writing. We examined the piece from beginning to end. We noticed the writer moved his writing in the following way:

• When they first got the chair

• How their son Nicholas used the chair

• How important the chair had become to the family—"not just a chair."

• Nicholas "now" (the present time—at four years old) in the chair

• Nicholas growing up, losing interest in the chair

• The chair in the future—finally reupholstered

• What all of this is making the writer think about, ". . . want to stop time and keep our little boy and his chair in our living room forever." Change is inevitable.

For the students, their thoughts on this piece were: change is hard; change always comes; it's hard for parents to watch their kids grow up.

From this analysis, the students noticed that Hank Lubsen didn't stop at telling the memories he had of his son playing in the old chair. If Hank Lubsen had simply told the story of the chair without telling what it meant to him, it would have been just an okay "old chair" story. If he had only told the meaning without telling the story of the chair, the piece wouldn't have been as meaningful to the reader. They concluded that he needed to tell *both* parts in order to impact the reader. Having our students come to this understanding through our analysis and discussion of the piece was only the beginning of the work for this cycle.

The students agreed that they were not yet exploring their topics completely or writing about the significance of their stories.

Extending the Work to Student Writing

We continued to do this work on big ideas throughout the beginning of this cycle with picture books, short texts, and poems where the big idea isn't always obvious. We tried to categorize our thinking by asking students to connect the story that the writer was telling to the big idea the author wants to convey. By doing this work with texts they were familiar with, we modeled how to look at the stories in their notebooks to begin to connect the writing to their own big ideas.

Minilessons

Developing Student Writing

Questioning the Writing

Learning to ask questions about our own writing is one of the ways of deepening our thought. We began this very important work with You Xiao Dan and continue to encourage students to reread their notebooks with these probing questions in their heads. We also want our students to be thinking about these questions when they are writing new entries. They should be asking these questions as a regular practice in their efforts to deepen their thought. We must model those questioning strategies in our conferences and minilessons. Please refer to You Xiao Dan's conference earlier in this chapter on page 116, and keep in mind that this work continues through all future writing cycles.

Modeling Trains of Thought

Judy modeled how she took the personal connection she made to *The World of a Child* and began to develop a series of entries. As she showed each of the entries, she jotted the big idea of each on a horizontal chart resembling a train. That is how the term "train of thought" came to be the term her class used to describe the work you do when you push your mind to see other possible ideas—letting the big ideas in one entry lead to big ideas for another, and so on, and so on. This modeling led to great conversations about the way a writer can look at his/her own writing and do the same. Judy stayed with this train of thought over the course of a few days, developing three entries off that first. You can see how far she strayed from the original idea of Meredith playing imaginary games in her room to the notion of change in her life. Not only did Judy model her train of thought, but also how she decided what she really was trying to say and let that idea drive her subsequent entries. See Figures 8-20a-d.

After Judy's model, the students began to see how they needed to look closely at their own writing to do the same. One of the things that supports our teaching is having a keen eye toward the students in the class who pick up on what we are trying to do. The support we get from using their work becomes an essential part of our minilessons and is shown in the following notebook entries.

Meredith spent a great deal of her young years in her own imaginary world, the world she created under blankets draped across bookcases, tucked into drawers, supported by chairs and storage crates. No board game, no doll, no puzzle, no book could captivate or lure her as the world she created under the covers. There were times I was invited in with a shout of "Mom, come see." But at other times, I was left to eavesdrop at the door. I delighted in the dialogue of friendly tea parties, marveled at her knowledge as she played teacher to an audience of stuffed animals & dolls, laughed at the silly verses she sang as she strummed the guitar she never actually practiced but substituted for a toy and sometimes, I was chilled to the bone as she played out a battle of wills we'd had days before. Oh, how I wish life was as simple for her now.

FIGURE 8–20A. *Judy's writing about her daughter.*

Dear Mer,

I'm sitting in my office trying to write. Not having much luck, though. So, I'm taking lots of breaks. During these, I find myself looking around this office. It's funny how today, I'm not seeing the piles of workshop materials that need to be organized. I'm not beating myself up for not exercising as I study the treadmill that sits closed against the wall. I am, however, haunted by the memories this room holds. I'm feeling melancholy and seem to be missing you. But how, I wonder, is that possible when I see you so often and we speak on the phone at least once a day. Of course I realize, I don't miss the adult you but the you I rocked to sleep in this room, the you who built tents with the bed and bookcase and invited me in for tea parties, the you who constructed imaginary worlds on this very floor using old scraps of yarn and Smurfs. I miss the sounds of Really Rosie as it played over & over again and the rhythmic tunes of Bob Marley and I even miss you laughing while I sang the wrong words. If I listen hard enough, I can still hear you chanting those made up songs you wrote when you were supposed to be practicing the guitar.

I want you to know you mean the world to me and I cherish each and every moment (good & bad, bad & not so much) we shared, each smile was special, each hug divine.

I love you and hope that someday, you'll share wonderful times with your children.

Mom

FIGURE 8–20B. *Judy's subsequent entry.*

I'm feeling very old these days. My hair is turning gray, my joints ache and I discover new lines on my face each day. I have a daughter who is 30 and a husband who will turn 60 in July. How can this be? How could time have passed so quickly? There was a time when everyone around me wasn't younger. I was the youngest teacher on the staff when I started teaching. I can still remember that feeling of naivety I felt when I was a young bride and Ira's business associates were older and had life's experiences – had traveled to exotic places. I felt worldly if I managed to get out of Brooklyn. Even when I gave birth to Meredith, I was the youngest mother in the playground.

All that has changed. Wherever I turn, wherever I go, everyone is younger. When my parents were my age, I considered them old. They were grandparents already. I look in the mirror and I see my mother. I don't feel old, though. I still love the same music and dance the same steps as I did at my Sweet 16. I still giggle like a school girl when my girlfriends & I get together. I still enjoy the same silly, sappy movies and cry just as easily, maybe easier.

So, what is considered old these days? Is it what's happening to your body or what's going on in your head?

FIGURE 8–20C. *Another journal entry from Judy.*

I've always resisted change. I've been afraid of it, I suppose. We've lived in the same apartment for 26 years. Testing new waters in a new place always seemed too scary. Even something as simple as changing hairstyles is traumatic for me. It took me five years to decide to get my hair permed. By the time I mustered up the courage to do it, straight hair was back in style. I don't understand the saying "The more things change the more they stay the same." I'm thinking I'm me feel like there is change coming and nothing is going to be the same. I'm thinking about retiring. My whole career has been the classroom. What will this change bring?

When you've maintained the status quo for so long, change becomes paralyzing. I admire people who have allowed themselves the flexibility to change jobs every few years, to move to new places and even change their appearance without the angst I feel when I'm faced with even the smallest change. I wonder if it's too late for me? Will I make the most of this new change in my life?

FIGURE 8–20D. *The last entry by Judy to demonstrate her "train of thought" sequence.*

Highlighting Student Work

Meet Eliza, a writer who:

- collected many well-written entries in her notebook about a variety of topics, but who was often simply retelling stories and needed to deepen her thinking. "The World of a Child in an Old Chair" inspired Eliza to write about her family purchasing a couch. After reading this mentor text, Eliza predictably retold the story of her family's experience shopping for a new couch.

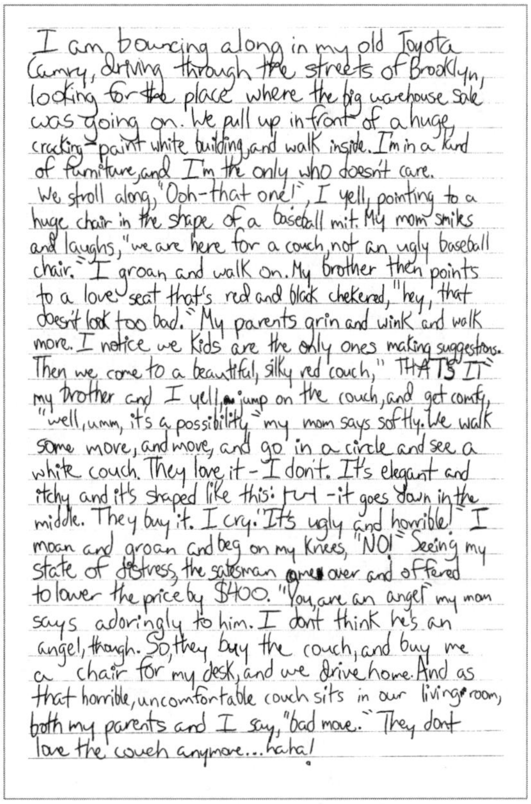
I am bouncing along in my old Toyota Camry, driving through the streets of Brooklyn, looking for the place where the big warehouse sale was going on. We pull up in front of a huge, cracking-paint white building, and walk inside. I'm in a kind of furniture, and I'm the only who doesn't care. We stroll along, "Ooh-that one!", I yell, pointing to a huge chair in the shape of a baseball mit. My mom smiles and laughs, "we are here for a couch, not an ugly baseball chair." I groan and walk on. My brother then points to a love seat that's red and black chekered, "hey, that doesn't look too bad." My parents grin and wink and walk more. I notice we Kids are the only ones making suggestions. Then we come to a beautiful, silky red couch, "THAT'S IT" my brother and I yell, jump on the couch, and get comfy, "well, umm, it's a possibility" my mom says softly. We walk some more, and move, and go in a circle and see a white couch. They love it - I don't. It's elegant and itchy and it's shaped like this: -it goes down in the middle. They buy it. I cry. "It's ugly and horrible!" I moan and groan and beg on my knees, "NO!" Seeing my state of distress, the salesman comes over and offered to lower the price by $400. "You, are an angel" my mom says adoringly to him. I dont think he's an angel, though. So, they buy the couch, and buy me a chair for my desk, and we drive home. And as that horrible, uncomfortable couch sits in our living room, both my parents and I say, "bad move." They dont love the couch anymore...haha!

FIGURE 8–21. *Eliza's notebook entry.*

Conference with Eliza

Teacher: We've been working on developing trains of thought off our notebook entries. How has that work been going for you?

Eliza: Well, I have been writing about my brother. First I wrote about what a pain he is. Then I wrote about the time he was sick and how I began to feel guilty about the times I was mean to him. Then I began to write about middle school and what that might be like. (She turns to those pages and shows the entries.)

Teacher: What are you working on today?

Eliza: I am rereading this entry about buying a new couch to see if I can find the bigger idea.

Teacher: What strategy are you using to help you do that?

Eliza: I'm just rereading.

Teacher: Sometimes, you can get to bigger ideas behind the story by identifying a part or a line that feels like it could get your thinking going. Is there a part in your entry that could do that?

Eliza: (Takes time to reread again.) This part here where I say, "Ha, Ha."

Teacher: What is that about?

Eliza: It's really saying, "I told you so."

Teacher: What do you really mean by "I told you so"?

Eliza: When they were buying that couch, I told them not to and they didn't listen to me. Now, they're sorry and every time they make a comment about how uncomfortable it is, in my head I think, "I told you so. You think you're always right. Sometimes you should listen to me about things."

Teacher: Just by identifying and thinking about the part that sticks out and what that means, you were able to take your thinking further. Let that new idea be the beginning of your train of thought and see where it takes you.

Eliza: O.K. I'll try.

By showing Eliza how to develop a train of thought, she was moved from telling the story of simply buying a couch to an entry about the role her parents play in her life, and ultimately to her perspective about how difficult it must be to be a parent. In her work with teachers, Sharon emphasizes that though we are raising the bar, all writers need to start some place, which may mean starting with the simple retelling of a story like Eliza did. The work in our minilessons and our conferences is to help our students go beyond retelling so they can get to their big ideas for those topics they choose to explore further in their notebooks. In future minilessons and share sessions we will highlight the strategy we taught Eliza to scaffold the work of the class.

This work raised the bar for all future notebook writing. Our students now knew how to dig deeper for ideas. It is interesting to note, when our students were publishing feature articles later in the year, the work that best supported their topic choices were those entries that were the outgrowths of the work with trains of thought. Eliza continued to stay with the topic of her parents and began thinking about how little time they actually have to spend together and subsequently published a feature article from that work. (See Chapter 11 for discussion of Feature Articles.)

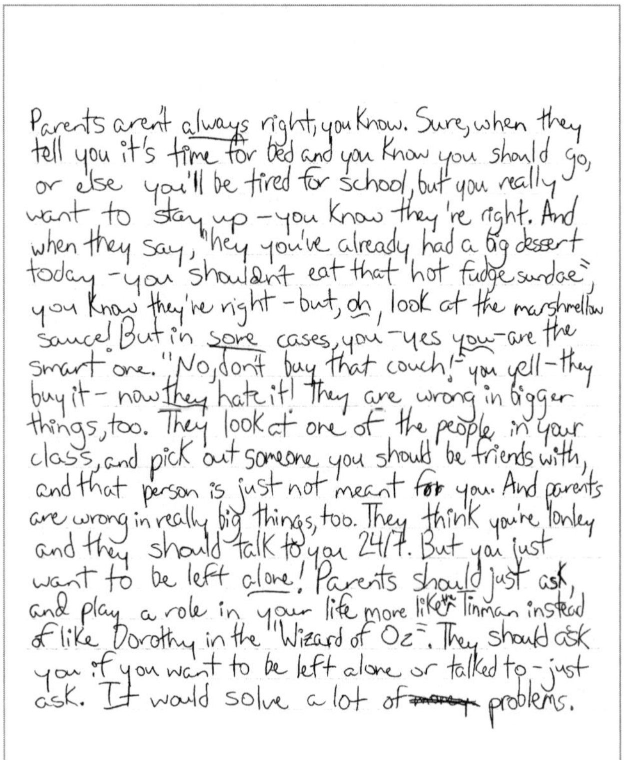

Parents aren't always right, you know. Sure, when they tell you it's time for bed and you know you should go, or else you'll be tired for school, but you really want to stay up—you know they're right. And when they say, "hey you've already had a big dessert today—you shouldn't eat that hot fudge sundae", you know they're right—but, oh, look at the marshmellow sauce! But in some cases, you—yes you—are the smart one. "No, don't buy that couch!" you yell—they buy it—now they hate it! They are wrong in bigger things, too. They look at one of the people in your class, and pick out someone you should be friends with, and that person is just not meant for you. And parents are wrong in really big things, too. They think you're lonley and they should talk to you 24/7. But you just want to be left alone! Parents should just ask, and play a role in your life more like the Tinman instead of like Dorothy in the "Wizard of Oz". They should ask you if you want to be left alone or talked to—just ask. It would solve a lot of problems.

FIGURE 8–22A. *Eliza's writing after the conference.*

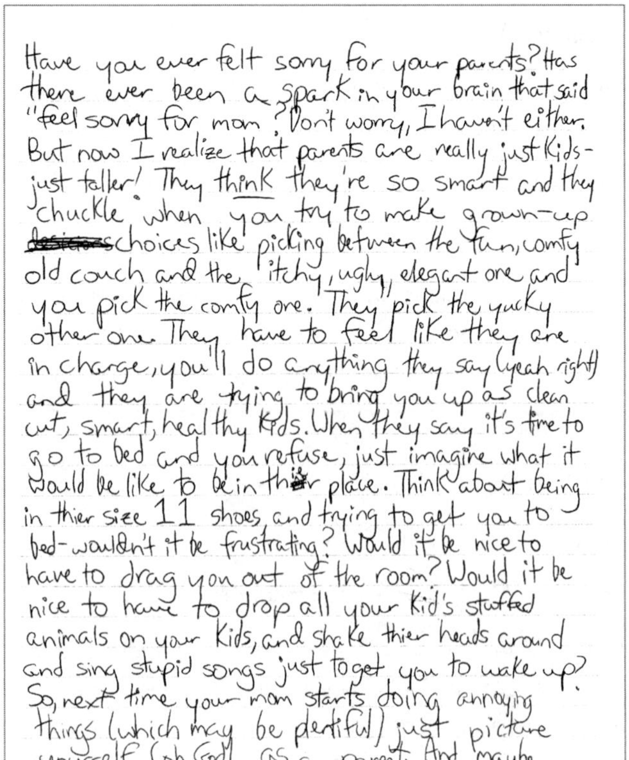

Have you ever felt sorry for your parents? Has there ever been a spark in your brain that said "feel sorry for mom"? Don't worry, I haven't either. But now I realize that parents are really just kids—just taller! They think they're so smart and they chuckle when you try to make grown-up choices like picking between the fun, comfy old couch and the "itchy, ugly, elegant one" and you pick the comfy one. They pick the yucky other one. They have to feel like they are in charge, you'll do anything they say (yeah right) and they are trying to bring you up as clean cut, smart, healthy kids. When they say it's time to go to bed and you refuse, just imagine what it would be like to be in their place. Think about being in thier size 11 shoes, and trying to get you to bed—wouldn't it be frustrating? Would it be nice to have to drag you out of the room? Would it be nice to have to drop all your kid's stuffed animals on your kids, and shake thier heads around and sing stupid songs just to get you to wake up? So, next time your mom starts doing annoying things (which may be plentiful) just picture yourself (oh God) as a parent. And maybe, maybe just cut them some slack.

FIGURE 8–22B. *Eliza's second entry in the train of thought.*

Finding Issues That Influence Our Lives

To support our students in seeing how their personal lives fit in with the bigger picture of issues in the world, we brainstormed issues that are important to them and developed a list. By doing this, it gave our students a bigger pool of ideas to draw from. We typed this list and gave it to the students to paste in the back of their notebooks or to keep in their writing folders. This should not be viewed as writing prompts, but rather as a way of helping students see the stories they have been telling in a different way. Our class developed the list shown in Figure 8–23.

FIFTH-GRADE ISSUES WE CAN WRITE ABOUT

- Sibling rivalry
  - being an only child
  - older sibling/role model
  - special issues concerning being a twin
  - middle child
  - youngest/picked on or babied/searching for identity in a large family

- Parent issues
  - disagree about things that affect you
  - being overprotective
  - enforcing rules that you think don't work or aren't fair
  - responsibilities of being a parent

- Hobbies and passions
  - time to spend practicing or collecting
  - being a team player
  - being on a losing team

- After school
  - time limitations
  - homework pressures
  - being overprogrammed

- Growing up
  - last year in elementary school
  - worries about middle school
  - setting expectations for yourself and meeting them
  - meeting the expectations set by others
  - having mixed feelings about growing up
  - understanding the difference between need and want

- World
  - situations in New York that affect our life
  - war in other parts of the world
  - how we can make the world a better place
  - understanding how the economy affects us
  - the issues of others less fortunate than us

- Money
  - allowance
  - being charitable
  - high prices of things we want

FIGURE 8-23. *The class-generated Bigger Ideas list.*

Highlighting Student Work

We invite you to follow Jonathan through some of the stages of the publishing cycle as he works to lift the quality of his writing and, as a result, comes to some big understandings. See Figure 8–24A–D. See our website for all of Jonathan's work from notebook entry to published piece and Writing Reflection. You will also find published work from other students that reflect the work of these cycles on our website, <www.heinemann.com/davis-hill>.

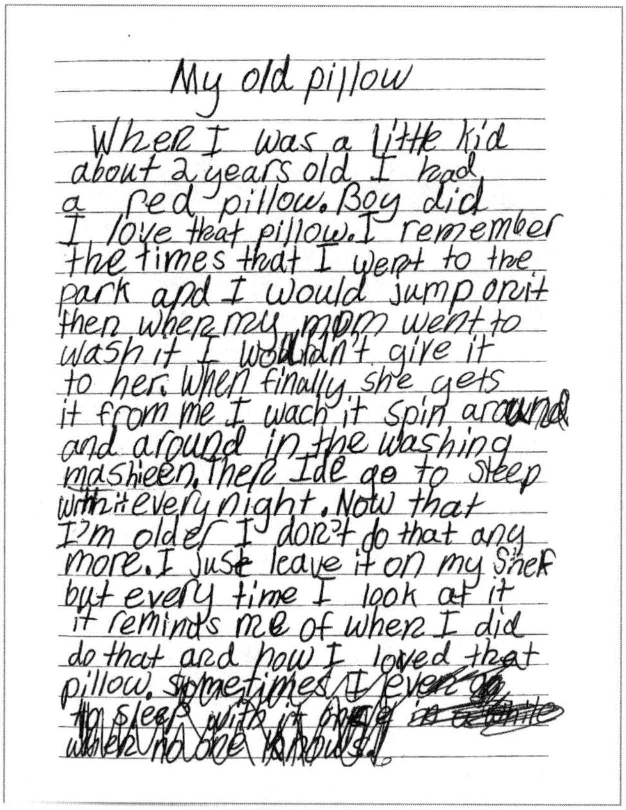

My old pillow

When I was a little kid about 2 years old I had a red pillow. Boy did I love that pillow. I remember the times that I went to the park and I would jump on it then when my mom went to wash it I wouldn't give it to her. When finally she gets it from me I wach it spin around and around in the washing masheen. Then I'de go to sleep with it every night. Now that I'm older I don't do that any more. I just leave it on my shelf but every time I look at it it reminds me of when I did do that and how I loved that pillow. Sometimes I even go to sleep with it every when nobody knows.

FIGURE 8–24A. *Jonathan's initial entry.*

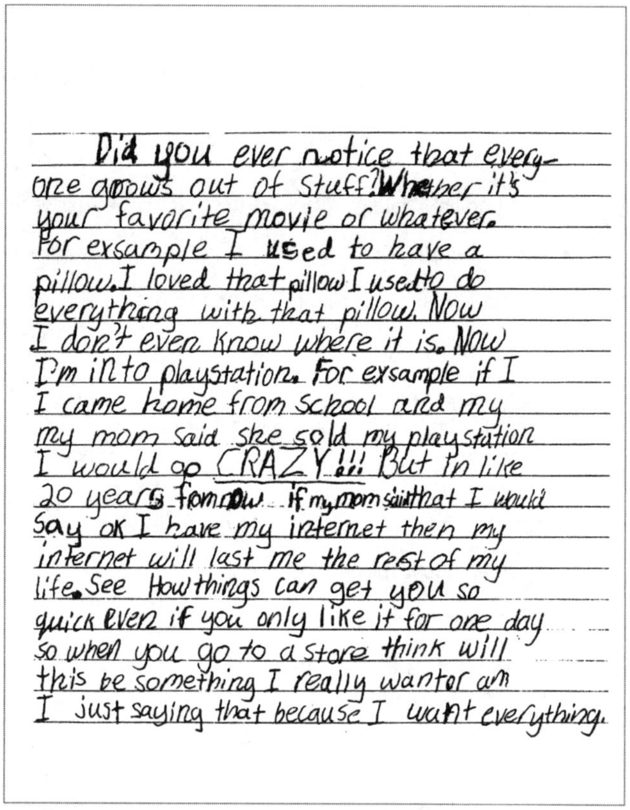

Did you ever notice that everyone grows out of stuff? Whether it's your favorite movie or whatever. For exsample I used to have a pillow. I loved that pillow I use to do everything with that pillow. Now I don't even know where it is. Now I'm into playstation. For exsample if I I came home from school and my my mom said she sold my playstation I would go CRAZY!!! But in like 20 years from now if my mom said that I would say ok I have my internet then my internet will last me the rest of my life. See How things can get you so quick even if you only like it for one day so when you go to a store think will this be something I really want or am I just saying that because I want everything.

FIGURE 8–24B. *Another entry on the same topic.*

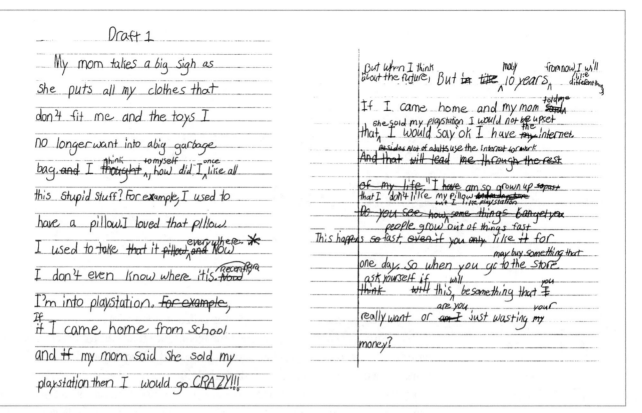

FIGURE 8-24C. *Jonathan's first draft.*

Jonathan C.

NOTHING LASTS FOREVER

My mom takes a big sigh as she puts my outgrown clothes and old toys in a big garbage bag. I think to myself, "How did I once like all this stupid stuff?" For example, I used to have a pillow. I loved that pillow. I used to take it everywhere. I took it to the park, to the laundry and to sleepovers at my sister's house. You would never find me without my pillow. Now, I don't even know where it is.

I watch as she tosses all my Legos and know something has changed. I used to spend hours building castles for my toy soldiers, wagons to carry my Lego people and imaginary space stations that I imagined one day I'd travel to.

Recently, I've gotten into Playstation. If I came home from school and my mom said she sold my Playstation, I'd go crazy. But when I think about the future, maybe ten years from now, I'll be into different things and my addiction to Playstation will just be a fond memory.

When you're a kid, you outgrow things really quickly; even things you really loved and thought you'd never give up. But in life, things are constantly changing. You get older, and your interests change. You never think of your Legos or your pillow, only what you're interested in now. Maybe all we can do is be thankful that we had it then and keep the fond memories long after you toss the things.

FIGURE 8-24D. *Jonathan's final, published piece.*

9

Mastering the Magic of Revision

There is magic behind good writing. It is called *revision*. Good writing happens when writers learn and consistently practice the techniques that lead to their best work. The writing process, though presented in stages with drafting followed by revision, is not really sequential. Revision first begins in the mind even as we attempt to crystallize our thoughts and write words onto the page. Even as our students compose drafts, revision begins as they sift through ideas, images, and phrases that naturally float through their heads. Once the words are down on the page, we expect our students to revisit their writing to improve the content and the craft. The work of revision is reconciling the differences between the intentions the writer has in mind and what is actually written on the page. In helping our students do this deliberate work, we teach them how to revise the content and craft their writing. A good time for focusing on craft studies is during the revision stage of each cycle.

Attending to the Mechanics

Knowing that revising can be messy work, we begin by providing writers with strategies to make the changes without having to do several rewrites. We teach them how to use various mechanical devices that allow them to add on, insert, delete, and reorganize information.

Making Changes	
REVISION PLAN	DEVICE
a) To delete and add text on the line in tight spots b) Adding text using the margins, top/bottom of the page, or separate page to add text	a) Cross out text using one line then use carets to make insertions b) Arrows, asterisks, letters, and numbers *Continued on page 129*

Making Changes, *Continued*	
REVISION PLAN	DEVICE
c) Adding new text or reorganizing text by using separate strips or larger pieces of paper. d) Earmarking designated portions of the text the writer wishes to keep, expand on, transfer to other places, or return to think about later.	c) Cutting and pasting, stapling the text to the relevant parts of the draft. d) Circling or underlining those parts.

focusing on the Content

Our students need to learn to reread their drafts with an eye toward identifying the key information they have presented. They must learn how to pay attention to developing and conveying the meaning they intend by presenting information with a clear focus, clarity of thought, coherence in the development and organization, and with accuracy.

Revision Strategies	
REVISION INTENTION	STRATEGY
Providing content that is focused	• Delete information that is not necessary. • Reread to see what is missing or what needs to be added to make your point. • Look for places where you have provided unnecessary information and delete it. • Reread notebook entries gathered around the topic and circle portions that need to be added to the draft. • Look for places where you have been vague and provide specific examples. • Try using some dialogue, not only narration, as a way of providing information. *Continued on page 130*

Revision Strategies, *Continued*

REVISION INTENTION	STRATEGY
Developing ideas and organizing information	• Reread to check the flow of information. Has all the information been included? • Revisit a flowchart to see how the draft holds up against your plan. • Work on transitions—does the writing move smoothly from one idea to the next, or one period of time to the next? • Find a part of the writing that is strong and build the rest of the writing from that. • Try beginning in different places other than what seems to be the natural beginning—try beginning at the place you would naturally save for the end. • Reorganize the information by circling chunks and rearranging them. • Put away your draft and start a new one.
Clarity—making your point	• Circle or underline parts that are confusing. • Ask someone else to read your draft and let you know where it is confusing to them.
Authenticity/believability	• Read to see if the information is believable.
Accuracy	• Read to make sure you have said what you want to say and that the information you have presented is accurate.

Focusing on Craft

Craft is how you say what you have to say. It is the writer's way of working with language in order to give each piece its own unique design. It plays on the reader's literary senses, creating sensory images, stirring emotions, setting the mood, and supporting the voice of the piece. With craft, the writer creates images, controls time, and brings life to the words on the page.

One aspect of craft is how words are arranged to structure sentences, paragraphs, stanzas, or the whole piece. Sentences don't always begin with the subject followed by the verb. How empowering it is when students come to know they can play around with the order of words in a sentence, the order of sentences in a paragraph, or choose to repeat a line as a way of structuring an entire piece!

A good storyteller must not only have stories to tell, but must also know the art of telling them well. So, too, a good writer must not only find good topics and organize her thoughts according to her intentions, but must also know how to artfully use words to transmit the very essence of what she is trying to convey.

Goals of a Craft Study

The following are our intentions for this study:

• Getting students to pay special attention to **how** they say what they want to say

• Developing their ability to read a mentor text for the purpose of noticing craft

• Identifying and naming a variety of crafting techniques

• Identifying the purposes of a variety of crafting techniques

• Internalizing craft study by:

  ◆ having specific intentions for craft in their writing

  ◆ practicing the techniques in their writing

• Trying out different structures for sentences, paragraphs/stanzas, the whole piece

Deciding Which Craft to Study

When we study the craft in various texts, we inevitably notice a wide variety of strategies that authors use. It is in our best interest to be selective about the ones we decide to invest our time and efforts in studying. The following criteria help us decide:

• Does a study of that particular craft hold great potential for lifting the quality of the students' writing?

• Are the techniques we choose developmentally appropriate?

• Is the purpose behind the craft applicable to the kind of writing the students are doing and their intentions as well?

- Do you notice that students are already making attempts at using the craft in their writing and therefore benefiting from a study focused on developing their understanding of its purpose and improving their expertise at using it?

- Do you have a collection of mentor texts that offer an abundance of examples of the craft?

Steps in a Craft Study

We start off by selecting a text familiar to our students. Their familiarity is important because we want to focus on the craft and not the story. So we make sure they have had the opportunity to enjoy the story and discuss it prior to using it as a text for a craft study. Using an overhead projector, we revisit the piece to carefully study the writer's craft from beginning to end. We teach students how to read the piece as *writers,* paying special attention to how the writer uses language. We clearly make the distinction that our focus at this time is on the *craft* and not on the *content.* We cannot take you through a craft study without referring to Katie Wood Ray and her book *Wondrous Words* and the impact of her work on our study of craft with students. Katie discusses how important it is to have the students identify the purpose of the craft and give it a name that makes sense to them, instead of overloading them with the conventional terms we were taught in our language arts classes. With this advice, the message is clear—what's important is understanding the purpose, and the name is secondary. To do a craft study we take our students through the following stages:

READING SO THE LANGUAGE RESONATES

- As we read the piece out loud, we ask students to notice which parts resonate.

- We invite students to read those parts out loud as we circle or highlight those portions of the text, then refocus our attention on each circled portion.

IDENTIFYING THE PURPOSE

- We think and talk about what the writer has done in order to make that part outstanding.

- We identify the purpose of that craft, or the effect it has on the writing.

NAMING WHAT THE WRITER HAS DONE

- We give a name to the techniques we have identified. The names may be informal such as those we invent in the class such as "show not tell" or names that have already been established such as "comparisons."

INTERNALIZING THE CRAFT AND ITS PURPOSE

- We practice the techniques in our writing in order to internalize what we have learned.

- We search out other texts for examples of the craft.

Minilessons

Craft Studies

- While examining a text, identify with the students as many craft strategies as they are able to notice from beginning to end. Create a chart with the excerpts from the text, describing the purpose of the craft and giving the strategy a name. (This list may be typed and given to students to place in their notebooks for future reference.) Students can then experiment with a variety of craft in their writing.

- Decide on the technique you want to focus on. Demonstrate how you find a place in your writing where you would like to use the technique. On a clean page, try to use that technique over and over again to improve the quality of the writing. After several attempts, choose the try that works best in your piece. Minilessons build on the work of the previous day by taking the students from simple examples to more complex ones.

- Use your own writing or student writing and circle or star places in the text that need to be revised. Establish what purpose you would like to achieve in your writing (slow down the reader, create an image, etc.), then decide on the craft strategy that best serves that purpose. Do several versions in front of the students, allowing them to see your process as you use that strategy. Have the students go off to find a place in their writing where they could try out the same strategy. It is important to emphasize that one trial is not enough. The children must make several attempts to practice the strategy, then they may choose their best effort.

Conducting a Craft Study

While exploring craft studies with students, Sharon searched for ways of giving students opportunities to identify a variety of crafting techniques, to understand their purposes, and to develop their own expertise through practice that is guided by minilessons and conferences. The table on page 134 highlights three effective approaches she has used to help us accomplish our goals.

Studying an Entire Text

When we study an entire text we present students with the opportunity to identify a variety of craft techniques in one piece of writing. By doing this, not only are we helping them begin to cultivate the habit of looking out for craft in the texts they read and to develop their awareness of the vast options they have for crafting their own writing, but we are also creating a context for them to practice what they have learned.

By following the previously outlined steps in a craft study, students are given the opportunity to try out some of the identified techniques and to develop their skills with the support of demonstrations and repeated practice. It is important that students understand the purpose of the craft and find places in their writing where they would like to achieve the potential outcomes of that particular craft technique. If they learn to craft without specific purposes in mind, then they often overuse the

Different Approaches to Doing a Craft Study

STUDYING AN ENTIRE TEXT	STUDYING A SPECIFIC CRAFT TECHNIQUE	STUDYING PURPOSE/EFFECT USING DIFFERENT TECHNIQUES
Scope: Wide and Shallow Students know a little about a lot of craft techniques	**Scope: Narrow with Depth** Students know a lot about a few craft techniques	**Scope: Narrow with Depth** Students know a lot about a few craft techniques
Read text as a writer Circle all the parts that stand out Identify the purposes Name the craft techniques Practice	Choose a particular technique to study Identify its purpose in the text Find the technique in other texts studying from simple to complex Notice if the technique is used for different effects Practice	Identify a particular purpose Study various techniques that achieve that purpose Practice using those techniques with the purpose in mind

techniques, which can make the writing superfluous and defeat the purpose of learning the craft in the first place.

We have used "My Grandmother's Hair" by Cynthia Rylant (see page 101), to help students learn how to study a text closely for craft. We have referred to this text in previous chapters and we use it once again in our craft study because of its familiarity to students and the great potential it presents for studying craft. From our close look at "My Grandmother's Hair," here are some of the crafting elements we identified together.

Craft Elements We Notice in "My Grandmother's Hair"

• Uses lists to give specific examples—"cats, baking powder biscuits, Sunday school class."

• Strings a series of adjectives to describe people and places well—"small white house," "thin blond-headed little girl," "... my skinny six-year-old legs..." "... gently, most carefully..."

• Gives people and places "proper" names—"Cool Ridge, West Virginia"; "Aunt Violet"; "Mrs. Epperly's big bull."

• Uses very specific verbs and strings them together—"twirling, curling, rolling..."

- Uses comparisons to create an image—"gray lock would be as tight as bed-springs . . ."; "covered her face like a lion's mane."

- Uses personification—". . . and would dance if you pulled on them . . ."

- Repeats words, phrases, lines to make a bigger point "sometimes we were quiet . . ." "sometimes my grandmother would shiver . . ." "Twirling, curling, rolling . . ." ". . . and make my little pink comb slide through it." "used my pen like a little pink comb . . ."

- Develops the end to make it more than just her own story about combing her grandmother's hair. It adds up to something important.

Studying a Specific Craft Technique

When we choose to study a particular craft technique in depth, we usually start out by studying it in its simplest form then move on to more complex examples. What we love about this kind of investigation is that once we start looking we are often surprised by what we find. This may lead to the reshaping of *our* thinking, and for our students, a widened window of possibilities. A study of comparisons, lists, and different ways of structuring a text are good choices for doing this kind of investigation. Let's look at some of the noticings from a study of comparisons.

STUDYING COMPARISONS

Young writers love to use comparisons but are often unaware of the purpose behind their use and how to write them well. Too often they use clichés such as "as quiet as a mouse," or comparisons that don't serve the purpose of making the image clearer for the reader. One of the first lessons we help them learn through our investigation is that comparisons help readers create images so they have to be made to things that are familiar to the reader. Comparisons must also be authentic. When one student wrote "my grandma's skin is as soft as a cushion," she was asked to think about what a soft cushion feels like and what soft skin feels like. It was then she realized the two just didn't compare the way she intended. Or when a writer writes, "clouds are like cotton balls," he may need to explain how they are like cotton balls. Is it the appearance of fluffiness, the texture, the lightness? The reader needs to know.

We also help students notice the kinds of words that writers use to make comparisons and how the words are arranged in sentences. For example, the preposition *like* is often used and though it appears somewhere within the body of the sentence, it may also be used at the very beginning as the first word in the sentence. We also help our writers understand the purpose of the comparison by discussing how our understandings are enhanced as a result of the comparison. This kind of in-depth investigation helps our writers appreciate the fact that comparisons work best when they create strong images in ways that are surprising to a reader. Take a look at the following chart which organizes some noticings from a study of comparisons.

Craft Study: <u>Comparisons</u>

TEXT/ AUTHOR	EXAMPLE FROM MENTOR TEXT	HOW DOES THE WRITER DO IT? (STRUCTURE OF THE COMPARISON)	WHY DOES THE WRITER DO IT?
Eleven by Sandra Cisneros	I want to be **far away** <u>like</u> **a runaway balloon.**	By describing a balloon with a single **word** "runaway."	To give an image of "far away" by comparing it to a runaway balloon.
When I Go Camping With Grandma by Marion Dane Bauer	The **moon floats low** in the bluing sky <u>like</u> **a balloon left over from a night party.**	By describing the position of the moon using a **phrase** "balloon left over from a night party."	To give an image of the moon—compare it to a balloon left over from a night party.
Owl Moon by Jane Yolen	The **snow** below it was **whiter than the milk in a cereal bowl.**	By using "whiter" as a comparative term.	To give an image of how white the milk is.
When I Go Camping With Grandma by Marion Dane Bauer	**A heron** wings over our heads. **Great blue shadow. Pterodactyl.**	With no use of "like" or other comparative terms.	To give an image of the large heron—exaggerating by comparing it to a pterodactyl.

Studying Purpose/Effect Using Different Techniques

This study helps students to not only become aware of the kinds of plans they can have for crafting their writing, but also the different techniques they can use to accomplish their plan. Writers learn that they have options.

We first choose a writing purpose and then study several mentor texts to notice different techniques writers use to accomplish that particular purpose. Next, we create opportunities for the students to try out the different techniques. See Figure 9–1 where Lia tries out lists, comparisons, and alliteration in an effort to describe her ice cream.

You may form study groups that allow students to work together to identify different techniques that accomplish the same purpose.

The following chart identifies various purposes and some of the techniques writers may use.

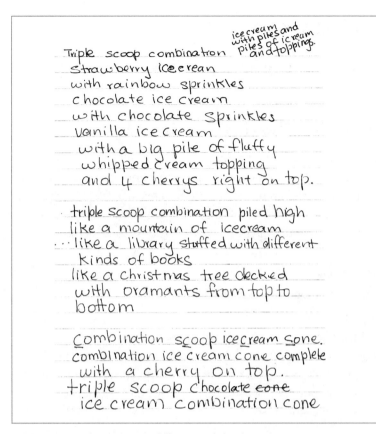

FIGURE 9-1. *Lia trying out different craft for the same purpose.*

Studying Craft with a Particular Purpose in Mind

PURPOSE	TECHNIQUE	
Describing: a place a person a mood/feeling	• Write with sensory details • Use strong verbs • Develop lists	• Use comparisons • Show not tell
Showing time passing or using time	• Show day passing into night • Show seasonal change through the piece • Show growth in the character • Use words that show time passing: *next, finally, eventually*	• Play with flashbacks • Explore a particular time sequence; similar to a series of snapshots • Sequence events in a logical order
Creating emphasis	• Use italics • Try exclamation points • Explore repetition	• Use a word or short phrase that holds importance immediately after a long sentence
Slowing down a moment	• Use sensory images to give details • Use comparisons • Use dialogue or internal thoughts to show what the character is thinking or feeling	• Show not tell—don't just say ". . . it was fun." Show how it was fun. • Experiment with punctuation—ellipses, dashes

Other Important Craft Studies

The following are additional craft studies we choose to do because of the powerful impact they have on helping students become better writers.

Studying How Writers Use Lists

Like our previous studies, we begin by circling and copying different lists we notice in the mentor texts. This crafting technique appears in so many texts and in so many forms! We noticed that writers often use three to four items in a list, although there can also be more or less. We discuss the effects of the use of various types of lists, emphasizing that purpose should always drive our decisions. Some of the purposes we discovered include:

- To give descriptions
- To draw attention or focus the reader on something
- To create rhythm
- To give the idea of how much . . . a lot of items

We discuss the structure of the lists and we practice them in our writing. To help our students grasp hold of the various structures we study lots of literature to find the different structures and purposes of lists. The following chart demonstrates how we scaffold this work for the students.

Craft Study: Lists		
TEXT/AUTHOR	**EXAMPLE FROM MENTOR TEXT**	**HOW AND WHY DOES THE WRITER DO IT?**
Come Sunday by Nikki Grimes	"I could admire them for hours–hats with feathers, bows and flowers."	Use of commas between items; *and* is used before the last item. *"Bows"* sandwiched by two longer words that have the same ending "ers." This gives the reader a better sound. *And* is used to separate each item in the series.
Great Aunt Martha by Rebecca C. Jones	"We went to the store and bought fish and carrots and spinach and prune juice."	*and* used between each item makes it seem like a lot of items.
Tulip Sees America by Cynthia Rylant	"The skies in Nebraska. They are everything. They are vast and dark and low and ominous."	*And* is used to slow the reader down to take in the vastness, the darkness, etc.
Great Aunt Martha by Rebecca C. Jones	"She hugged papa." "She hugged mama." "She even hugged me."	No commas, no *ands*–periods are used instead The hugs didn't happen quickly. This structure forces the reader to slow down between hugs.
When I Go Camping with Grandma by Marion Dane Bauer	"Grandma yawns, stretches, rubs her eyes."	Use of commas only, to separate items in the list. Shows the fluidity of grandma's motions—one runs into the other.

Our study of lists helps our students become more thoughtful about their own arrangements and helps them recognize the potential in using lists for improving the quality of their writing.

Studying Leads

The lead is an invitation to the reader to go with the writer on a journey. Since it is the hook or point of initial engagement and often determines whether a piece will be read or put away, students must learn to write them effectively. We teach our students that the lead sets the reader up for what they should expect from the piece. It is where the writer establishes voice and the purpose of the piece. By naming and trying out the different leads we notice in our mentor texts, we help our students develop their expertise in writing their own. The chart below shows different types of leads students have identified in some of our favorite mentor texts. Figure 9–2 is an example of how one student tried out different leads for the same piece of writing.

Craft Study: Leads	
TYPE OF LEAD	**EXAMPLE**
Begins with the title	"Seems like everything good that happens in my house happens in my momma's kitchen." *In My Momma's Kitchen* by Jerdine Nolen
Introduces the character	"Some say Leroy Paige was born six feet three and a half inches tall, 180 pounds, wearing a size fourteen shoe . . . It would take him eighteen years to grow to that size and about half that amount of time to realize that his hand and a baseball were a perfect match." *Satchel Paige* by Lesa Cline-Ranson
Begins and ends the same way	"There was once a small boy called Wilfrid Gordon McDonald Partridge and what's more he wasn't very old either." *Wilfrid Gordon McDonald Partridge* by Mem Fox
Creates a mood and establishes a sense of the time	"On a dusky January afternoon in 1925, Dr. Welch walked quickly toward the outskirts of Nome." *The Great Serum Race* by Debbie S. Miller
Describes the setting	"In the far, far north, deep in the wilds, a wolf pup named Hanni stepped carefully through the puddles of hot, stinky water. She was following her family to the top of Howling Hill, where the steaming water bubbled out of the ground. It was their favorite place to howl." *Howling Hill* by Will Hobbs
Speaks directly to the reader	"Gather around and listen as I share childhood memories of my brother, the Reverend Dr. Martin Luther King Jr. I am his older sister and I have known him longer than anyone else. I knew him long before the speeches he gave and the marches he led and the prizes he won." *My Brother Martin* by Christine King Farris
Starts with dialogue	"Lewis woke in the night. His mother heard him call. 'What is it?' She said, sitting on the edge of the bed. 'I miss Grandpa,' Lewis said." *My Grandson Lew* by Charlotte Zolotow
Creates an image that is important to the piece	"On Sunday afternoons, Sarah and I go to see Great-great-aunt Flossie. Sarah and I love Aunt Flossie's house. It is crowded full of stuff and things. Books and pictures and lamps and pillows . . . Plates and trays and old dried flowers . . . And boxes and boxes and boxes of HATS!" *Aunt Flossie's Hats (and Crab Cakes Later)* by Elizabeth Fitzgerald Howard

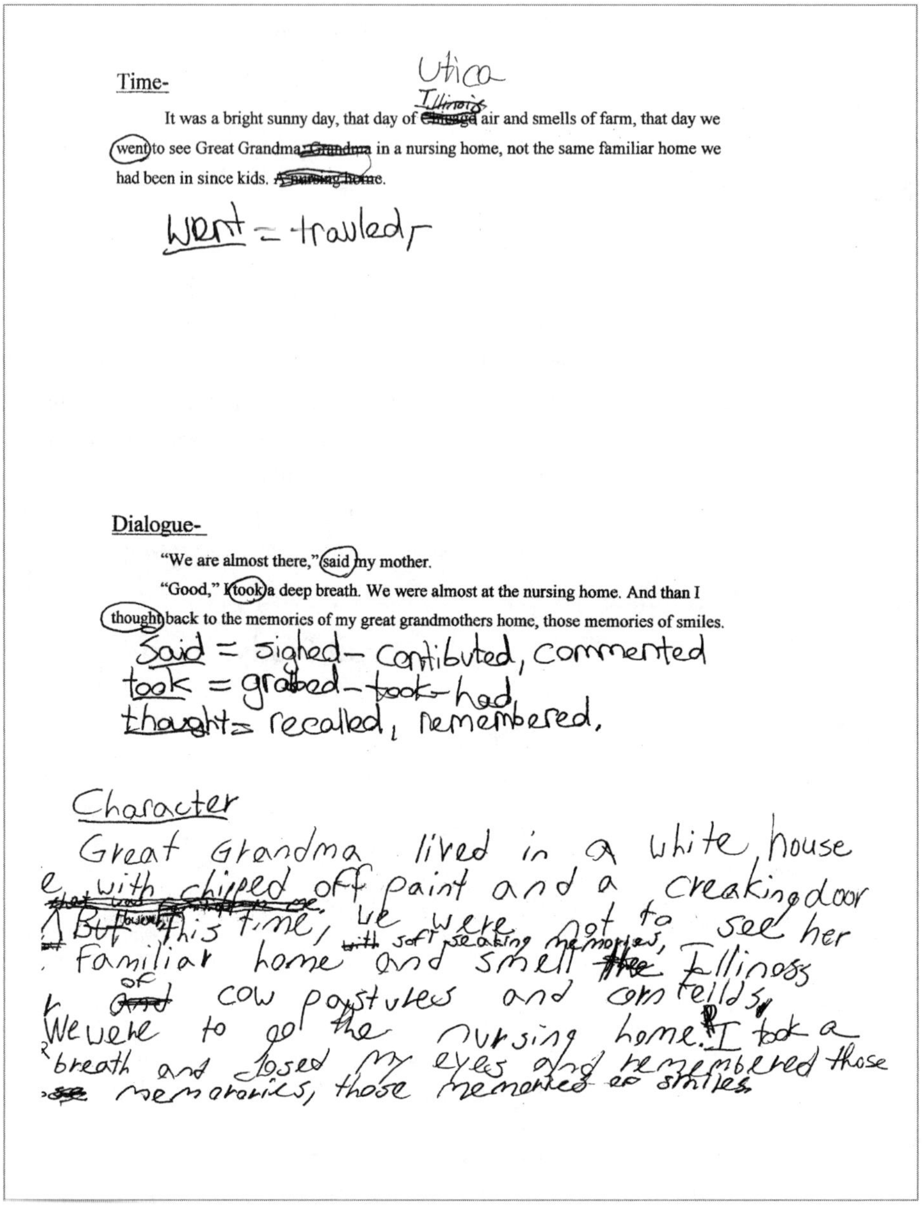

Time-

It was a bright sunny day, that day of ~~Chicago~~ Illinois Utica air and smells of farm, that day we went to see Great Grandma ~~Grandma~~ in a nursing home, not the same familiar home we had been in since kids. ~~A nursing home~~.

Went = traveled,

Dialogue-

"We are almost there," said my mother.

"Good," I took a deep breath. We were almost at the nursing home. And than I thought back to the memories of my great grandmothers home, those memories of smiles.

Said = sighed – contributed, commented

took = grabbed – ~~took~~ – had

thought = recalled, remembered,

Character

Great Grandma lived in a white house with chipped off paint and a creaking door But this time, we were not to see her familiar home and smell ~~the~~ Illinois of cow pastures and corn fields. We were to go the nursing home. I took a breath and closed my eyes and remembered those memories, those memories of smiles.

FIGURE 9–2. *Samantha trying out different leads.*

Focusing on Structure

When we speak about structure, we mean the various ways in which writing is organized to give the shape to an entire piece or portion of the text. Genre is one way to bring structure to our writing. We also bring structure to our writing by the ways in which we sequence events—what we tell in the beginning and where we end, whether the writing comes full circle (ending right where it began), how we use refrains to separate portions of text or make transitions, or the ways in which we structure paragraphs or stanzas in a poem.

The many picture books and short texts we read to our students offer an abundance of opportunities to study, name, and try out many structures. Katy Wood Ray in *Wondrous Words* has identified a wide variety of structures. Like anything else, structures go from simple to more complex. To help our students do this work, we first study the more simple structures that are linear and move on to more complex ones.

We find it helpful to students to have visual representations to help them plan and experiment with ways they may structure their writing. Figure 9–3 gives examples of some templates we have used to scaffold this work with students. Also see Appendix J.

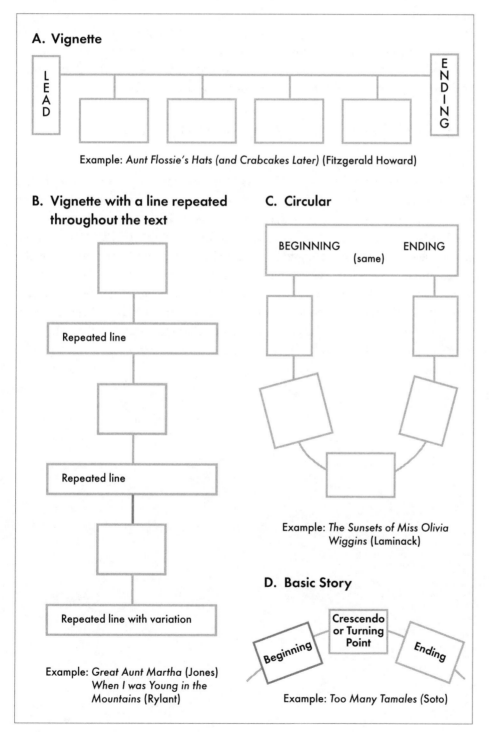

A. Vignette

Example: *Aunt Flossie's Hats (and Crabcakes Later)* (Fitzgerald Howard)

B. Vignette with a line repeated throughout the text

Repeated line

Repeated line

Repeated line with variation

Example: *Great Aunt Martha* (Jones)
When I was Young in the Mountains (Rylant)

C. Circular

BEGINNING   ENDING
(same)

Example: *The Sunsets of Miss Olivia Wiggins* (Laminack)

D. Basic Story

Beginning — Crescendo or Turning Point — Ending

Example: *Too Many Tamales* (Soto)

FIGURE 9–3. *Templates of simple structures.*

Focusing on Voice

Voice is established when the draft begins and the writer is paying attention to purpose, genre, and audience. By the time the revision stage comes, the voice of the piece has already been established and the writer can pay attention to fine-tuning the voice of the piece. Donald Murray in *Write to Learn* describes voice as "the person in the text; . . . what persuades the reader to listen and draws the reader on." Voice, Murray says, is the music of the piece and functions in the same way that the background music of a movie informs us of the meaning of what we are seeing. Writers sometimes show their early understandings of voice by writing, "In this piece, I am going to tell you . . ." or by putting in their commentary. Voice grows with the writer, and students must be taught to listen for it, to write with their voice and to let their voice in the piece be driven by the purposes they bring to the piece.

Looking Beyond What We Know and Expect

Our work with revision is always enjoyable for us and for our students. The more often we do this work, the easier it becomes. We are amazed at the things they notice that we sometimes may have missed. This is a nice reminder that we don't have to see ourselves as the experts, but instead can give the investigations over to our students and be willing to learn alongside them. Our excitement around this work comes from seeing the quality of the writing improve as the students understand and apply the techniques. Once students have the tools for revision under their belts, it is no longer a secret how to make a piece come alive. We feel especially rewarded when our students surprise us with techniques they find on their own, their way of telling us they really get it and they are well on their way to being good writers. Lia shows her love for ice cream in this well-crafted piece in Figure 9–4.

Ice Cream

By Lia A.

When I lick my ice cream
it wets my lips,
it tingles my teeth,
my throat gets really cold,
and my stomach grumbles for more.

Sometimes I am in the mood for
strawberry swirl.
Or sometimes I like the triple scoop
chocolate ice cream combination cone
with whip cream, rainbow sprinkles
and four cherries on top.
It's kind of like an everything bagel or
like a Christmas tree decked with ornaments
from top to bottom. So many combinations
stuffed into one ice cream cone.

Vanilla, Mmm! vanilla.
I remember when I went to Ben & Jerry's with my sisters
Becca and Julie and Mom.
I got vanilla ice cream with chocolate sprinkles.
It fell SPLAT!! on Julie's foot.
Her foot got so cold she started to cry.
I wanted to lick it off her foot because
I knew mom wouldn't get me another one.
I was so mad at myself.

I remember all those nights
when Vicky and I used to sneak
ice cream in the middle of the night.
Mom would always catch us
(we forgot to wear our slippers).
There was no carpeting on the kitchen floor, so our feet
always made that sticky sound
against the tiles. Only once we didn't get caught
(we remembered to wear our slippers).

Serendipity, my favorite ice cream parlor.
I get ice cream in the big glass bowl with
piles and piles of ice cream.
I lick it off the sleek, slender, spoon,
gobbling it up so fast
that mom always says,
"Lia, slow down! Or you'll get a headache."

Ice cream, it wets my lips and tingles my teeth.
It makes my throat really cold.
But my stomach will always grumble for more.

FIGURE 9–4. *Lia's well-crafted piece.*

Highlighting Student Work

We invite you to follow Suzannah through some of the stages of the publishing cycle as she goes from notebook entry to final piece in Figures 9–5a–e. See our website, <www.heinemann.com/davis-hill> for all of Suzannah's work through the publishing cycle. You will also find published work from other students that represent examples of other well-crafted published pieces.

My sister and I have shared a room since I was a baby. She had a little bed and I had a big crib. The room had green wall to wall carpeting that had marks of juice and cookies. for when my sister would try to sneak them in for me and her when we were hungry and already put to bed. When my sister was seven, she got a big green desk to put all her school work in. I always wanted a desk just like hers, so when I got older, my parents bought me a desk of my own. and then we could work next to each other. My sister and I shared a huge collection of stuffed animals that we would always pretend were real. We played a lot of imaginary games, pretending that the animals were people. We played movie star, maids, teacher and ballet dancers. Sometimes we would fall down from laughing so hard.

imaginary

FIGURE 9–5A. *Suzannah's original notebook entry.*

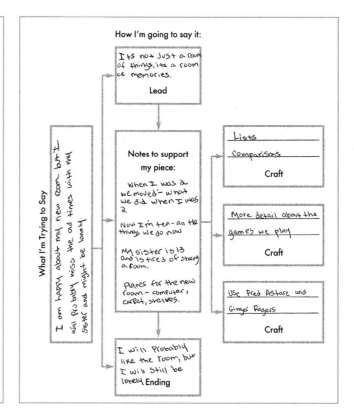

FIGURE 9–5B. *Suzannah's flowchart.*

Draft 1

My sister and I have shared a room since I was a baby. It's not just a room with desks and beds and stained carpeting.✳ It's a room full of memories. |

When I was two we moved upstairs.✳ ^(15th floor on 105th street) We moved in her little bed and my big crib. Since then ~~the~~ the walls have ✳seen us put on lots of make up, become our base as we ran relay races when our parents were not watching. They have felt us dance. ✳ (Add more about dancing)

Now that I am ten, my sister and I still share a room. We have made up games in that room. We have played with stuffed animals, pretending they were real people. ✳ We played maids, painters, and princesses, ^(or taboo) from far off lands.✳ At night, I look around the room and make movie mind pictures of us doing those things again. The camera rolling farther and farther back. Now that my sister is 13, she wants her own room, without too many Barbies. and more room on the shelves for her trophies. ✳ She says she is tired of me complaining about her messy desk, when mine is just as bad. She is tired of sharing the bathroom. ✳

My parents are changing everything for my sister and me. My sister is moving into my parents room, my parents ~~are~~ moving into our room. and I am moving into the study. So we will all have our own space. I will get new carpeting, my ~~~~ own ~~space~~ Computer, my own bookshelp and a dabble bed · for when I have friends sleep over. I am excited about all ^(of) this, but I am scared too. I will have my privacy, but I will probably be lonely.

FIGURE 9–5C. *Suzannah's first draft.*

FIGURE 9–5D. *Trying out revision possibilities.*

My Room, by Suzannah H.

It's not just a room full of games and stuffed animals and books. It's not just a room with desks and beds and a green stained carpet. It's not just a room where my sister and I sneaked in cookies and juice, hiding them in the space between our beds. It's a room full of memories. The room catches our spirit, like a mesh net catching a delicate butterfly.

When I was three years old, we moved up to the 15th floor on 105th Street. My sister and I shared our room and we moved in her little bed and my big crib. Since then those walls have heard us moan in our sleep. They have seen us put on loads of makeup, pretending to be movie stars with our friends. They have felt us frantically slap against them when they were our bases as we ran relay races across the room. And they have felt us dance, wall to wall, spinning and twirling until we fell down against them.

Now I am ten and my sister and I still share a room. We have made up games like maids, painters, and princesses from far off lands that speak different made up languages. We do really silly dances in that room, like ballet dances, and acting crazy dances, and ballroom dances, pretending to be Fred Astaire, sliding across the carpet with his partner Ginger Rogers. At night, I look around the room and make movie mind pictures of us doing those things again, the camera rolling farther and farther back in time.

Now that my sister is thirteen she is tired of the two boxes of Barbies that I don't play with anymore. She says that they take up too much space on the shelf for her trophies. She is tired of me hocking her about cleaning up her desk even though mine is almost as bad. She is tired of me begging her to play "maids" in which I play the part of the maid who is

new and knows nothing, and my sister, the more experienced maid, helps me. She is tired of sharing the bathroom where we both take hours grooming.

And that is why we are starting to look for wall-to-wall carpeting, double beds and wall paints that will match our stuff. That is why we are getting our own rooms.

Since I was three, we have had this room, the room in which we made up silly dances, played games, slept with piles of stuffed animals, the room full of memories shared with my sister.

I am excited to get my own room. I will get my own bookshelf. I will get a big new double bed for when I have friends sleep over. I will have my own pictures on the walls. I will have my privacy. But there will be one thing that I won't have, my sister to share my room with. I will probably be lonely.

FIGURE 9–5E. *The final piece.*

Extending Writing Possibilities

"Thoughts, ideas, stories, reports, and poems jump out of Carey's pen like flocks of birds across pages and pages of notebook entries. Through immersion in a life of real writing, she is empowered and feels she has some control over the world around her."

—KATE MANNING, MOTHER OF CAREY DUNNE
MNS GRADUATING CLASS, 2000

Poetry Study

By the later part of the year, our students are ready to take on more in-depth genre studies, which include intense immersion into the genre, inquiry into the specific features of the genre, and finally, writing in the genre. We have already discussed how genre studies fit into the structure of our year, but here we explain in greater detail the genres we cover in our class, starting with poetry.

Our students are exposed to poems everywhere, from the nursery rhymes they have heard and recited for most of their lives, to the songs and raps they enjoy with their friends, to the jingles that dance from their televisions at home. Poetry flashes on the subways and buses of New York City, it's quoted in the books our students read and admire, and poised among fancy drawings and illustrations in the greeting cards our students send to their friends and loved ones. A local phone company considered filling unsold advertising space in the phone book with poems. The customers surveyed about the idea loved it and looked forward to finding poems in such a surprising place. Most admitted that while poetry wasn't part of their regular reading diet, they enjoyed stumbling upon a poem.

Poetry is the most easily accessible genre for our young writers. Therefore, our classrooms should sing with the music of poetry. Our libraries should be crowded with collections that invite kids into the world of poems, brimming with anthologies that include poems that have great variety and appeal for all types of students, from our strugglers to our intellectuals. These books should include poems for animal lovers, sports enthusiasts, history buffs, nature lovers, and dreamers. We want our students to read poems about people who they admire and with whom they can empathize. We want the settings of some of the poems to be familiar, set in backyards and city parks, while others should carry our students to the exotic places kids dream about. We want the descriptions to be so rich in metaphor and the content so powerful that simply by closing their eyes our students are transported to a different place or time.

These collections should contain poems that rhyme, poems that are whimsical, and others that are poignant and moving. Some should be easy to read and others should present a challenge and become sources for powerful talk in the classroom and at the dining room table. They should be read and reread, recited and chanted. And, above all, they should suggest to our young writers that they can be poets, too. Indeed, we want our students to understand that they can reread their notebooks through a lens of poetry and try this exciting form of expression themselves.

Goals of This Study

Our intention during this study is to build on our students' previous experiences with poems by presenting explicit minilessons that help children notice their world in the way poets do. We don't ever want to give the children the idea that poems happen by accident. Our goal is to help our students:

• Become more familiar with the sound of a variety of poems through immersion in a wide range of poetry.
• Understand that they can prefer particular types of poems and yet push themselves to read poetry beyond their comfort zone; these poems can become the mentors that guide our students' own poetry writing.
• Become comfortable with the rhythm and pattern of the words by creating opportunities for them to read poems aloud and experiment with choral reading for an audience.
• Explore many different poems by carefully reading and responding to them.
• Identify the particular characteristics of poems by studying them closely and naming specific characteristics.
• Reread their notebooks and use the right side to experiment with poems.
• Discover that poets have intentions for their writing and that they must have intentions for their own poetry.
• Return to the mentor poems we study together to investigate the particular craft involved in writing poetry.
• Take risks as writers by experimenting with their "poetic license."

Year-Long Supports

Throughout the year, the children have had many experiences with poetry. They include:

• Studying those poems we chose as mentor texts to jump-start writing ideas for the notebook.
• Choosing to read poetry during the Reading Workshop.
• Revisiting the poems we enjoy together during Shared Reading lessons.
• Choosing a poem to share with the class. (Our good friend and mentor Georgia Heard reminds us that reading a poem aloud each day is a great way to bring more poetry into the classroom. So, heeding her advice, Judy begins by sharing one of her favorites. Each day thereafter, the students take turns reading one of their favorites. We make copies of these poems and put them in baskets on each table. Many students reread the collection during free time or independent reading time. They refer to them regularly, and some became mentors.)

- Experimenting with their personal narratives. Since the very first publishing cycle, each time students publish a personal narrative, they also use the content of the narrative to write a poem and publish that poem alongside the personal narrative.
- Reading poems each month in preparation for their poetry anthologies (see Chapter 4).
- Paying attention to words as they add to their personal thesaurus (see Chapter 4).

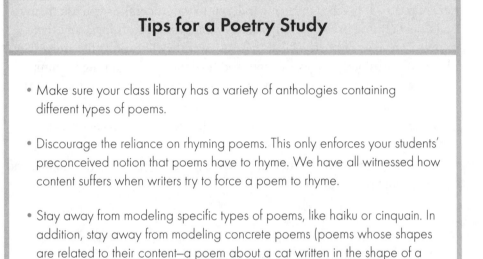

Tips for a Poetry Study

- Make sure your class library has a variety of anthologies containing different types of poems.

- Discourage the reliance on rhyming poems. This only enforces your students' preconceived notion that poems have to rhyme. We have all witnessed how content suffers when writers try to force a poem to rhyme.

- Stay away from modeling specific types of poems, like haiku or cinquain. In addition, stay away from modeling concrete poems (poems whose shapes are related to their content—a poem about a cat written in the shape of a cat, for example) or poems written for two voices. We want our writers to be free to create imagery, mood, rhythm, and not to be limited by structure.

- Don't overanalyze poems or fall into the old teacher model that suggests there is only one correct interpretation of a poem. Allow the children to take risks by engaging in natural conversations about the poems during which time they are encouraged to ask many questions.

- Have fun with this study! Poems are a natural expression of the way good writers observe the world.

Phase 1: Immersion

What the Teacher Is Doing

- Gathering poetry books and getting them into the hands of the students.
- Helping students collect poetry texts. Each of the students in our class had bags in which they kept the anthologies they collected. Many had two-to-four collections at all times; some were from our class library, some from the school library, some from local libraries, some borrowed from other classrooms, and some off the shelves from home. They carried them back and forth from home to school.

- Creating a list of the qualities of a good mentor poem. See our class-created list in Figure 10–1.
- Instructing children to put sticky notes on the poems they like and letting them know that some of those will become their mentor poems.
- Reading lots of poems aloud.
- Creating a list of instructions for reading a poem aloud. A sample list is shown in Figure 10–2.
- Helping students to discover what they are noticing about themselves as readers of poetry. It is very interesting to listen to the students as you ask them to talk publicly and in small groups about what they are learning about themselves as readers of poetry: what they discover they like, don't like; how they learn to read aloud with expression; and how they are beginning to think about what poems mean and what they think the poet intended for us derive from their poems.
- Making sure the time spent reading poems during minilessons doesn't eat into the writing time.
- Creating opportunities for students to write in their notebooks after sharing and talking about powerful poems.

QUALITIES OF A MENTOR POEM

- You love it.
- It touches you in a special way.
- You can read it fluently.
- You understand what the poet was trying to get you to understand.
- You can discuss it intelligently.
- The poem demonstrates qualities of good poetry and you can learn from it for your own poetry.

FIGURE 10-1. *Class-created guide to qualities of mentor poems.*

READ-ALOUD GUIDE

1. Read the poem two or three times silently or as many times as you need to so you don't stumble on any words.
2. Include the title and author in your reading.
3. Pay attention to the punctuation.
4. Find out the meaning of any words you don't know.
5. Pay attention to the line breaks and meaning and group words accordingly.
6. Decide where you need voice changes—louder, softer, whisper, angry.
7. Read it to someone, paying attention to his/her suggestions.
8. Read it aloud again and again until it sounds perfect to you and the person you are reading it to.

FIGURE 10-2. *Class-created guide for reading aloud poems.*

What the Students Are Doing

- Reading lots of poems, in school and at home, and placing sticky notes on those they like.
- Sharing their favorites with parents.
- Reading their favorites aloud, to the entire class if they choose, or in small groups.
- Gathering in small groups, choosing a poem that would be good for chanting or choral reading, and presenting their adaptation of it to the class.
- Writing in their notebooks as they become inspired by the poems shared in class and read at home. Some are beginning to write in poetry form, while others are still writing entries. However, as the immersion continues, their writing becomes more and more poetic as they take on the voice of poets.

The Result

Although students have been reading and writing poems throughout the year, this immersion is putting the wheels of a focused writing study in motion. We take the lead with the knowledge that they will continue with their independent investigations. Excited comments such as, "I had no idea there were so many types of poems" or "I used to only like rhyming poems" fill the room. The children's excitement is contagious as they share poems, dramatize them, and bring them into their homes.

Phase 2: Inquiry and Analysis

What the Teacher Is Doing

- Reading poems aloud such as "October Saturday," shown here in Figure 10–3, and asking the students to notice some of the features of poems.
- Responding to questions, such as those shown in Figure 10–4, that would help us come to know the poems better. Also see Appendix K.
- Helping students to begin filling in a class Poetry Study Chart (see Figure 10–7A and Appendix L).
- Providing opportunities for students to share the poems they are writing in an effort to notice the different ways people can be inspired by the same poem.
- Using his/her own notebook entries to model how writers move from narrative prose to poetry. See Figure 10–5a–b, Judy's Back to Brooklyn entries.
- Reading excerpts from books like *The Place My Words Are Looking For* and *Seeing the Blue Between* by Paul Janezcko, in which poets talk about the ways they get inspiration for poems and give advice on how to write good poems.
- Conferring to support the writing, asking questions like:

    1. What do you like about your writing?

    2. How are you being inspired by your mentor poems?

    3. Can you name what the poet you are studying is doing in their writing that is helping you create poems of your own?

4. Can you name what you are doing as a poet?

5. What strategies are you using to get ideas for the poems you are writing?

6. How are you making decisions about what is important in your note-book entry that should be included in your poem and what information should be left out?

What the Students Are Doing

• Writing new entries or poems in response to the personal connections they are making to the mentor poems shared in class.

• Using the right side of the notebook for thinking of entries and imagining poems that might spin off.

October Saturday

Bobbi Katz

All the leaves have turned to cornflakes
It looks as if some giant's baby brother
had tipped the box
and scattered them upon our lawn—
millions and millions of cornflakes—
crunching, crunching under our feet.
When the wind blows,
They rattle against each other,
nervously chattering.

We rake them into piles—
Dad and I.
Piles and piles of cornflakes!
A breakfast for a whole family of giants!
We do not talk much as we rake—
a word here—
a word there.
The leaves are never silent.

Inside the house my mother is packing
short sleeved shirts and faded bathing suits—
rubber clogs and flippers—
in a box marked SUMMER.

We are raking,
Dad and I.

Raking, raking.
The sky is blue, then orange then gray.
My arms are tired.
I am dreaming of the box marked SUMMER.

FIGURE 10-3. *A poem to launch our inquiry and analysis.*

- Trying to apply some of the features of poems to their own writing.

- Continuing to read and choose mentor poems, both in school and at home. Each time they do, they fill in a Response to Poetry Sheet to keep track of what they are noticing about each poem. Children either photocopy the mentor poems they choose or hand copy them, placing them in their folders with the response sheet attached.

- Using their personal Poetry Study Chart, as demonstrated during minilessons, to notice features of the mentor texts they are collecting.

RESPONDING TO POETRY

After you have chosen a mentor poem, fill in as much of the following as you can. Write small so you can fit your responses in the space provided. Attach it to a copy of the poem and keep it in your poetry folder.

TITLE OF POEM _October Saturday_   POET: _Bobbi Katz_

1. What was your first response to the poem?

The first time I read this poem I thought about how the seasons go by quicker than we want them to.

2. What personal connection(s) did you make?

It made me think about how my sister and I feel summer is the shortest season, because it goes by much faster than we expect. When the school year starts, we're never ready.

3. When you reread it, what else did you understand about it?

After rereading it, I realized that it was not only about seasons changing, but about how that affects families. (For example, raking together).

4. What did it inspire you to write?

I wrote about how I'm never ready for the first day of school and the feeling of fall sneaking up on you.

5. Which line(s) stood out and why?

"We do not talk much as we rake – a word here – a word there." This line shows that the feeling of togetherness can easily come without words.

6. What do you think the poet wanted you to get from his/her poem?

I think Bobbi Katz wanted the reader to take away how season changes can bring people closer together, which no one really thinks about.

7. What mood did it leave you in?

It left me wondering about seasons and how other people feel about them.

FIGURE 10–4. *Amanda's completed response sheet.*

I can remember, as if it were just yesterday, that pounding in my chest as we crossed the George Washington Bridge. We were returning to Brooklyn after a long summer in the Catskills. I recall with crystal clear clarity, the huge buildings looming tall and foreboding against a fall sky. Where were the grassy lawns, the tall trees whose broad leaves brought shade for our late afternoon club meetings? Where was the lake whose waters froze our ears even though only our toes were submerged? Where, oh where, would I go when I needed peace and quiet, to hear the crickets sing, to swing until my feet seemed in danger of hooking over the swing bar? No more summer, no more grass, no more country nights or dewy mornings. Fall had settled over Brooklyn, and so had we . . .

FIGURE 10–5A. *Judy's narrative prose.*

End of Summer

Back in Brooklyn
Summer's gone
Grass to concrete
Bare feet confined to socks and shoes
Itchy woolen clothes worn too early

Back in Brooklyn
Summer's gone
Evenings turn from crickets and stars
To homework and chores
Carefree dreams turn to worries.

Where has summer gone?

I want it back!
I need it back!

I am, alas,
Back in Brooklyn

FIGURE 10–5B. *Judy's poem.*

The Result

We find that this inquiry stage directly influences the quality of the poems students are writing in their notebooks. When Hallie declares, "I am discovering meaning beyond the beautiful language and it's helping me realize poems are more than just words," we know we are doing important work. The students are ready to take on some challenges and move out of the comfort zone some may have fallen into as they read and choose poems. Since we want the children's poetry writing to be more deliberate and for them to ultimately revise the body of work they are collecting, we want enough variety in their choices.

Phase 3: Moving Beyond the Comfort Zone

What the Teacher Is Doing

- Modeling mentor poems that are a bit more challenging and thought-provoking.
- Presenting opportunities for students to be reflecting on the body of mentor poems they have gathered so far (approximately 10), determining the qualities of those, reflecting on what they know about their taste in poetry, and trying to articulate the qualities of poems that might be beyond their comfort zone.
- Spending the next few days reading those challenging works. (See Figure 10–6 and Appendix M, "Knowing My Taste in Poetry Reflection Sheet.")
- Conferring with students as they are writing and being inspired by these poems.

Name Jordan

Knowing My Taste In Poetry

You have collected a number of mentor poems. Before you go further in your investigation, take time to review the Poetry Study Chart on which you have been keeping track of the length, topic, mood and craft of each poem. Use the questions below to help you categorize your choices so that you can draw some conclusions about your preferences.

1. What are you noticing about the length of the poems you have been collecting? Most of the poems I have collected have been short. The one I favored most was about a page long, but that was the longest one. I write long poems but like to read shorter ones because they are more straightforward.

2. What are you noticing about the topics or content of the poems? Do you tend to gather poems that are more story-like, about nature, etc. Try to name what you choose most. I chose poems about a lot of different topics. Most of my poems have been about nature and about feelings and things I can easily relate to. Then I can go off and write poems of my own.

3. Did you find yourself choosing poems you understood or related to easily or did you try to push yourself beyond your comfort zone? Explain? The poems I choose are easy to understand at first. Then I take time to think about the real meaning and always find some hidden meaning. I like to talk about them with my mom.

4. How do most of the poems you have selected leave you feeling? Most of the poems leave me feeling like I'm part of the rest of the world because the poems I chose are about things or feelings I know about. They usually leave me happy about my life.

5. What are the specific crafting strategies that seem to attract you to a poem? I like it when a poet uses unusual comparisons because if I read a really suprising one, it gives me ideas for my own writing.

6. Which type of poetry seems to inspire you to write more poetically? Name the poems and say how it has inspired you? Riding in a Railway Carriage by Robert Louis Stevenson inspired me because he used short images to illustrate the speed of a railway carriage. I tried to do that too, but came out with a different effect but a really great poem. An Untitled poem by Emily Dickinson inspired me because she was playing with words and that got me thinking about how to do that in my own writing.

7. Have you collected poems by totally different poets or are you attracted to one poet in particular? If so, what is it about that one poet's style that you like? I am attracted to Emily Dickinson and have four collected poems by her. I like the topics of the poems she writes and how she knows where to put comparisons that are unusual and suprising.

8. How will your conclusions influence your future inquiry? How will you decide to push yourself toward poems that are different or beyond your comfort zone? Will you focus on similar types? What do you think would be a good challenge for you now? I tend to read poems that are about experiences that I can relate to. My main goal is to push myself out of my comfort zone by reading poems that are about topics that can teach me something about the world. I will also try to read longer poems by adult poets. Most of the poems I read have been from anthologies that said they were for children.

FIGURE 10-6. *Jordan's response.*

What the Students Are Doing

- Gathering different anthologies that might contain poems of a different nature than those they have been reading.
- Identifying the qualities of these poems and filling in Responding to Poetry Sheets to help them keep track of their insights. In this way, we are confident their thinking will spill over into their writing.
- Writing responses to these more challenging poems.

The Result

At this point, the students have had many opportunities to read, analyze, respond, and write in connection to the poems they have studied. They have proven to themselves that there is life beyond the well-known Shel Silverstein and Jack Prelutzky. They are ready to move away from the templates we've provided to support their thinking and begin to apply this knowledge to the drafts of their own poems.

POETRY STUDY CHART

TITLE	POET	ANTHOLOGY TITLE	AUTHOR/EDITOR	LENGTH	TOPIC	MOOD	CRAFT
"October Saturday"	Bobbi Katz	The Place My Words Are Looking For	by Paul Janeczko	medium	end of summer	sad	• comparison—"all the leaves have turned to cornflakes" • continued the metaphor of cornflakes throughout the poem • repetition of words—"millions and millions," "crunching and crunching," "piles and piles," "a word here, a word there" • time passing—time of the year changing—time of the day changing . . . "blue, then orange, then gray" • alliteration—"short sleeved shirts" • contrast between the talking and the sound of the leaves • end refers back to a line in the poem
"Dragonfly"	Georgia Heard	Creatures of the Earth, Sea, and Sky	by Georgia Heard	short	a close look at a dragonfly	calm, peaceful, sleepy, relaxed	• sticks with one topic • wrote about something small • delicate subject helps create the mood • creates an image with a great comparison—stained-glass windows with sun shining through" • alliteration—"stops to sun itself" • great choice of specific verbs—"skims, blur, flicker" • list to create setting of the pond—"gnats, mosquitoes and flies" • great description lets you picture what is going on—"outspread wings blur with speed"

FIGURE 10-7A. *Poetry study chart.*

Phase 4: Drafting and Revising

What the Teacher Is Doing

- Returning to mentor poems to study craft more closely.

- Returning to the class Poetry Study Chart to study additional mentor poems with a deeper focus on craft. Also see Figures 10–7A–B.

- Encouraging students to study their own mentor poems and record on their Poetry Study Chart the features of each and the deliberate crafting moves the poets make.

- Modeling student writing on the overhead to talk about what these students have done as poets.

- Collecting a list of crafting strategies they've studied throughout the year and deciding how they fit into the revision work of poetry.

- Using his/her own writing to demonstrate craft strategies for revision.

- Categorizing the crafting techniques particular to poetry and providing students with samples; for instance, you might show students three or four poems that demonstrate how line breaks are used, three or four poems that demonstrate surprising language, three or four poems that demonstrate repetition, or three or four poems where imagery is apparent.

- Removing the line breaks from published poems and inviting students to try different ways to shape the poem. Ask your students to explain why they made their choices before revealing the poem and its actual construction. Then ask the children to discuss the ways in which different line breaks affect the way the poem is read and how it affects the meaning.

- Modeling how one might study a poem and apply each of the crafting strategies studied to revise their poems.

- Conferring with students as they revise their poems for publication. Help students make decisions about what might improve the rhythm, strengthen the voice of the poems, or tighten the structure of the poems they are writing.

What the Students Are Doing

- Moving out of their notebooks to draft poems. They divide the paper in half. On the left, they draft the poem. On the right, they try out revision strategies such as outlined in the chart below. Each time they make a change to the poem, they are naming the strategy they use and what they hope it will do for the poem.

- Using their Poetry Study Chart to review crafting strategies of mentor poets to help lift the quality of their own writing and revising their drafts accordingly.

- Revising their drafts using those specific strategies mentioned in the chart and the ones learned in the class study.

Dragonfly

By Georgia Heard

It skims the pond's surface,
searching for gnats,
  mosquitoes, and flies.
Outspread wings blur with
  speed.
It touches down
and stops to sun itself on
  the dock.
Wings flicker and still:
stained-glass windows
with sun shining through.

FIGURE 10–7B. *A mentor poem, "Dragonfly," by Georgia Heard from* Creatures of the Earth, Sea, and Sky: Poems. *Used with permission.*

Strategies for Revising a Poem
Helpful Conferring Conversations

Making Them More Thoughtful

• Write about things that mean a lot to you.

• Think about the issues in the world and include more of that in your poem.

• Ask questions about the poem that will help you get to the deeper meaning.

• Add specific examples.

• Decide about your intentions and be sure they are clear by the end of the poem.

• Make your comparisons authentic and to the point of your poem.

• Make sure you have enough detail to give good mind pictures.

About Crafting

• Read it aloud to see if the line breaks work for the emphasis.

• Experiment with line breaks and white space—try your poem a few different ways.

• Try using some repetition of words, sounds, or lines.

• Try using some surprising language.

• Experiment with using lists.

• Replace ordinary words with specific ones—for example, stronger verbs.

• Try different leads or endings.

• Try different titles.

• Try changing the order of your lines or stanzas.

- Using their personal thesaurus to find more poetic words that might lift the quality of their poems.

- Working with partners to help with revision.

- Asking partners to read their poems aloud to see if the poems make sense according to the decisions the poet has made about line breaks and punctuation.

The Result

This deliberate work with drafting and revising the poems throughout the Poetry Study supports the students' understanding that interesting content and surprising words are not the only tools of the poet; indeed, line breaks, white space, and punctuation all add to the successful revision of a poem.

Phase 5: Editing and Publishing

What the Teacher Is Doing

- Putting student poems on the overhead to edit and spurring conversations about the ways to edit poetry.

- Making all final edits.

- Helping students make decisions about the format of their poems for publication. Will it be in an anthology containing all the poems of the class and photocopied for each student? Will it be enlarged and illustrated to be hung throughout the school? Will the poems be given as gifts in the form of cards or framed in an attractive self-made or store bought frame, etc.?

What the Students Are Doing

- Self-editing, peer editing

- Deciding on how to illustrate the poems for publication

- Filling out a Poetry Reflection sheet that will allow them to reflect back on the process (see Figure 10–8F and Appendix N).

The Result

There is always great satisfaction at the end of any publishing cycle, but the excitement is sky high when we reach the end of our poetry genre study. We've invited our students into the world of poems and we all celebrate a job well done. We've helped inspire a class full of young writers who now regard themselves as poets. What better gift could we give them?

Highlighting Student Work

Please see Belinda's poetry work in Figure 10–8A–F as she goes through the entire process from initial entry to published work. See our website <www.heinemann.com/davis-hill> for additional student poems written during this study.

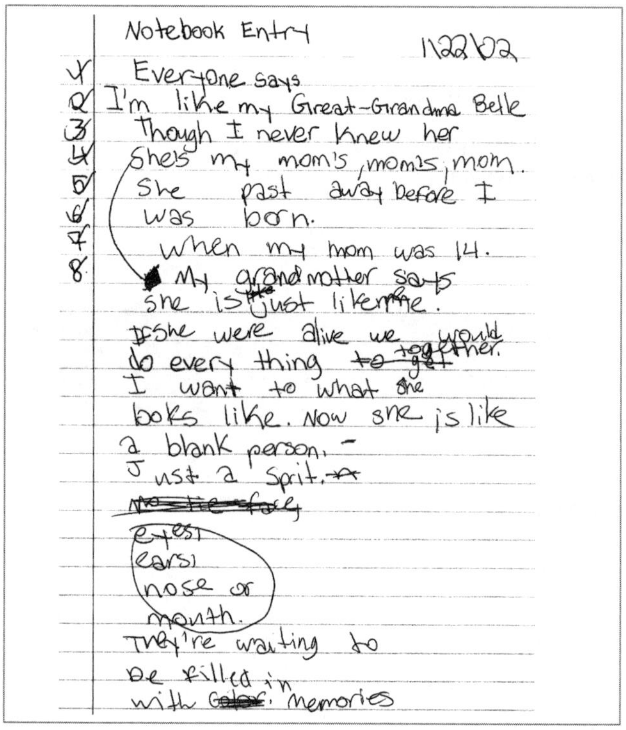

FIGURE 10-8A. *Belinda's notebook entry.*

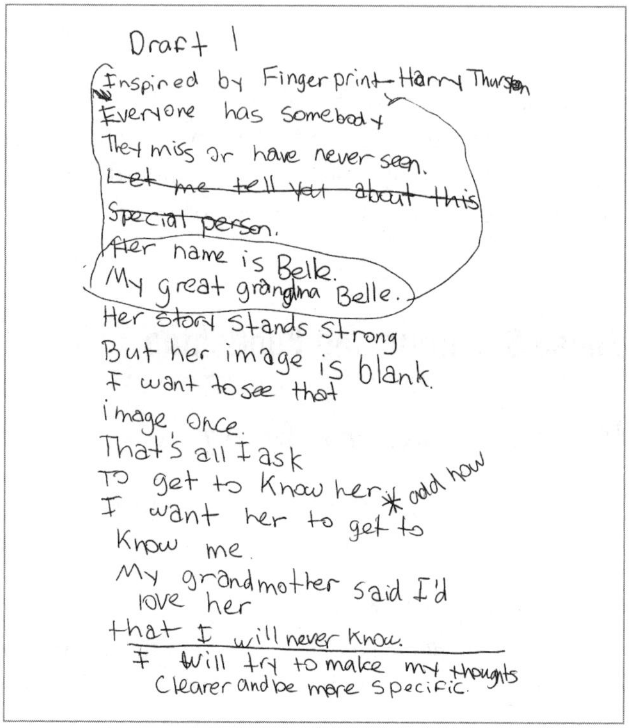

FIGURE 10-8B. *Belinda's first draft.*

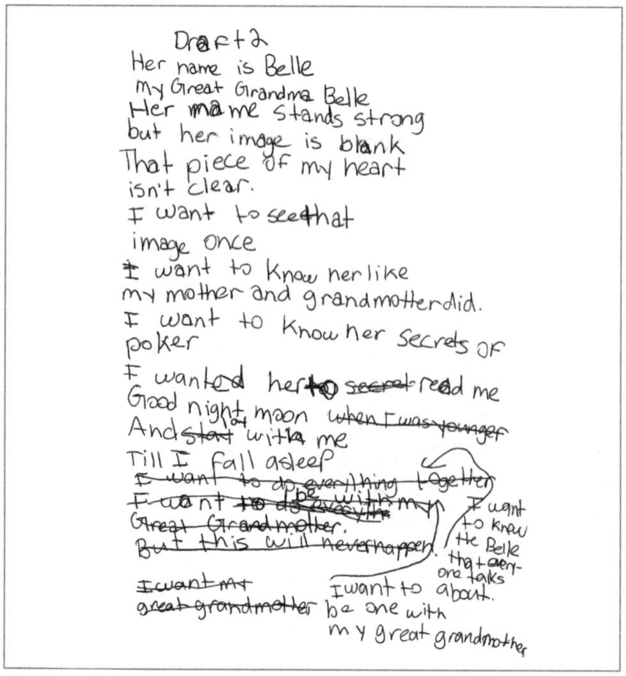

FIGURE 10-8C. *Belinda's second draft.*

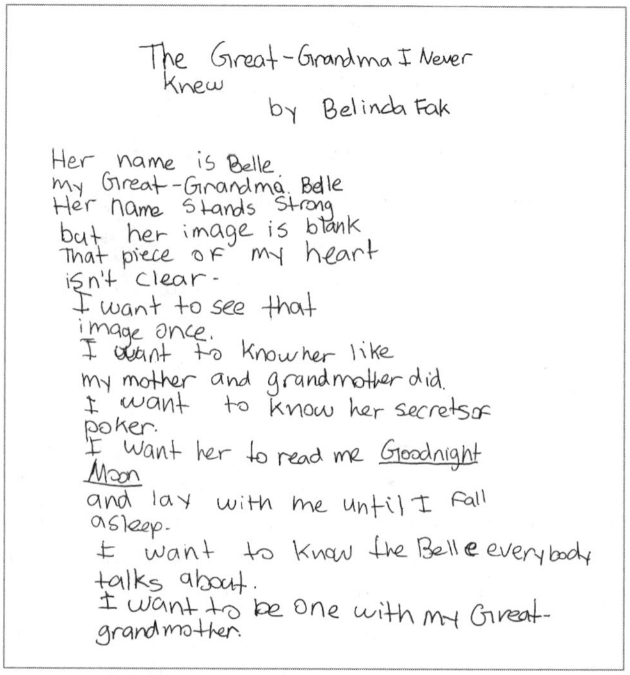

FIGURE 10-8D. *Belinda's poem.*

Poems by Belinda F

The Great-Grandma I Never Knew

Her name is Belle,
my Great-Grandma Belle.
Her name stands strong,
but her image is blank.
That piece of my heart
isn't clear.
I want to see that
image once.
I want to know her like
my mother and grandmother did.
I want to know her secrets of
poker.
I want her to read me Goodnight
Moon
and lay with me until I fall
asleep.
I want to know the Belle everyone
talks about.
I want to be one with my Great-
grandmother.

Alone

I want to be
locked in a castle
guarded by a fire-breathing
dragon.

I want to be riding my bike
through Central Park
while clearing my thoughts.

I want to be locked away
 from the rest of the world.

Alone,
 I unlock
secrets I've never known
about myself.

Mother Nature's Call

In the sky, in the summer sky
In the warm, pale pink and
lavender sky.
I see people driving a motorboat.
on my water.

In the sky, in the fall sky.
In the crisp, red and orange sky.
I see people picking juicy
apples off my trees.

In the sky, in the winter sky.
In the icy, white and gray sky.
I see skiers skiing down
my icy mountains.

In the sky, the spring sky.
In the awakening blue and green
sky.
I see moms & sons flying kites
in my glorious sky.

FIGURE 10–8E. *Belinda's published poems.*

POETRY REFLECTION

Belinda

As a result of this study, comment about how you've changed as a reader of poetry.

I've changed as a reader of poetry in many different ways. I used to think poetry was just a form of writing. Now I think it's more of a genre. With a special kind of writing that gets to your heart. I never read a lot of poetry till now. I never really liked poetry until I read more of it. I have more patience to reread them to get the meaning.

Comment on how the process you use to write original poems has evolved as a result of this study.

The process I used to write poems has evolved in some ways like spending more time on revision. When I read a good poem I start thinking about a good poem. I start thinking about writing what. It has inspired me to write.

For each of your poems, identify the quality of the poem you feel best about.

Title The Great Grandma I Never Knew
Comment I think I really used very descriptive lines I think people will not have to dig deeper to find out the meaning but they will relize that this is very important to me.

Title Alone
Comment It really shows people how much kids need to be alone sometimes. It is very descriptive about how I find my inner self. I like the way I used repeated lines and repeated the title at the end.

Title Mother Natures Call
Comment This shows my love for nature. and the outdoors. Everyone should care about the nature and this shows that I really do. I like the way I repeat the first line in every season and I like how I describe each season by naming what people do.

FIGURE 10–8F. *Belinda's poetry reflection.*

Feature Article Study

Our students at The Manhattan New School are encouraged to write for real reasons from the time they enter kindergarten. They've been writing letters, notes, lost and found fliers, brochures, signs, invitations, and various types of lists and notices. The list of their nonfiction writing is nearly endless. One of the signs of maturation as children move up through the grades is their increasing ability to step outside of themselves and their experiences and widen their view of the world. As they begin to develop some sense of their place and responsibility in the world, the Writing Workshop is a good place to help them deepen these explorations. By this time, our upper elementary students have had many experiences dipping into the wide pool of nonfiction reading material including books on various nonfiction topics, catalogs, newspapers, and magazines. Recognizing the fact that a vast proportion of the material adults choose to read is newspapers and magazines, we feel a responsibility to open up this world to our students. As we have mentioned before, we required that *Time for Kids* become a part of their regular reading diet, and have encouraged parents to get subscriptions to other magazines to support children's personal hobbies and interests. We also know exposure to these formats helps them see beyond themselves, enabling them to make important connections with the larger world. These reading experiences with informational texts can become the foundation through which our young writers begin to explore topics that lend themselves to these formats.

As Randy Bomer makes clear in his book, *Time for Meaning*, there are multiple genres, or types of writing within the world of nonfiction writing (including personal narrative, memoir, biography) and each genre fulfills a specific purpose. Part of our job is to help our students find the genres that fit the content and the intentions they have for their writing. Some nonfiction genres, because of their very nature, may require a significant amount of research in order for them to fulfill their purpose. Keeping our focus on teaching our students to become better writers, we cannot afford to overload the study with a focus on research skills. Therefore, we choose very carefully the nonfiction genres we study. The ones we choose must allow our students to write authentically, to use the writing they have collected in their notebooks as sources for topics, and to publish well-written pieces that are not heavily reliant upon research. The nonfiction-based personal narratives and poems the students have already written required them to do some personal research. A study of feature articles will probably lead them to do more research that requires them to step out of their personal world and seek information that may be more related to the content areas. Later, when the students are required to write research papers, this will serve as a good early foundation for that genre. With these considerations in mind, feature articles became the perfect genre to study.

What Are Feature Articles?

Feature articles are those written pieces we find in magazines where the writer provides information about a topic in an interesting and engaging manner and makes us care about the topic at hand. Often, feature writers provide an unique perspective on familiar topics, provoking us to think about the topic in a new way. Sometimes the reader receives "food for thought," gets advice, is persuaded to think differently, or is prompted or take action. The writer usually weaves in his/her direct personal experience with experiences and knowledge shared by others. The writer may need to engage in some minimal research that enables her to include facts or statistical information to help support her stance. Figure 11–1 is an example of this. The research, however, is secondary in our approach. As Randy Bomer suggests, we must keep in mind that our focus is helping students understand the form and the craft of the form; so, the research is not primary and shouldn't overshadow the purpose of doing the feature article genre study in the first place.

In order to write feature articles, students are taught to revisit the entries in their notebooks to explore, from different angles, the topics they have already written about. One of our goals is not only to help students find topics, but to find their particular passion in the topic . . . to develop their stance. This is the greatest challenge of the feature article study. We are upping the ante by pushing them to step beyond their personal experiences to see how those experiences might stand up to similar experiences of others. An example may be useful here: When one of our students, Luca, began rereading entries in his notebook, he was particularly struck by an entry about how lucky he is that his parents buy him everything he wants. As we worked on taking other stances, Luca decided to write about how parents may actually be doing more harm than good when they give their children whatever they want whenever they want it. Luca's writing was no longer limited to his personal experience, but he made it stand up outside of his immediate world. He took a stance, one that he had not thought about before, and his voice reached out to the world with a message—don't spoil your kids. See

our website <www.heinemann.com/davis-hill> for Luca's writing.

During the course of this study across the grades at The Manhattan New School, Sharon found the most challenging work for students was re-envisioning their entries from a personal to more universal perspective. We recognized this as the place students needed the most support. Through this process, however, they made discoveries, which helped to lift the quality of their thinking and subsequently the quality of their writing. Since we believe that writing is writing to discover, this makes a feature article study well worth every ounce of effort.

Too Much Homework?

It's a typical day for Molly Benedict. The 6th-grader gets home from Presidio Middle School in San Francisco, California. She does not break for cookies; she does not phone a friend. She even walks right past the TV. Molly heads straight for the computer in the basement and starts writing a page-long book report on *Harry Potter and the Sorcerer's Stone* by J.K. Rowling.

After half an hour of work and some helpful suggestions from her mother for improving the report, Molly has a quick snack and starts chipping away at more than 100 math problems. She moves on to social studies—labeling all the countries and bodies of water on a map of the Middle East. Then it's time for science. She studies the way blood circulates through the human body for an upcoming test. All that's left is practicing the piano, a little fine-tuning on that book report, dinner and—finally!—sleep.

Does Molly's schedule sound familiar? The amount of time American students spend on homework each week is at an all-time high. In 1981, 9-year-olds to 11-year-olds spent an average of 2 hours and 49 minutes on homework each week. By 1997, kids that age were doing more than $3\frac{1}{2}$ hours of homework a week. Kids 6 to 8 years old had an even bigger increase, from 44 minutes a week to more than two hours!

"I don't have a lot of time to do just whatever," says Molly. "My friends and I think it's a lot of work."

THE LOAD IS SO HEAVY, AND MY BACKPACK IS SO SMALL

What's up with piling on homework? Is it an evil plot that teachers cooked up on their summer vacations? Of course not. Parents and teachers want U.S. students to keep up with kids in other countries. They want them to be pre-pared for high school, college and a career.

Part of the homework load is aimed at getting kids ready for tests. Students today face many more achievement tests than students in the past, including new statewide tests in many subjects.

But even parents who believe their kids should study hard think homework can get out of hand. Kids are burned out, they say, and parents are

American kids spend more time than ever on homework. Will their hard work pay off?

exhausted from trying to help them. "Some days it's just a struggle," says Lynne O'Callaghan, a working mom in Portland, Oregon. Her daughter Maeve is 8 and has two hours of homework every night.

A few schools have answered homework complaints by making new rules. In Hinsdale and Burr Ridge, Illinois, school officials came up with an official homework policy defining how much work kids in each grade should bring home. That way families aren't surprised by the workload. Other schools assign all the week's homework on Monday, so that kids have the whole week to complete it at their own pace.

But overall, the older kids get, the more time they spend on homework.

WHOSE HOMEWORK IS IT, ANYWAY?

Homework can be as big a struggle for parents as for kids, especially when parents do the work! Most teachers like it when parents help out but not when they take over the whole job. That's not the point of homework assignments.

America's parents—and kids—weren't always so involved in schoolwork. In the early part of this century, many school districts declared a total ban on homework for younger students! Experts thought homework would make younger kids hate to study. But in the 1950s, as the U.S. struggled to keep up with other countries in science and math, teachers increased the workload. Homework became a way of life.

WHY HOMEWORK IS HERE TO STAY

For all the frustration it caused, homework really does help students learn. In the upper grades (7th and above), doing extra homework has been shown to help kids score better on tests. "Homework has benefits that go well beyond what's going on in school," says Harris Cooper, a University of Missouri psychology professor who has studied homework's effect on test scores. Kids learn to be organized, manage their time and master new skills without a teacher's help.

The real experts are the kids who do their homework every night. They realize that although their assignments can be too long, too hard or too boring, homework is here to stay. "With less work, I think we could learn what we're learning now," Molly says. "But I don't think it's too overwhelming."

FIGURE 11–1. *Sample feature article published by* Time for Kids, *January 29, 1999. Reprinted with permission.*

Goals of This Study

The notebook can be a tool for gathering ideas for any type of writing in any genre. In order to publish a well-written piece, the writer must have some experience with the topic as well as an understanding of the genre he/she wishes to write in. We have chosen to teach the genres that make the most sense for our writers; ones that help them meet city, state, and national standards as well as provide the foundation for all future writing. A focused study on feature articles is a challenging one and relies on the students' previous experiences. Writers must be comfortable with the process from notebook to published piece and should have had previous experiences doing other genre studies. We choose to study this genre with our students for the following reasons:

1. Students are able to rely on their personal experiences and exercise their choice of topic, but are also challenged to see their topics from other possible angles.

2. Teaching our students to write feature articles lays the foundation and is a perfect segue into essays and other nonfiction writing they'll be doing as they move on through the grades.

3. It supports the writing that students are asked to do in other curricular areas.

4. The research students are taught to do in their content-area studies will provide some support for the research they may do to write their articles.

5. It supports understandings required by our state standards.

6. The features of this genre present opportunities for students to come to new understandings of the qualities of good writing.

Our goal is to help our students:

- Learn the purpose of the feature article as a nonfiction genre.
- Identify and understand the characteristics of the genre.
- Organize and use the information they have gathered around a topic.
- Identify topics in the notebooks that may lend themselves to writing feature articles.
- Take different stances on personal experiences or topics in the notebook.
- Examine mentor texts for possible structures and crafting techniques.
- Explore layout possibilities for published pieces.

Phase I: Immersion

What the Teacher Is Doing

- Preparing a variety of different types of articles that appear in newspapers and magazines and deciding on the ones to be used in the study.

- Reading aloud from your own selection of feature articles then allowing students to enjoy and discuss the content. The goal is for students to begin appreciating

---

Tips for a Feature Article Study

- Make sure the students have had previous opportunities to study other genres before attempting the feature article study.

- Make sure students have published a number of times and understand the process of going from notebook to published piece.

- If you plan to have the finished pieces typed in the format of a magazine or newspaper article, consider the expertise of your students as well as the availability of technology for doing so. If necessary, make plans to ask for parent volunteers to type the articles.

- Start gathering articles ahead of time. See our website, <www.heinemann.com/davis-hill> for articles written by students. They may make perfect mentors. *The Chicago Tribune* has a KID'S NEWS website with timely articles perfect for this study.

- Use short, one-page articles that present many opportunities for learning instead of longer ones that can become more cumbersome.

---

the genre by becoming familiar with the kinds of topics writers choose to write about and how the genre fulfills their purpose.

- Revisiting feature articles you may have previously used for other purposes.

- Encouraging students to bring in other magazine and newspaper articles they think will support the study. It is important to create opportunities for them to further immerse themselves in the genre by reading and discussing the articles in small groups.

- Encouraging students to be tuned into the personal connections they make while reading or listening to these texts, and to facilitate writing notebook entries inspired by those thoughts.

- Having periodic conferences with students as they read feature articles and discussing what they like as well as what they notice about the texts. By now, the students have some understanding of how genre studies progress, and you may notice an overlapping of their immersion with inquiry. So, not only might they be discussing the content of the texts, but also noticing some of the distinguishing characteristics. We welcome this when it happens!

- Providing support through conferences for students who have begun to position themselves as "feature writers." Often these students are either exploring new possibilities for existing entries or writing new entries inspired by the feature articles they've been reading.

What the Students Are Doing

- Immersing themselves in the genre by reading articles at home, with partners, and in small groups during Writing Workshop. They are discussing the topics with peers, making personal connections, and getting a feel for the way the writing in the genre goes.

- Writing new entries in their notebooks as they are inspired by the topics they have read about in feature articles, events happening in the world, and everyday observations.

- Revisiting old entries to try out new perspectives that could lead to feature articles.

The Result

As students huddle over articles, we overhear snippets of conversation about the content that are quite lively since the articles we are sharing are timely and very relevant to their lives. While their ears are filling with the sound of the writing, some students are already beginning to notice some of the features.

Phase 2: Inquiry

What the Teacher Is Doing

- Rereading a feature article each day to allow students many opportunities to examine the text in order to notice, describe, and name the distinguishing elements of the genre. The following box on page 171 highlights the Elements of Feature Articles the students noticed.

- Creating a Feature Article Study Chart to help students examine the mentor texts we are using (see Figure 11–2). The following chart was completed in conjunction with a study of the feature article titled "Too Much Homework" from an issue of *Time For Kids* (shown in Figure 11–1 on page 167).

- Reading aloud feature articles and asking the students to imagine what the notebook entry might possibly have been had the writer kept a notebook. Draw from this discussion, helping students begin to imagine what feature articles might emerge from their own notebook entries.

- Helping the students practice taking different perspectives or different stances on a topic. Here are some ways of doing this:

    - **Example 1:** Find published pieces on the same idea to show how different writers have chosen to write about the same topic in different ways. While the topic is the same, each writer has a different purpose and has taken a different perspective.

    - **Example 2:** Using either student or teacher writing on an overhead transparency, the student gives examples of various perspectives he/she might take as the writer of this feature article. If the teacher is doing this work, it may be helpful to prepare the new entry ahead of time on a transparency then share the reasoning behind the new stance.

- **Example 3:** If you have established the ritual of collecting students' notebooks to get a sense of how things are going, take that as an opportunity to leave sticky notes on entries that seem to have the potential for exploration as feature articles. During conferences, further support the students in taking new stances.

- **Example 4:** Take a topic the class has had some experience with, and through interactive writing, take a new stance on the topic together.

- **Example 5:** Make a chart that displays the topics and the possible stances students are taking and display it publicly. This supports students in keeping the flow of ideas going and envisioning new possibilities.

What the Students Are Doing

- Selecting articles that could become additions to the class collection and discussing why they are good examples.

- Reading feature articles to add information to the class inquiry on the elements of features and using the list to help them with their writing.

Elements of Feature Articles

- Timeless—about an issue that could happen at any time. Sometimes a feature article can be the human side of a news event (i.e., about a family experiencing hardship after a hurricane).

- About people—(primary source) about issues and problems that affect all types of people at some time.

- Informs the reader.

- Usually we know the writer's take or perspective. Sometimes it is a detailed, anecdote-rich article.

- Uses interviews, quotes, or statistics (secondary sources) to support the writer's perspective.

- Could be a question the author sets out to explore.

- The writer is passionate about the topic and it shows.

- Portrays slice or window into someone's life or a topic pushed towards making a bigger point.

- Use qualities of good writing: the voice is clear and demonstrates authority of the subject matter.

FEATURE ARTICLE STUDY CHART

Text studied: *"Too Much Homework"* (*Time for Kids*)

LEAD	POINTS THE ARTICLE MAKES	PERSPECTIVE OR STANCE	HOW THE AUTHOR SUPPORTS THE POINT	KINDS OF INFORMATION INCLUDED	CRAFT
Introduces the person (Molly) focusing on details that support "Too Much Homework" "It's a typical day for Molly Benedict. The 6th grader gets home. . . . She does not break for cookies; she does not phone a friend. She even walks right past the TV." *Supports the point right away by showing her typical evening. Details her assignments.*	Kids are spending a lot of time on homework compared to previous years. Reasons why kids get homework. What some schools have done to offer some solutions. Parent involvement in homework. Benefits of homework.	Kids get a lot of homework, but homework may not be all bad. Does not make an argument that it is a bad thing. Gives some advice.	Gives several details about an evening after school for Molly. "Molly has a quick snack and starts chipping away at more than 100 math problems." **Makes comparisons between:** Kids in U.S. and kids in Taiwan. Kids in 1981 to kids in 1997. **Uses quotes:** "I don't have a lot of time to do just whatever," says Molly. "My friends and I think it's a lot of work." **Uses data:** "In 1981, 9-year-olds to 11-year-olds spent an average of 2 hours and 49 minutes on home-work each week." **Gives other perspectives:** "Feeling sorry for yourself? Cheer up! A first grader in Taipei, Taiwan, does as much homework as a 1st-grader in Minneapolis, Minnesota."	**People related information:** Gives a window into Molly's, her mom's, and other parents' lives around homework. **Research-related information:** Uses data. Quotes from parents and an expert. Gives a little on the history of homework from "total ban" to homework as "a way of life."	**Lists:** She does not . . . She does not . . . She even . . . **Asks the reader questions as an interesting way of providing information:** "Does Molly's schedule sound familiar?" **Uses exclamation marks to make interesting points stand out:** ". . . especially when parents do the work!" **Uses dashes and parentheses:** "All that's left is practicing the piano, . . . dinner and—finally!—sleep." "In the upper grades (7th and above), doing extra homework . . ." **Ends with an uplifting quote:** ". . . I don't think it's too overwhelming."

FIGURE 11–2. *A feature article study chart for "Too Much Homework."*

- Choosing mentor texts that they will use to help guide them through the process. They'll rely on these texts to study the kinds of information the writer has included, the structure, and the craft.
- Using the grid in Figure 11–3 to plan studies from notebook entry to feature article. Students share these possibilities in small groups and discuss how each plan would work as a feature article. Daniella's work below is a typical example of this planning.
- Writing entries in the notebook with feature articles in mind and practicing developing the voice and taking new stances.

The Result

From our immersion and inquiry, students begin to notice how paragraphs are set apart by subheadings and the ideas are presented in a more direct way than in poems or picture books. Students notice that the quotation marks are not an indication of dialogue taking place, but are instead quotes from sources that are used to support points the writer is trying to make. They are beginning to see that feature articles are "not a new species," as was so nicely framed by Antoine, but are very much related to the other genre we have studied.

FROM NOTEBOOK ENTRY TO FEATURE ARTICLE

DESCRIPTION OF NOTEBOOK ENTRY	POSSIBLE FEATURE ARTICLE TOPIC	STANCE/ANGLE/ PERSPECTIVE	RESEARCH NEEDS (STATISTICS)	INTERVIEW NEEDS: PEOPLE TO SURVEY WHO HAD SIMILAR EXPERIENCES—OTHER EXPERTS ON THE TOPIC
Date: 2-6-01 The things I'm afraid of.	Fear Drugs Peer pressure	I would take the perspective of a kid who has a lot of fears.	What kids are afraid of.	I would interview a psychologist to find out more about childhood fears.
Britney Spears and how I used to love her.	Role models	How kids find role models in rock stars or sport stars.	# of fan clubs for kids my own age.	Interview other kids to see who their role models are.

FIGURE 11–3. *Daniella's notebook entry-to-feature article grid.*

Phase 3: Developing an Idea

What the Teacher Is Doing

- Demonstrating how students may use webs or flowcharts to help decide what other information to include to support their stance. This is the next step once students have chosen the idea they plan to stick with and have spent some time writing their thoughts on that idea.
- Using mentor texts to help students notice the sources that authors use to support their stance.
- Demonstrating the importance of balancing personal experiences with other information.
- Helping students make decisions about which sources to choose to support their stance.

What the Students Are Doing

- Choosing the ideas they will stick with—ones they are interested in and know well enough to pursue.
- Collecting information to support their stance on the topic. Studying mentor texts to see what kinds of information are included. Deciding on what sources best support the writing they are doing. These may include:
  - Personal experiences
  - Information from surveys
  - Content obtained from reading other texts
  - Expert testimony/interviews
  - Looking more closely at their world through the lens of the idea

The Result

From having read many feature articles, the sound of the writing has begun to resonate with the students. They have tested out different stances on a variety of ideas and have identified the ideas for which they are most passionate. They are ready to explore such ideas as how unfair and unhealthy it is when kids have to tolerate parents who smoke, getting along with siblings, and parents with busy schedules who don't spend enough time with their kids. Their personal investment in their ideas has led the students to collect the information they'll need to compose their pieces.

Phase 4: Drafting

What the Teacher Is Doing

- Demonstrating how flowcharts may be used for helping students develop the focus of their piece and to organize their writing. (See Figure 11–4B, page 179.)
- Demonstrating how to use the information on their flowcharts to help them make decisions about what other information to include and what sources to investigate.

- Demonstrating how to use the information gathered about the topic to compose a draft.
- Using mentor texts to demonstrate:
  - Possible ways of organizing the piece
  - Possibilities for leads
  - Establishing voice
  - Development of the piece so the message is clear
  - Possibilities for endings
  - How to include quotes from others

What the Students Are Doing

- Deciding on a mentor text that will support them through the publishing process
- Using the mentor text and flowchart to help structure and organize their piece
- Trying out different leads
- Deciding on which information needs to be included and how to present it
- Composing drafts using the information they've gathered

The Result

Mentor texts are now becoming dog-eared from daily use. Favorite parts are underlined and marked with asterisks, and students return to them again and again to study the craft and practice it in their own writing. Energy is building as students share early drafts, offer suggestions, and appreciate each other's successes.

Phase 5: Revising and Crafting

What the Teacher Is Doing

- Revisiting mentor texts to study the craft more deeply. We add these to the Feature Article Study Chart (see Figure 11–2).
- Demonstrating the use of craft strategies using teacher writing, student writing, and mentor texts during minilessons.
- Demonstrating how students may use crafting strategies they already know to purposefully create various effects and lift the quality of their writing.
- Sharing techniques for writing titles.
- Identifying in mentor texts specific strategies the students are expected to develop as a result of having studied this genre. For instance, how the writer:
  - draws the reader into the article with phrases such as "imagine you are . . ." "have you ever . . ."
  - uses titles, subtitles, paragraph headings, and bolded excerpts to highlight information and "hook" the reader
  - uses play on words
  - weaves in quotations and research
  - makes transitions
  - develops the voice of the piece

- Supporting students in writing response groups by instructing students to:
  - ◆ use the expertise of students in their response groups.
  - ◆ notice reader response; for example, Does the reader chuckle in places you intended them to chuckle? Does he or she seem confused? Does the piece flow? Does he or she slow down or use his/her voice in the ways you intended?
  - ◆ ask the reader questions to determine whether or not the specific intentions he/she had for the piece have been achieved. Find out if the reader gets the point after reading: ask them to tell you the main points they got from the piece.

What the Students Are Doing

- Articulating their intentions and applying craft strategies that help them achieve those intentions and improve the quality of the writing. For instance, in a conference with Julie she indicated, "I want to emphasize this point, so I am going to repeat it in different places."
- Doing repeated practice of a particular craft to improve their understanding and skill.
- Finding places in their piece where they are able to meaningfully include the required craft elements for the genre as specified by the teacher. These would include: structuring the piece, making transitions, weaving in quotes and research, developing the voice.
- Independently trying out craft elements they have noticed in their mentor texts.
- Getting and giving support in writing response groups. Then using this feedback to make final revisions.
- Trying out possible titles.
- Making decisions about the inclusion of supporting diagrams, photographs, and drawing.

The Result

Through hard work, notebook entries have evolved into feature articles. You can see them evolve and hear them come together as students gather in groups and partnerships reading and listening to each other's drafts. The students are listening to make sure that stances have been supported, that transitions are smooth, and that the craft is effective. The energy is contagious as we get ready for the final stages of the process, where the students check to make sure the piece can stand apart from the author and still fulfill the author's intentions.

Phase 6: Editing

What the Teacher Is Doing

- Guiding students in reading and rereading the writing to make sure the thoughts are clear through the continued support of writing response groups.

- Selecting special features of grammar, punctuation, or interesting sentence structures based on the texts that you have chosen to study with students. A study of feature article elements promotes investigations around the following: ways of including quotes from other sources, the use of colons, semicolons, ellipses, and paragraphing. Set expectations for students to find ways of purposefully using what has been studied.
- Instructing students on how to read their pieces to check for the flow and to make sure the meaning is clear to the reader. Glitches in reading often mean glitches in writing.
- Making all final edits.

What the Students Are Doing

- Reading the pieces out loud to members of writing response groups as well as listening to others read their writing. Students make final edits based on these responses.
- Editing their own work and seeking the help of others when necessary in order to address spelling and punctuation issues.
- Trying out some of the new conventions addressed in minilessons.
- Fine-tuning the title and subtitle.

The Result

The pieces have been read over and over again by their authors and a few of their peers. With the message clear, the writing crafted, and the editing checks completed, it's time to focus on the layout and the final presentation.

Phase 7: Publishing the Articles

What the Teacher Is Doing

- Using mentor texts to guide students in making decisions about how the articles will be presented—looking at various features of layouts, use of space, columns, etc.

What the Students Are Doing

- Planning and trying out different layout possibilities
- Rewriting pieces in best handwriting or typing them on the computer
- Doing illustrations by hand or pasting/scanning pictures on the computer
- Completing an Assessment Sheet (see the website, <www.heinemann.com/davis-hill> for Daniella's assessment. Also see Appendix Q.)

The Result

The clever titles and relevant issues ring out loud and clear in the room and serve as irresistible invitations for all to read the articles. The writing is so real and the voices resonate with authority because students have written about topics tied to their own lives; what's more, they have applied the qualities of good writing.

Highlighting Student Work

Daniella ponders the meaning of a role model. Let's take a look at some stages of her process from notebook entry to final piece in Figures 11–4A–D. For all of Daniella's work through this process, please see our website <www.heinemann.com/davis-hill>. You will also find other examples of student feature articles on the website.

February 26 2001 Monday

I'm a kid and I see things I really shouldn't be seeing. Not because I want to seem older but because I can't help what I see. Last year when I went to Cortland, I played a game with the rest of my teamates. What the message in there was, I never understood until now! It's showing that a woman or girl's purpose in life is to show off themselves in becinie to men And also be beatiful to men. It also shows to boys that their purpose in life is to race cars and fix cars and be rich. But that is not a good message that kids 10-12 or older should learn because it's not true and also it's not appropriate. Does anyone realize what that means anymore? Do the video game makers know that they are the causes for unappropriate actions now a days? Or is my Idea of appropriat diffrent from everybodys everybody's perspective of appropriate. My idea of

appropriate is not watching Jerry Springer and and all of the other shows out there that are crazy like Jerry Springer's show.

Kids my age look for a role modles in life that are good for them. The problem is what is appropriate for the role modlos to do may not be appropriate for 10 and 11 year olds to do. People like Britney Spears are giving boys and girls impressions like these. She gives girls the impression that in order to be sucessful in life, they have to be beautiful to men and wear short shirts and so on. She sends boys the message that they have to look for someone who wearing like a girl who wears becinies.

Bad
[Britney Spears] ── [Mam]
│   │
Eminem   │
[TLC]   [Dad]
│   │
[Vitamin C]   [Grandma]

FIGURE 11–4A. Daniella's initial notebook entry.

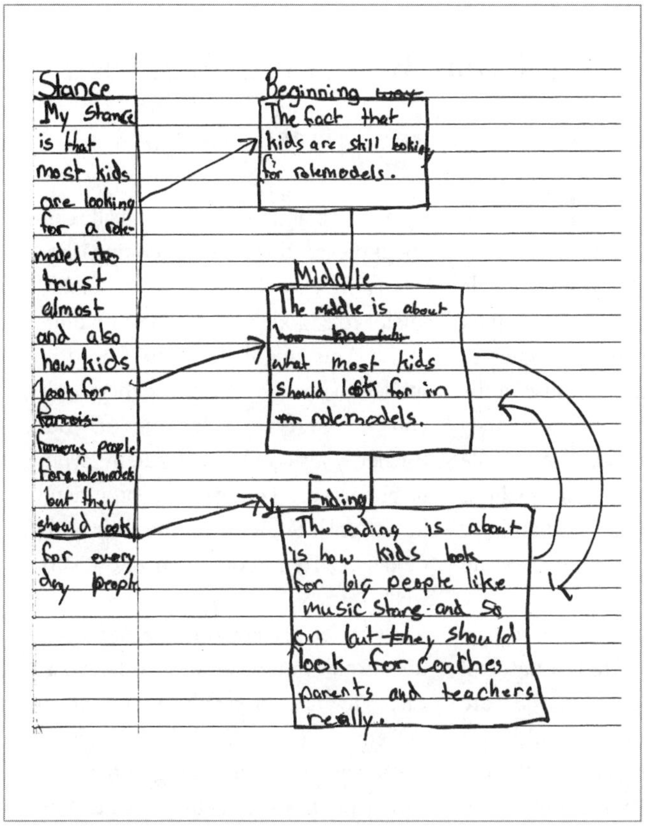

Figure 11-4B flowchart

Stance
My stance is that most kids are looking for a role-model to trust almost and also how kids look for parois- famous people for rolemodels but they should look for every day people.

Beginning
The fact that kids are still looking for rolemodels.

Middle
The middle is about how ~~kids look~~ what most kids should look for in rolemodels.

Ending
The ending is about is how kids look for big people like music stars and so on but they should look for coaches parents and teachers really.

FIGURE 11–4B. *Daniella organizing her ideas using a flowchart.*

Figure 11-4C draft page 1

Have you ever met someone and after talking with them you felt like you met your rolemodel? Did you ever think that the person that your sitting next to at dinner could be your rolemodel? The one who helps you with your math homework after your teacher spasifically said "Do this math homework on your own no help!" Or maybe your rolemodel is the coach you love to death but everyone else thinks that he stinks? You're probably wondering "hey whats with these questions?" Well most kids are still looking for a good rolemodel. Someone who cares about being a good role model for kids. Daniella, someone a friend of mine who goes to manhatten New School. I've has had a bad experiance with a bad role-model. Britny Spears she used to love her so much that I'm sure that if She keeped off liking her, her mom and would have gotten sick of her begging and she would have bought the CD. "The reason you I should't don't like Britany Spears is obvious for me," says Daniella "She is a a bad rolemodel for kids and, She strips" takes most of her clothes of on stage, and she tells girls that in order to be secessfull they have to wear little or no clothes." Daniella first realized this when one saturday in

FIGURE 11–4C. *Daniella's draft, page 1.*

Daniella's draft, pages 2 and 3

august, ~~three~~ six days after ~~away from~~ her birthday she was working with her mom on math. Daniella was afraid of bees at that time so she keeped getting up from my her seat. "I couldn't help it, I keeped getting up and moving away from the bees, no matter what my mom ~~would~~ say." Then Daniella's sister, ~~rushed~~ called her in because Britany Spears was on tv. "I thought it was something good but I knew as soon as I saw it I was in shock at ~~what~~ what I saw which was Britany Spears with almost nothing on." "It was on my mind all the time but finally I got on with life and decided to just move on." Its been a year since Daniella has hummed wistled or sang any Britany Spears songs she doesn't even think about her that much.

Do all rolemodels have to be rockstars? ~~That is not~~ The answer to that is no because rockstars and music stars and others at sometime some how disapoint you (like Britany Spears). Christiana Wishing who goes to at Daniella's YMCA says that "the best role model is someone who cares about being a good rolemodel for kids," like her-self she says.

"My rolemodel is my second coach called Robert." "My role model is Rob also because he helps me get better at my strokes and he doesn't curse or say or do bad things." Says Daniella, Christiana's friend. Not everyone thinks that They think he is crazy and mean.

The one thing kids should remember is when your looking for a good rolemodel look for someone they know and love not someone they don't know and are famous. Its not a crime to flip backwards over the Backstreet Boys, or clap and sing along with Christina Aguilera when she is on the radio but from what Daniella has experianced and ~~taken~~ from what Christina believes, they both recommend ~~pe~~ every day people they love and know.

Daniella's draft, pages 2 and 3.

Role Models Are Not In The Stars . . . They May Be In Your Backyard

Don't just look to the "Stars" for role models. . . look in your "Backyard"

By Daniella H.

Jennifer, a fourth grader is listening to her new Britney Spears C.D., "Oops I did it Again". Like many kids her age, she deeply admires Britney Spears. Jennifer watches her every moment she can on television, she listens to her on the radio, she dresses up like her and she even tries singing like her. In fact, Jennifer wants to be just like her. Jennifer sees Britney Spears as her role model.

"Role models are important to have," says Valerie the guidance counselor at the Manhattan New School. The problem begins she says, "when kids choose the wrong role models, choose role models for the wrong reasons or when role models behave inappropriately and cause big disappointments to those who believe in them."

"I used to adore Britney Spears," says Julie, a fifth grader who goes to school in Queens, New York, "until one morning when I dropped everything I was doing and ran as fast as I could to see Britney singing my favorite song on television." Julie described how shocked she was when she saw Britney Spears. "My idol was on stage wearing barely any clothing. I was so disappointed."

When asked why she adored Britney, Julie said that Britney was beautiful, popular and successful so she wanted to be like her. When she saw her on television with barely any clothing on, Julie wondered about the message Britney was sending to young kids like her. The message that you had to wear as little clothing as possible in order to be beautiful, popular or successful. Julie did not like that message.

Like Julie, many kids look up to famous people for role models, but they should be careful about which role models they pick and why they pick them. Some famous people are great to be picked as role models because of the things they do or because of what they have accomplished. If we choose role models, we have to pick the qualities about the person that are good and not pick the person just because they are famous and popular.

"Role models don't have to be perfect . . ." says George Brett, a baseball player. We can't forget that they are humans too and they should not become our idols. But after all, role models can be as mystifying as an undiscovered disease. So, it was not wrong for Julie to have chosen Britney Spears as a role model. But what she should have done was to find out more about her. If she did a little research, she might have found out that Britney wanted to be a singer since she was a very small girl. She worked towards her dream and was successful. Julie should admire that quality instead of just wanting to be beautiful like Britney.

Do all role models have to be people whom you may never have met like rock stars, movie stars, sports personalities, famous people on television or in magazines? Absolutely not! Sometimes famous people can be disappointing because not all famous people feel the same way as George Brett. He recognizes the need for role models more than ever in these troubled times, and if he can help the game's image with his behavior, he'll gladly accept the role as a goodwill ambassador.

Some famous people don't really care about the fact that kids are looking up to them as role models. So instead of looking for role models in the stars you don't know, you might want to find role models in your "backyard". . . the people you see everyday. How about your teacher, your coach, your parents, your neighbor, your family doctor or a friend in school? Sometimes the best role models can be people you know very well.

"One of my favorite role models is Rob, my swimming coach," says Melissa, a team member of the Flushing Flyers in Queens, N.Y., "because he doesn't go crazy over one kid doing something wrong and he doesn't curse. He has a lot of patience with me and other kids when he is helping us perfect our strokes, and he is always there come rain or shine."

So think carefully about the people you choose as role models. It's not a crime to flip backwards over the Backstreet Boys or scream and clap and sing along with Christina Aguilaira. But from what Julie has experienced, we can say maybe the best role models are those you know and love in your everyday lives. So take a good look at the good qualities your mom, your dad, your teacher, your coach or your neighbor have, and let them be the role models for you.

And, if you choose a star or famous person, make sure you find out about them—what are the qualities that make them successful or admirable? Then be free to love them and let those qualities be the reason why you would choose them as role models.

FIGURE 11–4D. *Daniella's final feature article in published form.*

Picture Book Study

It wasn't such a long time ago that upper elementary school teachers hadn't yet tapped into the potential of picture books for the teaching of writing. We loved to read them aloud to our students because they could relate to the stories and identify with the experiences. Then, along came *writing process* and the notion that we must provide mentor texts for our young writers. It became obvious that trying to model the qualities of good writing from a novel was a futile effort. Our students needed to use mentors that were more like the kind of writing they could produce. Of course, everyone agreed that picture books provided just the supports they needed. Their length, use of illustrations, predictable form, and simple story line lent themselves to perfect models. We could refer to them over and over again, and, we certainly loved reading them aloud to our students. Soon, we found beautiful baskets and filled them with our favorites and made them a staple of our Writing Workshop.

Goals of This Study

Our intention during this genre study, as it is with all the studies we write about, is to build on our students' previous experiences with the genre, in this case picture books, by presenting explicit minilessons that help our students study the genre with the particular lens of crafting a piece of writing in the genre. We are aware that there are many different types of picture books. When we choose to do a picture book study, we think of books such as *When the Relatives Came* by Cynthia Rylant or *A Chair for My Mother* by Vera B. Williams. These are the rich story books we begin to gather to study more closely with the children. These types of stories match well with the style of entries we have been encouraging children to collect in their notebooks. They are about what they know best and lead to the richest retellings. It is also important that we stress to the writers the importance of imagining the illustration that would compliment their writing in this genre. They must ask themselves if they have created an image vivid and detailed enough to be illustrated. It is a barometer writers use to judge if their writing meets the criteria for a picture book. It is also our intention to support students as they:

- Become familiar with the qualities of picture books through immersion and inquiry into the genre.
- Identify entries in their notebooks that have the potential to be developed into picture books.
- Study the craft used in picture books and apply it to their own writing.
- Make decisions about which picture books provide the supports they need as they go through the stages of the writing process.
- Clarify their intentions for what they want to say and how they want to say it.
- Develop an understanding of the purpose of illustrations in picture books and verbalize their intentions for the use of illustrations in their own work.

Year-Long Supports

Throughout the year, and every prior year at our school, the students have had many experiences with picture books. That is why we chose to make it one of our genre studies. The students have:

- Listened to us read their favorite picture books, discussed personal connections, and written about them in their notebooks.
- Gone to the shelves to read picture books for ideas when they were facing the blank page.
- Studied picture book texts for particular craft techniques during our study of revision throughout the year.
- Read favorite picture books over and over again with their reading buddies from the younger grades.
- Filled their notebooks with pages of entries waiting to be reread and studied for this writing project.

Phase 1: Immersion

What the Teacher Is Doing

- Gathering picture books and putting them in baskets around the room so the students can easily access them when it is time for Writing Workshop.
- Rereading the picture books that have become mentors to the class.
- Generating ideas from the children as to what makes a good picture book. Our class-generated list follows on page 184.
- Reading the book flaps to find out if the book's events come from the author's life. If so, generating conversations about what parts seem real and what parts might have been intentionally added for the sake of the story.

Tips for a Picture Book Study

- Don't attempt it too early in the year. It is best when children have published a good number of smaller pieces and have many revision strategies and craft techniques firmly planted under their belts. As they read many picture books, they'll easily identify the craft they've been learning all year long.

- A self-published picture book can take a very long time to complete if you consider that the art and illustration can take a very long time to get through. We suggest considering the writing portion of the work as your genre study. Although you must support the art as the students make decisions, schedule the completion of the artwork as homework after that. Set the children up with a schedule of work so they can complete a certain number of drawings a night as you move on with your next writing cycle. If you try to hurry the students' artwork to fit it into the time frame of a writing cycle, the quality of their work will suffer. If you give the time necessary to really work on art in class, your writing will suffer and you will spend precious Writing Workshop time completing the art. Set aside several regular check-in dates for peer conferring and share times.

- Consider purchasing already bound, hard-covered books as you did for the poetry anthology project. Remember, you can purchase "Bare Books" inexpensively from a company called Treetop Publishers. They come in a variety of sizes. You can order just the right size to match the type of writing your children are doing. The children will take them very seriously because they are hard covered and much like the ones they might find in a bookstore. Of course, you can make your own books if you have the materials and know-how and think your children would enjoy that process.

- Give each student an oversized zip-lock plastic bag. Since the books are white, they get dirty easily. The bags help keep them clean until the work is complete.

- Consider the type of publishing celebration you'd like to have. (See Chapter 7.) With this end in sight, set a flexible date for the celebration. As you move along in the study and get a better sense of the possible completion date, firm up your plans. Remember to remind the children of the deadline. Too many of us neglect to set deadlines and the study can go on way too long.

- During the celebration, make preparations for readers to write reviews. You can have them write directly on the back cover of the Bare Books (permanent marker works great) or create a comment sheet that can be pasted on the back or inside of the back cover. These reviews serve as a permanent reminder of the caliber of the work they have done during this project.

- Encouraging students to read as many picture books as possible, branching out to try different types other than those they are familiar and comfortable reading. This is an opportunity to expand their repertoire.
- Conferring with students as they read picture books and promoting discussions about what they like about the books. These conversations help support the writing as the children move further along in the study.
- Conferring with students about what is already in their notebooks and supporting them as they make proper choices for subjects for picture books.
- Taking home notebooks and using sticky notes to identify entries that you think could be developed into good picture books. The simple act of jotting a note to a student suggesting that you could imagine this idea being developed into a picture book and sharing your ideas in a conference empowers the writers and helps guide them into making the right choices. By doing this, you can do some advance troubleshooting. With large classes, it is difficult to confer with each student before they have made a choice about an idea for this project. This teacher review can avoid a student developing an idea that might not be rich enough to be realized as a picture book.

QUALITIES OF A GOOD PICTURE BOOK

- The story is one we can relate to.
- The characters are like us or remind us of people we know.
- The lead gets us interested immediately.
- The writer creates images we can visualize.
- The writer uses crafting techniques we can name.
- We want to know what is going to happen next.
- There is an element of surprise in the story.
- The story is rich enough to make you want to turn the pages.
- The story has some believability to it.
- There is a predictable format that the reader can follow.
- The writer's intention is clear.
- The illustrations add more to our understanding of the text.
- The dialogue sounds like the words of real people.
- You understand why the writer is telling you this story.
- The end is satisfying.

What the Students Are Doing

• Reading lots of picture books.

• Bringing in their favorites from home and sharing them with classmates.

• Writing entries, some that may be inspired by picture books they have read.
Figure 12–1A is used in support of this work. Keep in mind that many students
write new entries but many revisit entries, allowing this immersion to influence
their thinking on an old idea. Figure 12–1B is Julia's new entry inspired by
When I Was Young in the Mountains.

Getting Inspired By A Good Picture Book

Name: Julia

Title of
Picture
Book: When I was Yung in the ~~Man~~ Mountains   Author: Cynthia Rylant

Topic: When the author was young in the ~~man~~ mountains

Type of Illustrations: they go with the words – one Se scene with no really big background

1. **Read the picture book**

2. **What did you love about it?**
I loved the way that this book had no ~~dialog~~ dialogue. It was just the author speaking to the reader. I also loved how Cynthia Rylant picked out the things that stood out most to her when she was ~~yo~~ young in the mountains.

3. **Reread your notebook. Did you revise an entry? How did this picture book inspire you to revise your entry the way you did?**
~~Yes, I revised an entry.~~

4. **Did you write a new entry? How did the picture book inspire you?**
Yes, I wrote a new entry. This picture book ~~inspr~~ inspired me to write an entry almost like it. ~~This book~~ The only thing I did was change the setting to Arizona.

5. **Do you have an idea for a picture book of your own yet? If so, how do you imagine it might go?**
One idea for my picture book is expanding on my entry. It would go something like this: "When I ~~expi~~ experienced Arizona...." Then I would go on to ~~say~~ talk about the things that were special to me.

FIGURE 12–1A. *A response form for picture books.*

The Result

On the one hand, we are trying to create this sense of relaxation and enjoyment around the reading of these texts. On the other hand, we want the students to have a sense of their responsibility to begin to set up mental files that will allow them to be poised and ready to begin the work that lies ahead.

2-17-02

off of "When I Was Young in the Mountains" by Cynthia Rylant
Possible idea for picture book

When I experienced Arizona, I tasted a town like citing and tex-mex food. I swam in a hexagon shaped pool, and ate in a restaurant with an Irish name, but no Irish food.

When I experienced Arizona, Dad said to get in the car and I packed my books. Mom sat next to Dad, and my Brother sat next to me. We all looked out the window and saw the city buildings turn to dry desert and cacti.

When I experienced Arizona, Mom pointed out mountains and we ooohed and aaahed at the towering forms of nature.

When I experienced Arizona, I looked down from a Mesa mesa only to gave gaze upon a shimmering city, and a distant town. Dad had paid for the jeep ride up and down the mountain.

When I experienced Arizona, I had my hair tied back and my sunglasses on and I watched the air-planes take off and land as the sun went down.

When I experienced Arizona, we were awe struck at nature's rock carved canyon. There was a trail, too. And we took it. It hugged the side of the canyon, and we could see as far and wide as the canyon went.

When I experienced Arizona, I waved to a friend on the otherside. I didn't know who I was waving too but there was a light, and the bright angel moon hung in the night sky.

When I experienced Arizona, I took a trip, an unforg unforgettable trip. And when I returned to the city, I read about my experience in Arizona.

FIGURE 12–1B. *Julia's entry inspired by the picture book* When I Was Young in the Mountains *by Cynthia Rylant.*

Phase 2: Inquiry and Analysis

What the Teacher Is Doing

- Using the Picture Book Study Chart to highlight with the students the features of the mentor picture book studied together that day. (See Figure 12–2 and Appendix S.)
- Giving students opportunities to share entries they think might become picture books and encouraging them to tell the stories to the class. When students are encouraged to tell their ideas first, before they have even written them down, it becomes easier when they write. Getting immediate feedback from other writers is important, too. This is the opportunity for classmates to tell each other what they think would enhance the story.
- Conferring with writers about what strategies they will use to develop their ideas for a picture book.
- Helping students outline their story and deciding where they need to collect more ideas.

What the Students Are Doing

- Returning to the picture books they read and choosing mentors. Filling in their personal Picture Book Study Chart as they notice the features of the books they choose.
- Rereading their notebook to choose an idea, then developing their ideas by talking to family members, looking at old photographs, doing research about a place they are writing about, talking to classmates, making observations, etc. Hopefully, this study of text characteristics will help as they gather more ideas for their book.
- Searching the notebook to decide if other entries can become part of the picture book. For example, if a student has decided to write a picture book about his experiences with his best friend who has moved to Philadelphia and has three or four notebooks entries that are about these visits yet he finds he doesn't quite have enough to flesh out the book, then perhaps entries from the notebook that don't address his best friend might be "reworked" or "invented" to fit the story. Perhaps he might have an entry about something he does with his father or brother (for example, playing chess), but for the sake of the picture book, it can be reinvented as something he might do when visiting his best friend. It is what William Zinzer has called "inventing the truth."

The Result

The students have made decisions about the ideas that would lend themselves to picture books. They have been developing those ideas in an effort to flesh out their stories. They have tried them out on classmates and listened to suggestions about what to add. As they prepare to begin their drafts, they know they are about to begin a long-term commitment that will include dipping back into the pool of mentor texts to help make deliberate decisions about such things as shape, leads, language, illustrations, and endings.

PICTURE BOOK STUDY CHART

TITLE/AUTHOR	STRUCTURE	USE OF TIME	LEAD	REPETITION	OTHER CRAFT	ENDING	ILLUSTRATIONS
Someplace Else by Carol P. Saul	• different vignettes with each child she visits • beginning and end connected	• nonspecific but feels like a few weeks elapse with each vignette	• gives setting at present and poses a question that connects to the title	• repeated dialogue pattern within each vignette • title: Someplace Else is repeated throughout the text • "All her life . . ." repeated throughout the text	• great transitions from vignette to vignette— "houses gave way to tall buildings" • great lists—"She went to museums and theaters and stores and restaurants" • describes specific details of each place she visits • rhyming names	• repeats the title and answers the beginning of the book question	• across both pages • matches the text • very soft colors
Daddy Played Music for the Cows by Maryann Weidt and Henri Sorensen	• follows the main character as she grows up • music is the thread that links the different events that happen	• about ten years pass • important events mark the passing of time— learning to read, first day of school, birthday parties . . . • illustrations help reader see the passing of time • lines like "all that year . . ." "in second grade . . ." "for my eighth birthday . . ."	• repeats title and gives the barn setting and music playing from the radio	• "As daddy played music for the cows" ends each scene	• uses specific names of people, places, and song titles, even the cows have names of famous singers • dialogue true to the voice of the character • strong verbs— whirled, twirled, chickens did the two-step	• end circles back to the beginning "while daddy played music for the cows"	• full spread across two pages • text in small box inset in the illustration • soft colors • shows the character getting older to help the reader get the feeling of time passing

FIGURE 12-2. *The class-created picture book study chart.*

Phase 3: Drafting/Envisioning the Structure of the Picture Book

What the Teacher Is Doing

- Presenting minilessons about how to draft the gathered material into a structure they have become familiar with from their prior studies and during the inquiry stage of this study. See Chapter 9.

- Helping children organize their thinking and make decisions about how to structure the drafts by looking at picture books with different structures.

- Sharing the writing of students who are well on their way to developing a picture book, allowing them to think aloud as they make decisions about the text. Such decisions might be about when to begin and end a page.

- Conferring with students about organization of ideas and supporting their thinking about what is still missing.

- Instructing children on how to write or type up their drafts; for instance, leaving spaces to indicate page breaks.

- Encouraging students to try organizing their ideas in different ways and then making decisions about which structure works best.

- Instructing students on how to fold pages of $8\frac{1}{2}'' \times 14''$ unlined paper in half to become pages of a mock book they will use for planning pages and revisions.

What the Students Are Doing

- Organizing their ideas into a typed text version of a picture book. This means they make decisions about where the pages might turn based on the structure they have adopted.

- Writing one or two drafts so they can work out the design and organizational challenges involved in actually putting the book together.

- Cutting and pasting each page onto the left-hand side of the mock book, leaving the right side empty so they can return to it for future revision work.

The Result

This envisioning sets the stage for the revision work that is about to come. They need to see it in order to see how to make it better. However, it is very likely that as they were drafting, organizing, and reorganizing their ideas, they were already thinking about the techniques they have learned and studied in the mentor books that would lift the quality of the drafts.

Phase 4: Revision

What the Teacher Is Doing

• Conducting very specific minilessons on particular aspects of craft. For this, you gather the mentor texts and organize them based on the craft being studied. For example, when studying leads, refer to the picture books studied, talk about the various leads, try to name them, and discuss why the author might have made the decision to begin the book that way. Encourage the students to return to their mock book, use the right-hand side of it to try two or three different leads for their book. Help them to note what they would like the reader to get from the lead and allow their intention to guide their choice of lead.

• Conducting minilessons on other craft strategies that would lift the quality of picture books. For example, study the transitions authors use in the mentor texts, list them, name them, discuss why the author chose to transition in that way, then encourage the students to go back to their mock books to study how time is passing in their text and try different transitions. Other strategies to study include determining how to:

  ◆ decide on and craft an ending
  ◆ create lists to add detail
  ◆ create comparisons to make the images more vivid
  ◆ use strong verbs to be very specific about the action
  ◆ make the story more personal by adding authentic dialogue
  ◆ craft a "best fit" title

• Conferring with the students as they are applying the different craft strategies; trying to identify those who are doing exemplary work; and forming partnerships and groups around what they are doing well as a way to support the work of the others who might need more help than you can provide.

What the Students Are Doing

• Practicing the craft strategy modeled during the minilesson and learned from their personal mentors. This work is done on the right side of their draft book. They try two or three different ways to revise their work by applying that strategy. See Jordan's work in Figure 12–3 and Driton's work in Figure 12–4.

• Sharing work with partners and groups to gain support and help with their writing.

The Result

Although the students have done a great deal of revision work to improve the quality of the text, the visioning the students do as they make decisions about art may influence their writing and force them to go back into the text as they realize that word images must match the visual images. During this next phase when art becomes the focus, it is a good time to go back into the texts to edit the work and make sure the spelling, grammar, and punctuation are correct before the writing becomes final.

The girls with the sparkly
hairpieces and fancy clothes.

The girls with sparkly scrunchies
and applying fake make up

The prissy primadonna girls
with their sparkly barrets
and patten leather shoes applying
fake make up

the rough tough boys.
wrestling on the
playground floor.

the rough tough boys
with baseball caps
wrestling on the playground
floor.

The rough tough boys
with their baggy pants and
backwards base ball caps
wrestling on the play ground
floor.

In one corner of the playground there were girls with the sparkly hairpieces and fancy clothes. In the other corner were the ruff tough boys. Wrestling around on the playground floor.

FIGURE 12-3. *Jordan's mock book, highlighting her craft work.*

p. 2

I feel lucky some times with my dad when I go places like Florida and we spend all the time in the world together, but when we are home in New York he is working all the time when we do our activities together like when I go on a ride in the car to places with my dad for fun, but the cell phone rings and he says "I got to go to work so I will drop you off at home." Or when my dad and me go for a bike ride in the park and he says, "I have to go to work because the guys need help."

I wanted the
reader to get
how busy my i,
father is in
New York

① In New York he is always working
ethier contracting, helping tenants because
he is a super, and fixing up a
apartment.

② In New York he is always a
busy bee working all day long on
Construction sights, A super, A contracter, fixing
Floods, leaks, and plumbing.

FIGURE 12-4. *Driton's mock book, showcasing his work on choosing a lead.*

Phase 5: Studying the Art and Editing the Text

What the Teacher Is Doing

- Conducting minilessons to support the editing of the writing.

- Returning to the mentor texts used to study craft and studying the art and the intentions of the illustrators as they make choices for layout and design. This would include choice of medium, choice of size, choice of color, decisions about how the illustrations will support the writing, and where the writing goes in connection to the text.

- Conferring with students as they edit and making any final edits if necessary.

- Conferring with students as they make decisions about art and layout.

- Securing supplies and encouraging students to try out different illustrations in various mediums that best express the mood of the book. Our colleague Joanne Hindley asks her students to choose a very descriptive line from their texts, fold a large piece of white construction paper into four sections, then create the same illustration in four different mediums, testing to see which works best.

What the Students Are Doing

- Self-editing and peer-editing their writing.

- Picking a mentor text to use as the model for the art they will be doing.

- Doing some sketches in their mock books to try out their choices.

- Experimenting with different mediums.

- Making decisions about layout, title design, and cover design. Will they cut and paste the typed version of their book or will they hand write it onto the pages of the finished book? Will they get help with the illustrations or will they do them alone? Will the cover be one of their favorite pictures from the book or will it be a completely different design?

- Transferring the work in their final book.

The Result

As it is when we read published picture books, we find that some illustrations carry the text, while with other picture books, it's the words that take our breath away. It will be no different for your students. Your artists might have gorgeous products while the writing may be a bit weak. Your writers might craft stunning stories, but fall short with the illustrations. Either way, the products are wonderful achievements and each should be celebrated.

Phase 6: Publishing

What the Teacher Is Doing

• Keeping track of the artwork the children are doing at home.
• Setting due dates for the work.
• Setting up check-in days where everyone brings in the artwork they are doing for a share and receives support from others in the room.
• Setting up a publishing celebration.
• Celebrating the work of the writers.

What the Students Are Doing

• Keeping to the established schedule for completing the artwork
• Completing the Picture Book Assessment (see our website, <www.heinemann.com/davis-hill> for Sophie's assessment and Appendix T)

The Result

The reward of this study is in the finished product and the pride the students feel when they listen to the comments of others and read the reviews of their self-authored and self-illustrated picture books. This work is evidence of the learning that has occurred all year to support this long-term effort.

Highlighting Student Work

You can follow the evolution of Sophie's picture book in Figures 12–5A–H from her first notebook entry to her final draft, some attempts at crafting from her mock book, and the final typed text of her picture book. For Sophie's picture book, see the website, <www.heinemann.com/davis-hill>. You will find typed versions of other student picture books on the website as well.

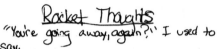

Rocket Thoughts

"You're going away, again?," I used to say.

"Look, Soph, I went away 3 weeks ago. That a long time ago."

"I know, but it seems like such a short time."

"Don't worry, Soph, you can send me Rocket Thoughts."

"Okay, dad." And that was good enough for me.

The nights when my parents were away, cold dark, bitter winter nights, or hot, steamy, humid summer nights, any time of year at all, I would lay awake in my bed. Knowing they weren't there. Knowing I was alone.

Then I remembered, I could send a message to my mom or dad anytime I wanted.

I would take my finger, gently put it to my forehead, and "write" the message that I wished to send. Then, I would keep my finger on my head, think about the place I wanted it to go, and send it off like a rocket. And somewhere in my mind, I knew it was in the right hands.

Through the period of time that my parents were separated, I relied on Rocket Thoughts. I would send them to my mom and dad all the time. And they would always get where they were supposed to be.

In those thoughts, I could say anything, to anyone in. It was like a journal. No, more like passing secret notes.

Now I'm 11. I have other things that I think about: Friends, school, basketball, piano, all new things. My parents are back together, so I don't need to worry about them.

Even though my life is different, and even though I'm older than I used to be, and even though I know Rocket Thoughts are pretend, I still believe that there is still a little majic that makes Rocket Thoughts real.

FIGURE 12–5A. *Sophie's original notebook entry.*

Babysitting Harlo

I loved to babysit. I didn't even care about the money I got. What I did care about, was Harlo. I loved him bouncing a ball with him, or counting with him, or watching T.V. with him. I loved to do everything with him. I loved babysitting. Except for one time. It was the time I found out he was moving. I tried not to get upset, I tried to keep cool. But inside my feelings were bubbling up, from my toes to my head. But I didn't let them go. Anger, sadness, excitment, all different feelings, for all different reasons, swelled inside me. I felt like I was going burst. But I didn't. I kept my outside calm.

The next time I went to his house everything was wrapped in plastic. The only thing we could do is watch T.V. We watched T.V. until my mother came. My mom and Harlo's mom talked about his new address, his new house, his new life.

I overheard them talking until Harlo's mom came out and gave me his new address. Harlo "wrote" his new address for me, too. It was all scribbles.

As I reluctantly left the house apartment for the last time, I gave Harlo a hug and promised to visit.

(Bye,) I thought, (forever) "I'll miss you." I turned back and mummbled. Then I realized, I just said good bye, forever.

FIGURE 12–5B. *An entry in Sophie's notebook that is indirectly related but informs her later picture book.*

Rocket Thoughts

I would stare up at the ceiling swirling cracks into pictures. I would wait, wonder when mom and dad would be back. Would they still bring me back the leftovers from dinner? And then I would remember, Rocket Thoughts.

To send one, I would slowly take my little five year-old finger, place it to my head, and pretend to write the message I wished to send to them.

A message would say something like, "Hi, mom! How's dinner? Love you, Sophie." or "Hey, dad! Hope your show is going well! Love you! Bye!" It could say anything from A to Z.

After I was finished writing, I would roll up the thought in my mind and send it off like a rocket. And that's how the name came to be.

I would send one when I was in bed, when I was in school, even when I was on a sleepover. Anywhere. Just to remind my parents that I loved them.

I would send one to them because I had something to tell them, or because they told me to, or just because.

They would send them to me when they were having a parent's night out, or performing, or even when they were teaching. Just to remind me that they loved me.

They would send them to me because they had something to tell me, or because I told me to or just because.

The times, reasons, even the Rocket Thoughts themselves have changed over time. Now I'm older, and I don't send them every night. Now I know that they were make believe.

But even though I'm older, and even though I know that they are kind of pretend, I still send them because I still believe in the magic that makes them real.

Rocket Thoughts

FIGURE 12–5C. *Sophie's evolving story in draft form.*

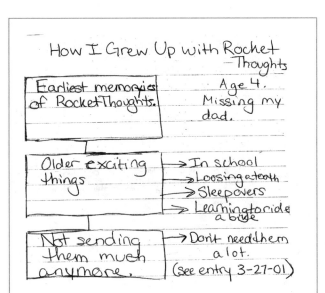

FIGURE 12–5D. *Organizing with a flowchart.*

I would stare up at the ceiling swirling cracks into pictures. I would wait, wonder when mom and dad would be back. Would they still bring me back the leftovers from dinner? And then I would remember, Rocket Thoughts. ✗

Ever since she I can remember her my parents have been teaching or performing they've been Going out at night or sometimes even over night. And ever since she I can remember, I've she's missed it them and worried about them.

Ever since she can remember, Sophie's parents have been teaching or performing. They've been going out at night. Sometimes out to dinner, sometime out to the movies, or sometimes out out the the theater. Sometimes even staying overnight. And ever since she can remember, whenever they did, she missed them and worried about them.

FIGURE 12–5E. *Working on different leads.*

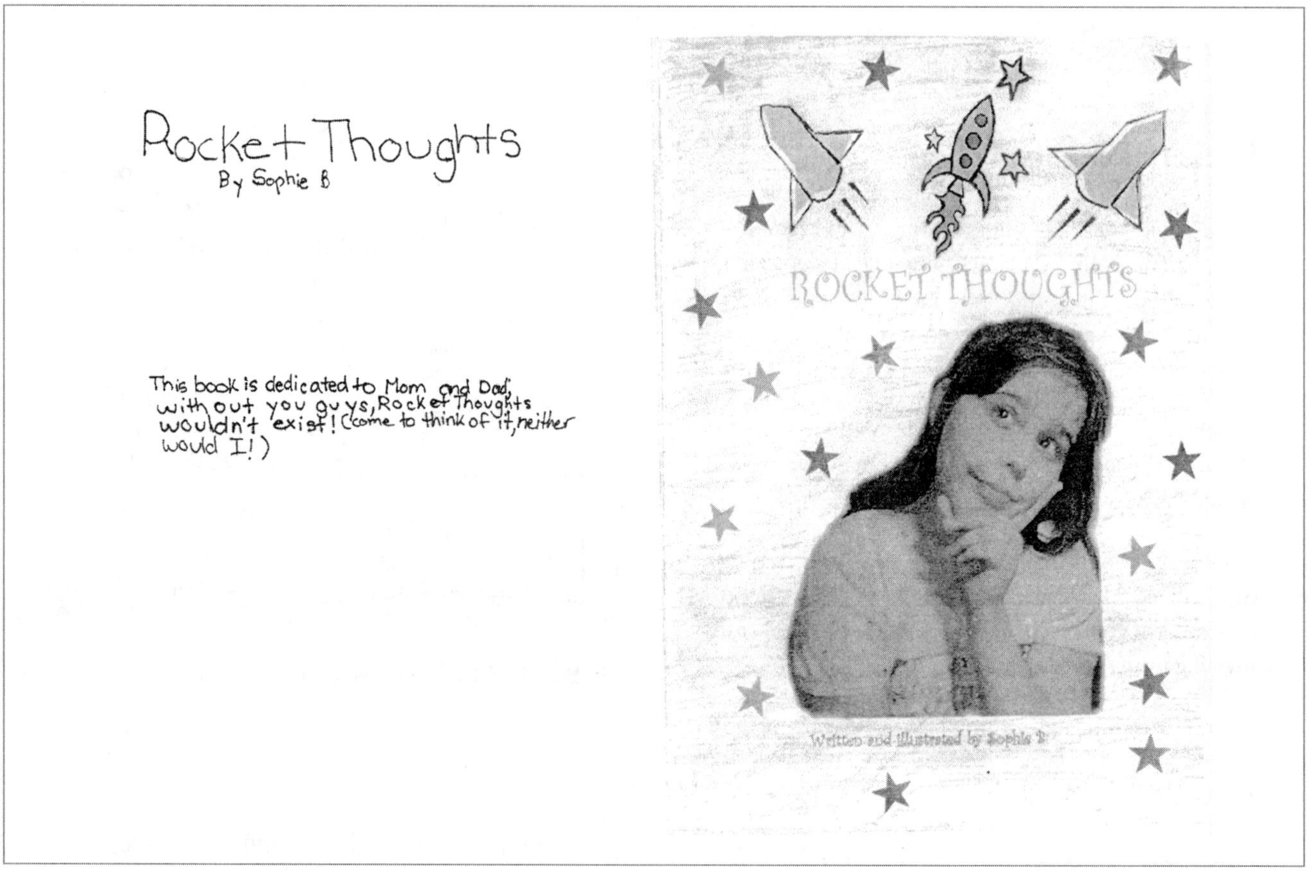
Rocket Thoughts
By Sophie B
This book is dedicated to Mom and Dad, without you guys, Rocket Thoughts wouldn't exist! (come to think of it, neither would I!)
ROCKET THOUGHTS
Written and illustrated by Sophie B

FIGURE 12–5F. *The cover and inside page of Sophie's book.*

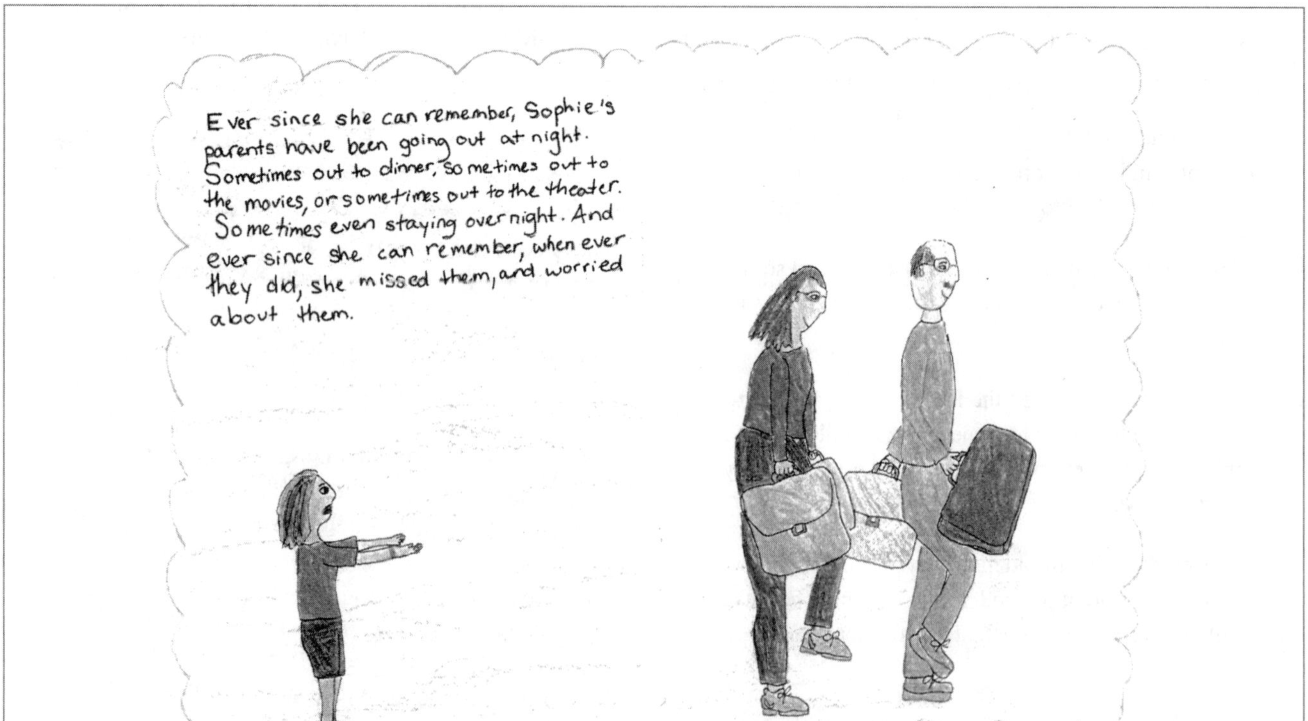
Ever since she can remember, Sophie's parents have been going out at night. Sometimes out to dinner, sometimes out to the movies, or sometimes out to the theater. Sometimes even staying over night. And ever since she can remember, when ever they did, she missed them, and worried about them.

FIGURE 12–5G. *The interior of Sophie's book.*

Rocket Thoughts

By Sophie B.

Ever since she can remember, Sophie's parents have been teaching, or performing. They've been going out at night, sometimes even staying overnight. And ever since she can remember, whenever they did, she missed them and worried about them.

One of those very nights, when Sophie was four or five, her dad was on a three day business trip to Washington D.C. and she was crying. Her mom was doing everything she could.

She tried distracting Sophie with one of her favorite stuffed animals, Eddy, and her Tinker Toys . . .

She cried louder.

She tried cooking Sophie a big, steamy pot of spaghetti and dumping a truckful of sauce on it, just like Sophie liked it . . .

She cried louder.

She even tried turning off Sesame Street and singing Sophie to sleep with "Chim, Chiminey" her favorite song from the movie, *Mary Poppins* . . .

She cried even louder.

Finally, Sophie's brilliant mother thought of the one thing that would make the waterworks stop: She called them, Rocket Thoughts.

She showed her how to write one (even though Sophie couldn't write yet). She told her to take her index finger, slowly put it to her head, and pretend her finger was the pen, and her forehead was the paper. She told Sophie to write whatever message she wished to send her dad.

She showed her how to send one. How to roll, twist and curl the thought up in her mind, strap on its seatbelt, and send it off like a rocket to her dad or wherever she had set the destination.

Sophie soon grew to love sending Rocket Thoughts. She also grew into a six year old, who sent Rocket Thoughts because she got elected class student council representative.

And a seven year old, who sent Rocket Thoughts when she spelled "because" right on her spelling test.

And an eight, nine, ten year old, who sent Rocket Thoughts to her mom when her dad taught her how to ride a bike. Who sent Rocket Thoughts to her dad when she hit the high note in the school concert and he couldn't be there. And to both of them when she went to sleep away camp and felt terribly homesick.

And finally an eleven year old, who sent Rocket Thoughts to wish them good luck on a show, or for no reason at all.

Now at eleven, and one-half, Sophie has started baby sitting for a five year old who apparently is very close to his parents. He cries every time they step out of the house!

One time it was getting bad. Sophie was trying everything she could . . .

She tried distracting him with his Legos and his favorite stuffed animal, Bunny . . .

He cried louder.

She tried slicing some apple for him, and smearing the slices with peanut butter, just the way he liked it . . .

He cried louder.

She even tried turning off the Tele-Tubbies and playing his favorite book-on-tape . . .

He cried even louder.

Finally, Sophie thought of the one thing that would make him stop sobbing. The one thing that would help him feel close to his parents once again, as it had for her. The one thing she knew only she could pass on. Sophie called them . . .

Rocket Thoughts.

FIGURE 12-5H. *The typed version of* Rocket Thoughts.

13

Open-Choice Investigations

In the latter part of the year, the energy is high. The students have come off genre studies, are invested in writing, and anxious to move at their own pace. With each cycle, the Writer's Workshop has taken the students from generating ideas in the notebook through the writing process and on to publishing personal narratives, poems, feature articles, and picture books. Some students have sent passionate letters and emails to friends, relatives, politicians, and business executives. During this time they've come to understand that writers must have intentions for their writing and those intentions drive the form for the type of publication. Students have been part of partnerships, response groups, and study groups in an effort to push their thinking and lift the quality of their writing. Our upper-grade students have served as mentors for younger students and been instrumental in easing them through their own writing process. Bulletin boards, baskets, and portfolios are brimming with writing that demonstrates our students' growth as writers.

Goals of Open-Choice Investigations

Our work in all subsequent cycles centers on three primary goals:

- To nurture independence when making decisions about forms for publishing

- To encourage writers to publish multiple genres from one entry

- To encourage writers to apply what they know about the organization of a genre study to design one that meets their personal needs for publishing

You have read about how we scaffold our students' development as writers by providing appropriate mentors, conducting minilessons that teach the writing strategies our writers need to accomplish this work, and conferring with individuals and groups in an effort to teach toward the process. You have read about how we conduct genre studies in an effort to broaden the field of possibilities for their thinking.

During these final cycles of the year, we invite the students to flex their muscles and make their own choices about the writing they will undertake. Up until this point, although they have always had choice about their writing topic and content, we have chosen the genre to focus on. Now, we expect that they will be experienced enough not only to make decisions about topic and content, but also to make choices about the appropriate genre.

Many students inevitably return to their notebooks, explore topics, and publish in genres they feel particularly drawn to: personal narratives, poems, feature articles, and picture books. Some will choose to work on revising pieces they published earlier in the year. Some will even return to works published in previous grades and apply their new writing skills to the revision of those pieces. Some find inspiration in research and begin investigations sparked by the work we did in the content area.

Others, however, attempt to look at the entries in their notebooks and make decisions about which ones might be a possible source for multiple publishing. In other words, students will reread their notebooks and deepen their thinking by taking a single entry and publishing it in many ways according to their purpose. Again, we expect them to make their own decisions about which form best fits their intentions.

By the time our students are ready to undertake this work, they have studied rich examples of different genres. They are ready to use written language in the way they use oral language, adjusting it for different purposes and different audiences.

To help our writers see the possibilities, we provide them with the topic chart in Appendix U to help frame their thinking.

Examples of Open-Choice Investigations

Zack

Zack chose to explore a notebook entry he had written about having a lazy eye. Zack had identified this entry as a possibility for further development earlier in the year, but never returned to it to gather more thinking around that topic. During this open cycle, Zack deepened his thinking as demonstrated in the following chart he developed.

Open-Choice Investigation Topic Chart

TOPIC OF NOTEBOOK ENTRY	FACTS	QUESTIONS	OPINIONS	POSSIBLE FORMS FOR PUBLISHING
I have a lazy eye	• I was born that way. • I can get surgery but I don't want it. • I'm different from everyone else I know. • I don't notice it anymore. • I am confident in myself now • People tease me.	• What do people think of me now? • What will people think if I have the surgery? • Why do people tease me? • Why do I think the surgery is being fake? • Why do my mom and dad constantly bring up the topic? • What would the surgery do? • What would people I admire do in my position? • Would there be side effects to the surgery? • How have I managed to build my self-esteem?	• People tease me because they don't feel good about themselves. • Surgery would be fake. It wouldn't be me anymore.	• Advice column Title: How to Develop a Strong Self-Image • An article for a kids magazine Title: Self Conscientious Is Everywhere • Report Title: Correcting the Lazy Eye • Personal Narrative Title: My Lazy Eye

Zack published a personal narrative about having a lazy eye. He researched the procedure that would correct the problem. He interviewed his doctor and wrote a report on the procedure and delivered a speech to the class about the steps involved and the potential risks. Finally, Zack worked on an article about how he went from being teased to developing a positive self-image in spite of the visible lazy eye.

Oliver

Oliver chose to explore an entry about loving to dance. Oliver had already published a personal narrative off this notebook entry. He revised it into a poem and revised it again to enter it into his poetry anthology. The chart below tracks Oliver's thinking as he continued to work in this open-choice cycle. (See Appendix U.)

Open-Choice Investigation Topic Chart

TOPIC OF NOTEBOOK ENTRY	FACTS	QUESTIONS	OPINIONS	POSSIBLE FORMS FOR PUBLISHING
I love to dance	• Even as a toddler, I would dance around the house • I go to National Dance Institute (N.D.I.) every Saturday • Love going to dance even when it cuts into other social time • The LaGuardia High School theater is my favorite place • Jacques D'Ambois started the National Dance Institute	• Why don't boys choose to dance? • Why do a lot of boys think basketball or baseball are boy's sports? • Are there as many boys in N.D.I. as girls? • Do more boys drop out of N.D.I. than girls? • Why does my friend Julian want to quit? • Why are so many people against boys dancing?	• Dance should be for everyone • Jack shouldn't drop dance or basketball • Because of freedom of speech, people can say what they want even if it hurts other people • People can say what they want about boys in dance but I don't have to listen	• Biography about Jacques d'Amboise • Article about how boys are stereotyped and teased if they dance • Persuasive letter to convince Jack to stay in dance • Essay for admission to middle school • Review of the movie, Billy Elliot • Picture book about the evolution of a dancer from toddler to young man

The following series of writing in Figures 13–1 to 13–9 shows Oliver's notebook entry written at the very beginning of the year and all the published work that followed. You can clearly see the benefits of returning to the notebook to dig deeper and develop thinking about ideas in different ways. Oliver's need to write about dance went far beyond the expectation we put on him to publish in school. This passion and persistence left Oliver with a world of written possibilities to get his voice heard. Now, he truly understands that writing is life's work and not school work.

Dance

When I was little any music that was flicked on I'd wobble up on to my feet bouncing on the spot itching to get sturdy legs so I could dance my heart out. There I would stand holding on to the side of my crib bouncing to Louie Armstrong or James Brown, always thinking about dance, always loving it.

I still dance, and still love it, any music that plays now my feet move to. My heart is full of dance and my feet are made of music I was born upsidedown from dancing to much and move to the night music while I sleep. Dancing is part of my life and my life is only a small part of dance.

I'm nothing without dance, and when days dance practice is cancelled, I slump around all weekend with an empty heart.

When I dance I try to express my feelings only by doing what my heart tells me to and thats the only thing I need to do t obe happy.

Dancing is my life because I was born dancing.

FIGURE 13-1. *Oliver's first notebook entry on this topic.*

Dancing Heart

When I leap from patch of light
to patch of light,
soar in waves of dancers,
and flip over colors flashing on the stage,
the feeling that beats in my dancing heart
is my love and my energy
mixed together in a warm sun of happiness
shining around a dance.

—*Oliver D.*

FIGURE 13-3. *Oliver's poem from an initial published piece.*

Dancer's Delight

When I soar through the air,
whirl through patches of light
and flip over waves of dancers,
the feeling I get is all my love
energy and emotions about dance
mixed together,
forming a warm sun inside me.
Magical moments to last
forever.

FIGURE 13-4. *Oliver's poem revised for his poetry anthology.*

A Dancing Heart

When I started dancing I got a feeling of amazement at each twirl and leap I did. When I flipped, whirled and jumped it was more than just a feeling I got, it's tons of love and energy mixed together forming a warm sun of mixed thoughts that welled up and burst, and exposed my inner emotions.

Dancing with the National Dance Institute is a great honor for me because I know that no other activity offers costumes filled with colors like crimson, sapphire and turquoise that could wipe out any shadow, frown or sadness from sight. Only dance offers leaping off the floor, twirling through waves of dancers and weaving around the stage in patches of light. But when I was picked for the S.W.A.T. team for N.D.I., I knew that dance had finally weaved its way into my heart.

The reason I keep dancing is because I know how hard my life without dance would be. Saturdays would drag by. The days would seem like weeks, and the empty space in my heart would take over. Dance is my way of showing my feelings a different way, a showy way, a way that everyone can see.

Although I might have to stop dancing, I will always think of dance as a wonderful memory that N.D.I created for me.

—*Oliver D.*

FIGURE 13-2. *Oliver's initial published piece.*

La Guardia High School Theatre

When I think of the big theatre at La Guardia High School, my feet get all twitchy, and I think about how my dancing life began there. When I was picked for the National Dance Institute (NDI) Swat Team, I knew that dancing would fill a big space in my heart, a space as big as the giant theatre, where the seats stretch out before you like a sea, and the people fill the seats like clouds fill the sky.

The stage is humongous and I guess if you stood on it by yourself you'd feel like you were suddenly, magically miniaturized right there on the wooden boards. But one never has to worry about that. The stage is always filled with dancers from schools from Chinatown, Harlem, Staten Island, the Bronx and Brooklyn.

The extraordinary thing about this room is that everyone in it loves to dance. They always cheer you up if you are sad, because the happiness of dance seems to rub off them and on to you.

Above us there are lights like giant flashlights connected to metal poles. They shine with the warmth of the sun and after a while, the stage is like the beach on a sticky, summer's day. But we don't mind, we keep dancing. When the lights are on us, it's so dark

in the audience, the room seems smaller because you can't see the people. But the audience, the silent audience, waits in the dark for the dancers to emerge into that light.

The colorful costumes and majestic scenery throw scarlet, gold, violet and azure across the stage. The bright colors make you want to dance like you've never danced before. The scenery is attached to long, clear ropes, impossible to see from the audience. One minute a ship will sail across the stage while the next, a treasure chest will fall from the ceiling, pulled, as if by magic, by stagehands from behind the scenes.

There are wings on the side of the stage. These are red velvet drapes soft as moss, that hang down from the ceiling. They make you invisible to the crowd when you're getting ready to dance onto the stage. Nobody knows you're behind those big curtains until you spring from out of nowhere surprising the audience so they jump from their seats.

Below our feet is the orchestra pit. Down there, bass drums as big as boulders and trumpets play so loud and so long that you feel it in your chest and your muscles, your skin and your blood. The singers sing from so

low to so high that you can just about see their vocal cords popping. The music echoes through the whole room. It vibrates the floorboards and rings around the orchestra pit, under our feet, up and down the red carpeted aisles and out the door into the corridors of the school.

When the music passes through my ears, into my heart and reaches my feet, I automatically start to dance. When we leap, I feel like I'm flying higher than the giant ceiling, higher than the singers' voices could reach, and when we land, the applause echoes off the high lights and the red velvet curtains and the wooden floor boards and keeps on ringing throughout the whole room.

I don't really love this room so much because of what it looks like, I love it because of who's in it, what's in it, and what happens to me there.

—Oliver D.

FIGURE 13–5. *Oliver's essay for admission to middle school.*

Jacques Amboise: A Dancing Man

Jacques Amboise is a very good model for boys who want to dance. Some boys are teased for wanting to dance. Some people say that it's wrong for a boy to dance, that dancing is for girls. They mock boys who dance. But they have never seen dance the way Jacques teaches it, they've never seen dance through the eyes of an NDI dancer.

NDI stands for the National Dance Institute. It's a program for kids in schools who love to dance. Jacques started it because when he was little, he danced with the New York City Ballet, and was teased for it in his neighborhood He wants everyone to experience the wonder of dance. "Approach a little boy and say 'dance,'" says Jacques, "and a part of him would say in this secret voice 'yes I'd like to' and another part of him would say 'I'd have to wear my sister's leotard and the other boys would laugh at me.'"

So Jacques started NDI with only six boys. They showed up and looked at him expecting him to hand them a bat and ball. But they were swallowed up by dancing once the lessons began. As the kids learned to dance, Jacques learned how well he could work with children, and soon the number of children grew from six to eighty in the first performance, and later to eight hundred boys and girls.

He teaches dance the way boys like it. Stomping, punching, and jumping to good music. Its not pointy shoes and frilly tutus and prissiness. After dancing with Jacques kids always feel as tired and sweaty as you feel after a good basketball game. Now Jacques is 69 years old. He has wavy silver hair and dancing eyes. He stretches out tall as his personality is large. He can jog up eight-flights of stairs to get his energy going and he never rides up the elevator.

—Oliver D.

FIGURE 13–6. Oliver's biographical sketch.

Teasing

Have you ever been teased? I have. And so have 9 out of 10 5th graders I talked to. Many admit that they tease to, but hate it when someone else teases them. Some kids are teased for wearing glasses, others for being a bit too fat. All types of teasing are cruel but it happens to every one.

I'm teased sometimes because I'm a boy and I love to dance. All the other boys say dancing is for girls. They think I'm dumb for dancing. They call me a girl and they mock me, copying the fake ideas of dance, the ones about pink frilly tutus and fluffy dance shoes. When they get bored of teasing me they go to the person next to me wearing glasses, and I see them snatch his glasses and call him Four Eyes.

Many people are teased about things you think are dumb to tease about, like being too tall or too short or having a different accent. But even thought they're dumb reasons, they all are still teased about them. They call tall people Lighthouse, or shout "how's the weather up there?" The short people are called midget or pipsqueak and even the people with accents are asked "What planet are you from?"

It's hard to ignore the teasing, but there are some strategies I could show you that really help. One thing I do is think about how they know nothing about what it's like to be teased, and they tease only to impress people. But it's not impressive, it's cruel. Another thing I do, is try to think of all the amazing things you can do if you get past getting teased. You could do so many things if you ignore what they're saying. Teasing can't be stopped, but you can stop listening to the teasing if you try and remember the strategies I used, to get past the cruel things about teasing.

—Oliver D.

FIGURE 13–7. Oliver's feature article on teasing.

Dear Jack,

Basketball is no reason to quit dancing with N.D.I. If you're really quitting because you're a boy and you don't think it's right for boys to dance, I think you should reconsider.

Boys have always danced and still do. They grow famous for dancing. If you're being teased now, here's some advice: just ignore them. They have no clue what it's really like.

Just imagine what your life would be like without dance. I know dance means a lot to you. Definitely you wouldn't quit for any other dumb reason so think of getting teased another dumb reason.

If you had a choice between playing basketball and dancing, you would choose dancing because this is your only chance to dance your heart out. You can play basketball anywhere but a chance to dance with the National Dance Institute, is a once in a lifetime opportunity.

Don't quit,
Oliver D.

FIGURE 13-8. *Oliver's letter to persuade.*

Billy Elliot

A Review by Oliver D.

Billy Elliot is a wonderful movie about a boy who learns how to express his feelings through dance. Billy is introduced to dance when he goes to an after school boxing program and watches a group of girls doing ballet. He stays late after boxing practice and dances with the girls in the class. Billy discovers the wonder of dancing from that class and from then on he skips boxing and secretly dances with the ballet group.

His father is a miner in Newcastle, a town whose people are very poor. The only job people can get is coal mining. Billy's father doesn't approve of boys dancing. He thinks only girls should dance. When he catches Billy dancing, instead of boxing, he is extremely mad. He hits him and insists that Billy not dance. Billy decides to run away and stay with his dance teacher. During Billy's stay at the teacher's house, a

friendship develops between the teacher and him, and she persuades him to go home. On the drive back to Billy's house, the teacher offers him private lessons, free of charge, so once again Billy Elliot dances in secret. During one practice the teacher persuades Billy to audition for a ballet called Swan Lake. Billy has to convince his father to let him go, and finds that the only way to show him is to dance and make him watch. Finally, his father sees that his son has amazing talent, and he gives in. So Billy goes to London for the audition and when one of the judges asks him how he feels when he dances, he reveals his deepest secret of how dancing lets his heart go free, and makes him feel like he just disappears. He feels fire in his body when he dances.

Billy Elliot, by Greg Brenman and Jon Finn, made me feel a personal connection to Billy Elliot. In the world today there is a stereotype applied to dancing. Boys are not encouraged to dance the

way girls are, even though some men have become the greatest dancers of all time. Most ballets need men and women for the parts, and yet boys feel embarrassed to begin to study dance. This is because they fear being teased and laughed at. They are afraid of being called sissies by other boys. I am often teased because I dance. I am jeered at and mocked, but I don't listen. Like Billy I try to ignore the remarks and make it through and usually I do. The movie taught me to think about confidence and be proud of myself for dancing, and always to listen to what you believe and be yourself. This movie was very powerful and showed reality through a different perspective; through dance. When I get teased I try to think of mentors that help me. *Billy Elliot* is a new mentor for me and I will look at the ways he got through tough times and try to use his example in my own life.

—*Oliver D.*

FIGURE 13-9. *Oliver's review of* Billy Elliot.

Conclusion

When Writing Spills Out of the Writing Workshop

The true test of whether Writing Workshop has made a difference is not whether all of our students become professional writers (although we would be honored to know that some of them do), but whether writing becomes a tool they use for responding to the world—to comfort, to convince, to pay tribute, to commemorate, to celebrate, and to speak out. Above all, we hope our students will understand how to use writing as a tool for making meaning, enabling them to come away with deeper understandings of themselves and their world.

When writing spills out of the classroom and into the students' lives, they find reasons to use their writing to take messages far beyond the reach of their voices. This reminds us of Kevin, a fifth grader who has lots of opinions and openly shares them. On this particular occasion, he cared enough about what he had to say that he put his words into action in a letter to the former Soviet President, Mikhail Gorbachev (see Figure C-1 on page 206).

Several weeks later, Kevin received a response via a phone call from former President Gorbachev. The following exchanges, translated by Kevin's mother, Gala, are excerpted from the conversation.

PP: Hello, may I please speak to Kevin?

KM: Yes, this is me.

PP: Hello, Kevin. This is Pavel Palazhchenko, the assistant to President Gorbachev, he would like to talk with you.

KM: President Gorbachev? The real one? Is this a joke?

PP: This is no joke, Kevin.

MG: Kevin, good afternoon.

KM: Good afternoon, Mr. President.

(Conversation about translation.)

MG: Kevin, I want to thank you for such a nice letter. It is very warm and nice . . . I am stunned by it: that such a story might happen in real life!

205

Dear President Mikhail Gorbachev,

My name is Kevin Morrell and I am 10 years old. I live in New York City and I am a 5th grader at the Manhattan New School.

We never met, but I know that you know my grandfather, Boris Batsanov, who was the chief-of-staff of the Soviet Prime Minister for many years. I called my grandfather this morning and told him that you are in New York, but unfortunately I will not have a chance to meet you personally. My grandfather Boris told me that I should write you a letter, because what I was going to tell you is really very important!

Here is my story.

My dad and mom are former enemies. In the 80s my mom was in the Soviet military, she was a journalist of Pravda covering military events. My dad was a captain of the American Air Force. He flew F-15. He served at the American Air Base in Okinawa, Japan. My Mom worked at the Soviet Far East and often flew with Russian bombers. She told me that several times she saw American fighters on the radars of her plane. I know now that it could have been my Dad, whom she saw, in the air, on the opposite side.

Russia and America hated each other. And my dad and mom had to hate each other too.

I also know, that if they were ordered to, my parents could have shot each other and if they did not miss, they even could have killed each other.

But it happened so, that my mom and dad met (in Siberia), fell in love and got married. And I want to thank you, dear Mr. President, for it. Because, if you did not start Perestroika, my parents would have never been able to meet in the Siberian ski and be together afterwards.

You helped my family to be happy.

I just wanted you to know that living here, in New York, I often think about you and always wanted to tell you thank you for what what you have done for my family.

I want to wish you all the best in your life and your work as well.

Sincerely,

Kevin Morrell

FIGURE C–1. *Kevin's letter.*

KM: Oh, I am so happy that you read it. I wrote it very quickly, but to tell the truth I have been writing it for a very long time—all my life.

MG: You don't say!

KM: I thought that if it was not for you, I probably would not have even existed.

MG: That's right.

KM: And my family would not have existed either.

MG: You are right, Kevin, you know, truly, your project would have been jeopardized.

KM: My grandfather built the Berlin Wall when he worked in Germany.

MG: No, really?

KM: When grandpa came to visit me in New York, I took him to the park near the Intrepid and showed him the pieces of the Berlin Wall. My grandpa built that wall and you tore it down.

MG: You see, Kevin, you are a witness of a new life! You see what happens when we all become normal people, when there are no walls between us, when we have hope for a better future, thank God.

KM: When we can move forward.

MG: Exactly! You are right.

KM: I would like to tell you about my school. It is called The Manhattan New School. I think that this school would make you happy.

MG: Really?

KM: The thing is that in my school there are children from 48 countries and they speak 56 languages. Arabs and Jews, Catholics and Protestants, and we all live in friendship. We are together building and creating plans for the future.

MG: You see, Kevin, all of this shows that children will be able to build a new world. I wish for you, your mom, and dad happiness and good luck. And please pass along to the children in your school who speak so many languages a hello from me and a wish for them to build a new world. Be strong, dedicated in this endeavor.

KM: . . . I promise, I will tell them everything.

MG: Good. I give you a strong hug.

KM: Thank you, President Gorbachev, we will build a new world, I promise.

Kevin certainly never expected a telephone call from Mikhail Gorbachev! But what a remarkable moment for him. We can be certain that he understands the power of writing as a tool to reach and, perhaps, influence others far beyond his own family, circle of friends, school, and neighborhood. Kevin demonstrates that writing is too big to be contained within the confines of the Writing Workshop or even within a school. What's more, Kevin understands that writing is not just about passing the city and state tests and delivering tidy five-paragraph essays. It means more even than the beautifully crafted essays, memoirs, personal narratives, poems, and letters that grace the walls of The Manhattan New School or the lovely self-written picture books shared with appreciative family members and younger children. While this writing matters, we know we have made a real difference when we witness the ways in which our students use their writing to shape their lives and the lives of others they care about. What they ultimately do with their knowledge of writing as the result of participating in our classroom and in a daily Writing Workshop is the true test of our teaching. As dedicated teachers of writing, we wait and watch for what happens long after the published pieces are lifted from the bulletin boards or the applause in an Author's Celebration dies down. When Writing Workshop has spilled over into the lives of our students, they may, like Kevin, use writing as a tool to craft a safer, more understanding world. At this point, we can smile, turn off our classroom lights, and anticipate the next day we're privileged to spend teaching and learning alongside our student writers.

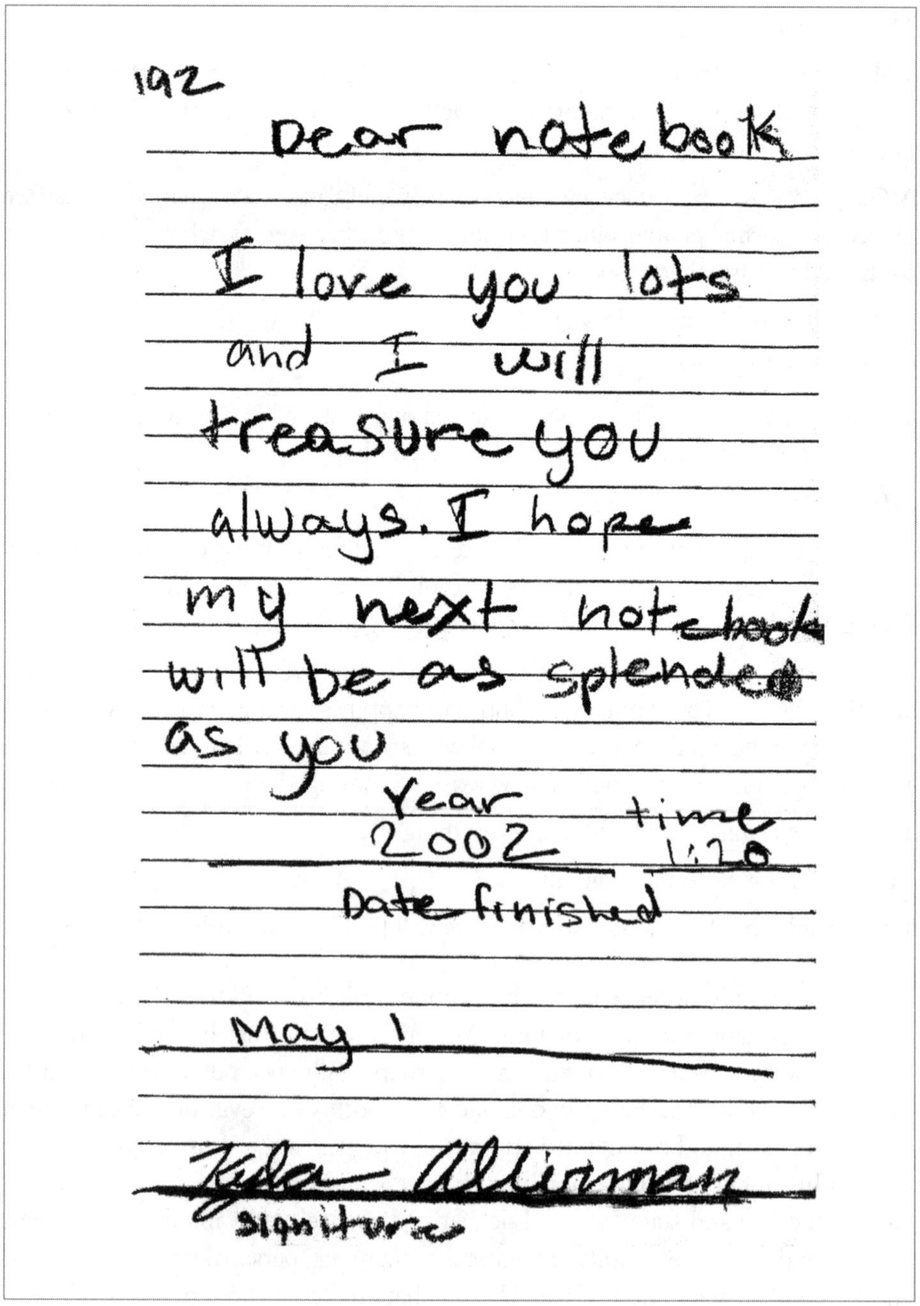

192

Dear notebook

I love you lots and I will treasure you always. I hope my next notebook will be as splended as you

Year 2002   time 1:20
Date finished

May 1

Kyla Alinman
signiture

FIGURE C-2. *Our sentiments exactly!*

Afterword

The No-Nonsense Guide to Teaching Writing is a gift to all of us who love to pull a chair alongside students and to become part of their writing worlds. It is a book that will move off of our bookshelves and next to our beds, into our bookbags and into our classrooms. It will grow worn with jottings and a bit messy with protruding post-its. The voices of Judy and Sharon will stay in our heads as we use their book in study groups and in quiet moments of reading.

Sharon and Judy prove over and over that listening to children, studying their work, knowing literature, understanding craft, and reflecting periodically are the essential tools of developing a writing curriculum. Principals, teachers, and staff developers will recognize their own teaching within this book and also learn ways to enhance their practice. We should all have moments of gasping and laughing, crying and joy when we read our students' writing. These moments lead us to turn to our colleagues to think through instruction, to rethink what we practice, and to ask questions about change. Judy and Sharon's book will support us in that work with their experience, insight, and reflective practice.

I have been awed for many years by the teaching of Sharon and Judy. They are truly gifted educators who teach with the most generous of hearts. I close this book just to open it again with a new group of friends to linger over every chapter. And I hope the same for all of you.

Jacqui Getz, Principal, The Manhattan New School

Appendices

Editing Checklist

SPELLING

1. I have found misspelled words and tried spelling them in the margin.

TRICKY WORDS

2. I have checked to see if I used the correct homophone.

- there, their, they're
- your, you're
- used to
- which, witch
- then, than
- could have

- to, too, two
- weather, whether
- past, passed
- except, accept
- its, it's

DOES IT MAKE SENSE?

3. I have reread my work to make sure I have not left out any words I intended to write.

4. I have checked to make sure my sentences are not too long. If they were, I have either rephrased them or made them into more than one sentence.

PUNCTUATION

5. I have placed **periods, commas, questions marks,** and **exclamation marks** in places where they belong.

6. I began each sentence with an uppercase letter.

7. I have used uppercase letters for names of people, places, and proper nouns.

8. I have indented each new paragraph as my thoughts shifted.

Student Weekend Writing Assessment

Name _____   Week of _____

Reflecting on the goal I set last week, I can say _____

_____

_____

_____

This week:

_____ I have written at least 6–8 entries.

_____ Each of my entries are at least one page long.

_____ I edit my entry each night when I am finished writing.

_____ I have at least three different types of entries (memories, observations, opinions, etc.)

_____ I have added at least two new writing ideas to my "Things I Can Write About" list.

_____ I have worked on improving my writing. I worked on_____

_____

_____

_____ I have reread my entries and have found at least one new idea from an old one.

_____ I have written more thoughtfully about something I have written about before.

_____ I have shared my writing with someone else and have carefully considered their feedback.

_____ I have written at least one entry off an article I read in *Time for Kids* or *Junior Scholastic* or any other magazines or newspapers I have read… (wonderings, opinions, questions).

I am using this coming week to focus on _____

_____

_____

_____

_____

I plan to do this by:

_____ speaking with peers _____ conferring with teacher _____ finding a mentor piece

Parent's Signature _____   Peer Signature _____

Name_____

Writer's Reflection

The notebook entry I chose to publish was about _____

_____

_____

_____

_____

As I drafted and developed the idea, I realized that what I was really trying to say was _____

_____

_____

_____

The craft strategy I used to lift the quality of my writing was _____

_____

_____

_____

My favorite part of this piece is _____

_____

_____

_____

It is my favorite part because _____

_____

_____

_____

One thing I have learned about good writing that I will apply to all my future writing is _____

_____

_____

_____

_____

Conference Recordkeeping Sheet

WRITING CYCLE _____

Notebook Checklist

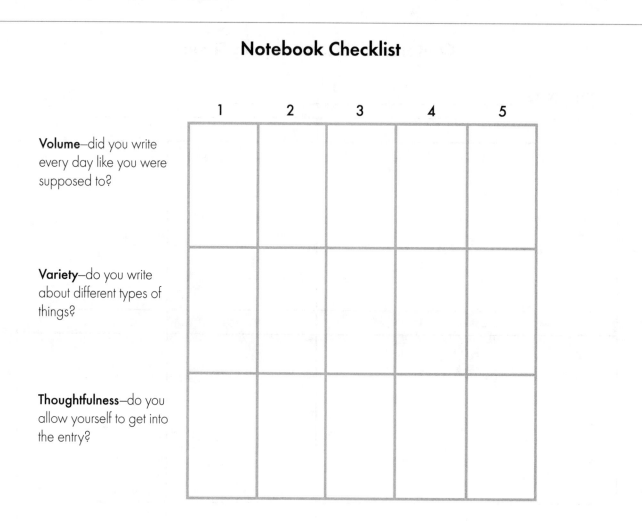

	1	2	3	4	5
Volume—did you write every day like you were supposed to?					
Variety—do you write about different types of things?					
Thoughtfulness—do you allow yourself to get into the entry?					

_____
Checklist date

_____
teacher signature

Writer's Response

_____
writer's signature

Do you agree with my evaluation?

How can I help?

What will you do?

MINILESSON PLANNING SHEET FOR CYCLE ON: _____

FOCUS FOR THE WEEK	DAY 1	DAY 2	DAY 3	DAY 4	DAY 5
WEEK:					
WEEK:					
WEEK:					
WEEK:					
WEEK:					

DAY-TO-DAY MINILESSON PLANNING SHEET

Cycle: Focus:

Week:

DATE: **MINILESSON FOCUS:**   **TEXT/MATERIALS:**

        Teaching Points   **Practice**   **Homework**

                Share

DATE: **MINILESSON FOCUS:**   **TEXT/MATERIALS:**

        Teaching Points   **Practice**   **Homework**

                Share

DATE: **MINILESSON FOCUS:**   **TEXT/MATERIALS:**

        Teaching Points   **Practice**   **Homework**

                Share

DATE: **MINILESSON FOCUS:**   **TEXT/MATERIALS:**

        Teaching Points   **Practice**   **Homework**

                Share

DATE: **MINILESSON FOCUS:**   **TEXT/MATERIALS:**

        Teaching Points   **Practice**   **Homework**

                Share

THINGS TO THINK ABOUT FOR NEXT WEEK

Flowchart: What I'm Trying to Say

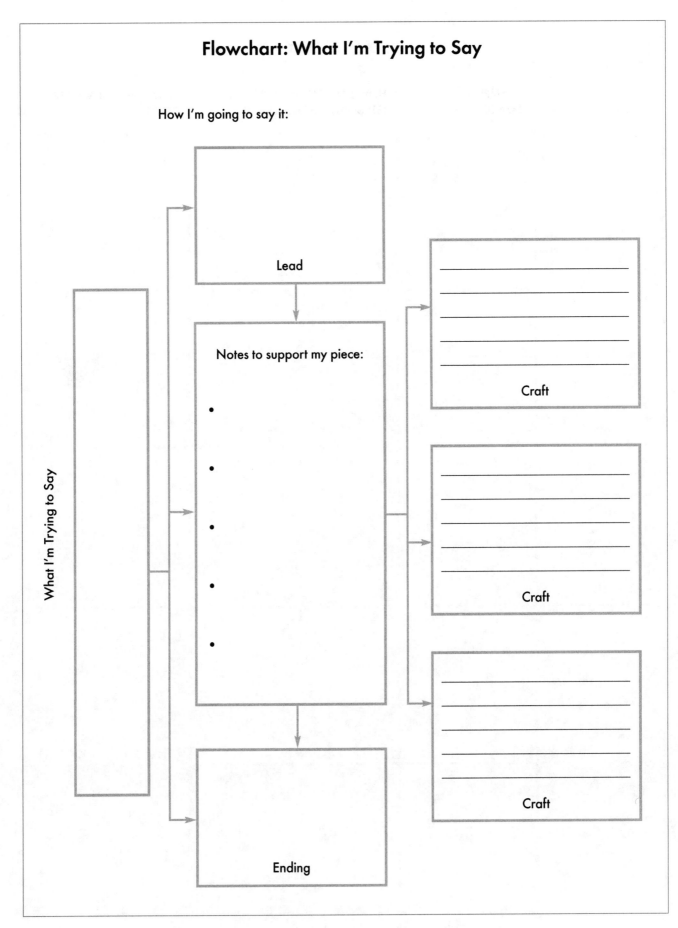

How I'm going to say it:

Lead

Notes to support my piece:

-
-
-
-
-

What I'm Trying to Say

Craft

Craft

Craft

Ending

CRAFT STUDY

TEXT/ AUTHOR	EXAMPLE FROM MENTOR TEXT	HOW DOES THE WRITER DO IT? (STRUCTURE OF THE CRAFT)	WHY DOES THE WRITER DO IT?

Structure Templates

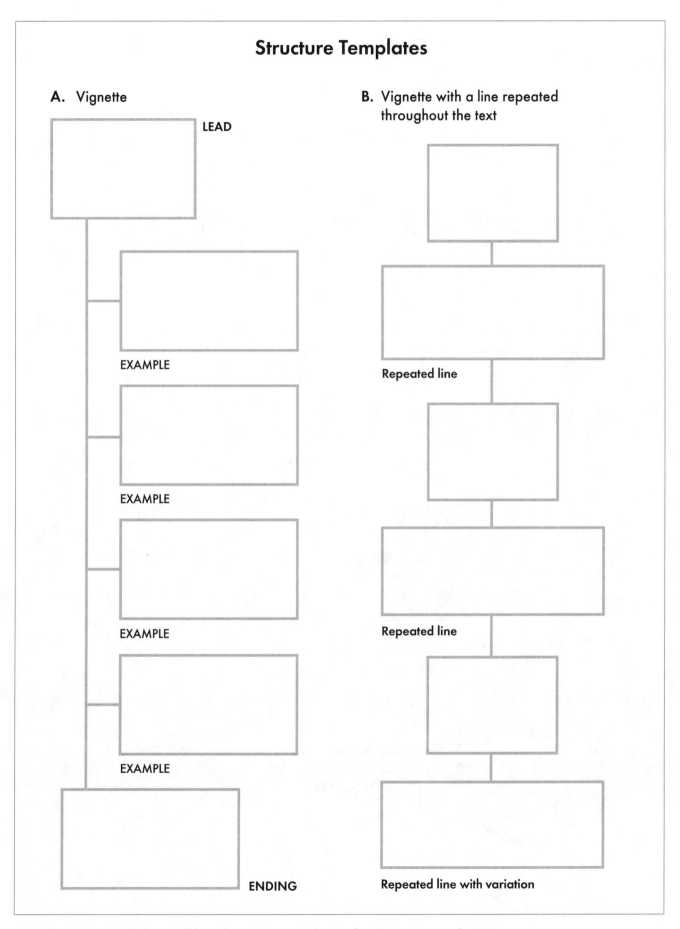

A. Vignette

LEAD

EXAMPLE

EXAMPLE

EXAMPLE

EXAMPLE

ENDING

B. Vignette with a line repeated throughout the text

Repeated line

Repeated line

Repeated line with variation

Structure Templates

C. Circular

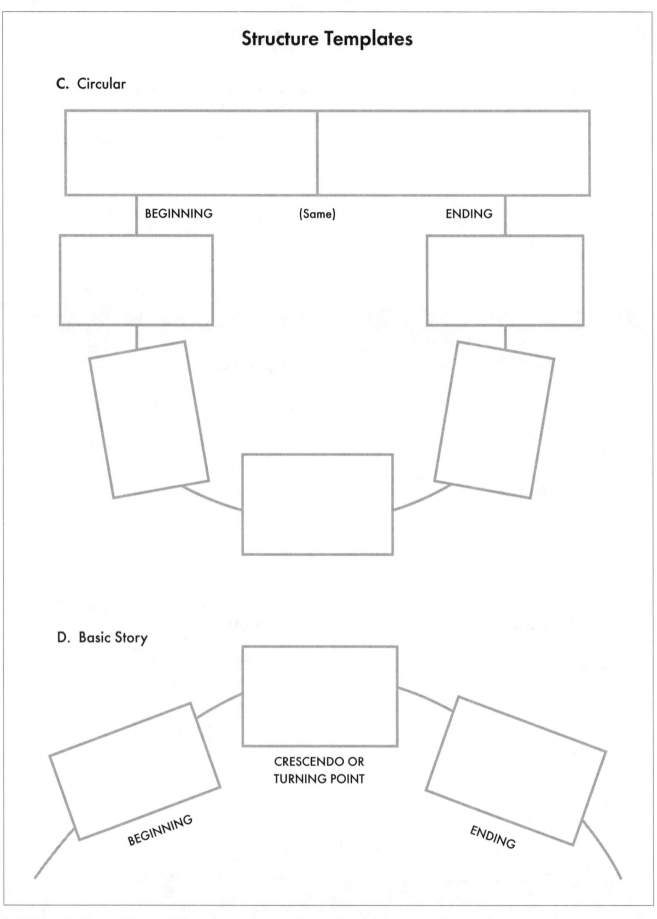

BEGINNING   (Same)   ENDING

D. Basic Story

CRESCENDO OR
TURNING POINT

BEGINNING

ENDING

Responding to Poetry

After you have chosen a mentor poem, fill in as much of the following as you can in the space provided. Attach it to a copy of the poem and keep it in your poetry folder.

TITLE OF POEM_____ POET_____

1. What was your first response to the poem?

2. What personal connection(s) did you make?

3. When you reread it, what else did you understand about it?

4. What did it inspire you to write?

5. Which line(s) stood out and why?

6. What do you think the poet wanted you to get from his/her poem?

7. What mood did it leave you in?

POETRY STUDY CHART

TITLE	POET	ANTHOLOGY TITLE	AUTHOR/EDITOR	LENGTH	TOPIC	MOOD	CRAFT

Knowing My Taste in Poetry

You have collected a number of mentor poems. Before you go further in your investigation, take time to review the Poetry Study Chart on which you have been keeping track of the length, topic, mood and craft of each poem. Use the questions below to help you categorize your choices so that you can draw some conclusions about your preferences.

1. What are you noticing about the length of the poems you have been collecting?

2. What are you noticing about the topics or content of the poem? Do you tend to gather poems that are more story-like, about nature, etc.? Try to name what you choose most.

3. Did you find yourself choosing poems you understood or related to easily or did you try to push yourself beyond your comfort zone? Explain.

4. How do most of the poems you have selected leave you feeling?

5. What are the specific crafting strategies that seem to attract you to a poem?

6. Which type of poetry seems to inspire you to write more poetically? Name the poem and say how it has inspired you.

7. Have you collected poems by totally different poets or are you attracted to one poet in particular? If so, what is it about that one poet's style that you like?

8. How will your conclusions influence your future inquiry? How will you decide to push yourself toward poems that are different or beyond your comfort zone? Will you focus on similar types? What do you think would be a good challenge for you now?

Poetry Reflection

Name _____

As a result of this study, comment about how you've changed as a reader of poetry.

_____

_____

_____

_____

_____

_____

_____

_____

Comment on how the process you use to write original poems has evolved as a result of this study.

_____

_____

_____

_____

_____

_____

_____

_____

For each of your poems, identify the qualities of the poem you feel best about.

Title_____

Comment _____

_____

_____

_____

_____

_____

Title_____

Comment _____

_____

_____

_____

_____

_____

Title_____

Comment _____

_____

_____

_____

_____

_____

FEATURE ARTICLE STUDY CHART

Text studied:

LEAD	POINT THE ARTICLE MAKES	PERSPECTIVE OR STANCE	HOW THE AUTHOR SUPPORTS THE POINT	KINDS OF INFORMATION INCLUDED	CRAFT

FROM NOTEBOOK ENTRY TO FEATURE ARTICLE				
DESCRIPTION OF NOTEBOOK ENTRY	POSSIBLE FEATURE ARTICLE TOPIC	STANCE/ANGLE/ PERSPECTIVE	RESEARCH NEEDS (STATISTICS)	INTERVIEW NEEDS: PEOPLE TO SURVEY WHO HAD SIMILAR EXPERIENCES—OTHER EXPERTS ON THE TOPIC

Feature Article Assessment

Feature Article Title _____

Reflecting on my favorite article, I can say it exemplifies the elements of the genre in the following ways:

It _____

_____

_____

It _____

_____

_____

It _____

_____

_____

The feature article that helped me the most was _____

It helped me in the following ways: _____

_____

_____

_____

_____

_____

_____

_____

The qualities of good writing that I think I used well in my article are: (name the quality and then quote the lines from your article)

_____

_____

_____

_____

_____

_____

_____

_____

_____

_____

After publishing this feature article, I can say that the most important thing I learned about writing is _____

_____

_____

_____

_____

_____

_____

_____

_____

_____

_____

_____

Getting Inspired by a Good Picture Book

Name _____

Title of Picture Book _____ Author_____

Topic _____

Type of Illustrations _____

1. Read the picture book.

2. What did you love about it?

3. Reread your notebook. Did you revise an entry? How did this picture book inspire you to revise your entry the way you did?

4. Did you write a new entry? How did the picture book inspire you?

5. Do you have an idea for a picture book of your own yet? If so, how do you imagine it might go?

PICTURE BOOK STUDY CHART

TITLE/AUTHOR	STRUCTURE	USE OF TIME	LEAD	REPETITION	OTHER CRAFT	ENDING	ILLUSTRATIONS

Picture Book Assessment

Name _____ Title of My Picture Book _____

The characteristics of my picture book that make it most comparable to other picture books we've studied are:

_____

_____

_____

_____

The picture books I used as mentors are:

Title: _____ Author: _____

Quality of good writing I admire: _____

Example from mentor text: _____

_____

Example from my book: _____

_____

Title: _____ Author: _____

Quality of good writing I admire: _____

Example from mentor text: _____

_____

Example from my book: _____

_____

Title: _____ Author: _____

Quality of good writing I admire: _____

Example from mentor text: _____

_____

Example from my book: _____

_____

My favorite part of the picture book I published is:

_____

_____

_____

_____

It is my favorite part because:

_____

_____

_____

_____

The biggest challenge for me in writing this picture book was:

_____

_____

_____

_____

I have learned many things about being a good writer from this study. They are:

_____

_____

_____

_____

_____

_____

_____

_____

_____

_____

_____

OPEN-CHOICE INVESTIGATION TOPIC CHART

TOPIC OF NOTEBOOK ENTRY	FACTS	QUESTIONS	OPINIONS	POSSIBLE FORMS FOR PUBLISHING

Bibliography

Professional Books

Anderson, Carl. 2000. *How's It Going? A Practical Guide to Conferring with Student Writers.* Portsmouth, NH: Heinemann.

Angelillo, Janet. 2002. *A Fresh Approach to Teaching Punctuation.* New York, NY: Scholastic.

Atwell, Nancie. 1998. *In the Middle: New Understandings About Writing, Reading, and Learning.* Portsmouth, NH: Heinemann.

Bomer, Randy. 1995. *Time for Meaning.* Portsmouth, NH: Heinemann.

Calkins, Lucy. 1994. *The Art of Teaching Writing.* Portsmouth, NH: Heinemann.

Fletcher, Ralph, and JoAnn Portalupi. 1998. *Craft Lessons: Teaching Writing K–8.* York, ME: Stenhouse.

———. 2001. *Writing Workshop: The Essential Guide.* Portsmouth, NH: Heinemann.

Graves, Donald. 1994. *A Fresh Look at Writing.* Portsmouth, NH: Heinemann.

———. 2000. *Writing: Teachers and Children at Work.* Portsmouth, NH: Heinemann.

Harvey, Stephanie. 1998. *Nonfiction Matters: Reading, Writing and Research in Grades 3–8.* York, ME: Stenhouse.

Harwayne, Shelley. 1992. *Lasting Impressions.* Portsmouth, NH: Heinemann.

———. 2001. *Writing Through Childhood: Rethinking Process and Product.* Portsmouth, NH: Heinemann.

Hindley, Joanne. 1996. *In the Company of Children.* York, ME: Stenhouse.

Heard, Georgia. 2002. *The Revision Toolbox.* Portsmouth, NH: Heinemann.

Lane, Barry. 1993. *After the End.* Portsmouth, NH: Heinemann.

Murray, Donald. 1990. *Write to Learn.* 3rd ed. New York, NY: Holt, Rinehart and Winston.

Ray, Katie Wood. 1999. *Wondrous Words: Writers and Writing in the Elementary Classroom.* Urbana, IL: NCTE.

Snowball, Diane, and Faye Bolton. 1999. *Spelling K–8: Planning and Teaching.* York, ME. Stenhouse.

Poetry Anthologies

Field Tested at the Manhattan New School

Cullinan, Bernice, editor. 1995. *A Jar of Tiny Stars: Poems by NCTE Award Winning Poets.* Photographed by Marc Nadel. Honesdale, PA: Boyds Mills Press.

DeFina, Allan A. 1997. *When a City Leans Against the Sky.* Honesdale, PA: Boyds Mills Press.

Dotlicht, Rebecca Kai. 1996. *Sweet Dreams of the Wild.* Honesdale, PA: Boyds Mills Press.

Dotlicht, Rebecca Kai, Jan Spivey Gilchrist. 1998. *Lemonade Sun: And Other Summer Poems.* Honesdale, PA: Boyds Mills Press.

Fletcher, Ralph J. 1997. *Ordinary Things: Poems from a Walk in Early Spring.* Illustrated by Walter Lyon Krudop. New York, NY: Atheneum.

———. 2001. *Relatively Speaking: Poems About Family.* Illustrated by Walter Lyon Krudop. New York, NY: Scholastic, Inc.

———. 2002. *Poetry Matters: Writing a Poem from the Inside Out.* New York, NY: HarperCollins Publishers.

Florian, Douglas. 1999. *Winter Eyes.* New York, NY: Greenwillow Books.

George, Kristin O'Connell. 1999. *Little Dog Poems.* Illustrated by June Otani. New York, NY: Houghton Mifflin Co.

———. 2002. *Swimming Upstream: Middle School Poems.* Illustrated by Debbie Tilley. New York, NY: Houghton Mifflin Company.

Graves, Donald. 1996. *Baseball, Snakes and Summer Squash: Poems About Growing Up.* Illustrated by Paul Birling. Honesdale, PA: Boyds Mills Press.

Heard, Georgia. 1997. *Creatures of the Earth, Sea, and Sky: Poems.* Honesdale, PA: Boyds Mills Press.

Helldorfer, M. C. 1994. *Gather Up, Gather In: A Book of Seasons.* Illustrated by Judy Pederson. New York, NY: Viking Penguin Publishers.

Hopkins, Lee Bennett, Editor. 1996. *Opening Days.* Illustrated by Scott Medlock. New York, NY: Harcourt Brace & Co.

———. 2000. *Sports! Sports! Sports! A Poetry Collection.* Illustrated by Brian Floca. New York, NY: HarperCollins Children's Books.

Hughes, Langston. 1994. *The Dream Keeper and Other Poems.* Illustrated by Brian Pinkney. New York, NY: Alfred A. Knopf.

Janeczko, Paul B. selected by. 1991. *The Place My Words are Looking For: What Poets Say About and Through Their Work.* Designed by Molly Heron. New York, NY: Simon and Schuster Children's Books.

———. selected by. 1998. *That Sweet Diamond: Baseball Poems.* Illustrated by Carole Katchen. New York, NY: Simon and Schuster.

———. selected by. 2000. *Stone Bench in an Empty Park.* Illustrated by Henri Silberman. New York, NY: Scholastic Inc.

———. Editor. 2002. *Seeing the Blue Between: Advice and Inspiration for Young Poets.* Cambridge, MA: Candlewick Press.

Newman, Fran. selected by. 1960. *Round Slice of Moon and Other Poems for Canadian Children.* Ontario, Canada: Scholastic/TAB.

Nye, Naomi Shihab. 2000. *Come with Me: Poems for a Journey.* Images by Dan Yaccarino. New York, NY: Harper Collins.

———. 2002. Reprint. *Flag of Childhood: Poems from the Middle East.* New York, NY: Aladdin Paperbacks.

Singer, Marilyn. 2002. *Footprints on the Roof: Poems About the Earth.* Illustrated by Meilo So. New York, NY: Alfred Knopf.

Soto, Gary. 1990. *A Fire in My Hands and Neighborhood Odes.* New York, NY: Scholastic Inc.

Stevenson, James. 1995. *Sweet Corn: Poems.* New York, NY: William Morrow and Co.

———. 1998. *Popcorn: Poems.* New York, NY: Greenwillow Books.

———. 1999. *Candy Corn: Poems.* New York, NY: Greenwillow Books.

———. 2001. *Just Around the Corner.* New York, NY: HarperCollins Children's Books.

Worth, Valerie. 1994. *All the Small Poems and Fourteen More.* Illustrated by Natalie Babbit. New York, NY: Farrar, Straus and Giroux.

Yolen, Jane. 1995. *Water Music: Poems for Children.* Photographed by Jason Stemple. New York, NY: Boyds Mills Press.

———. 1997. *Welcome to the Green House.* Illustrated by Laura Regan. New York, NY: Putnam Publishing Group.

Picture Books

Field Tested at the Manhattan New School

Aliki. 1996. *Those Summers.* New York, NY: HarperCollins.

Ackerman, Karen. 1988. *Song and Dance Man.* Illustrated by Stephen Gammell. New York, NY: Scholastic Inc.

Bauer, Marion Dane. 1995. *When I Go Camping with Grandma.* Illustrated by Allen Garnes. BridgeWater Books.

Bernhard, Emery. 1996. *The Way of the Willow Branch.* Illustrated by Durga Bernhard. San Diego, CA: Gulliver Books/Harcourt Brace.

Borden, Louise. 1999. *A. Lincoln and Me.* Illustrated by Ted Lewin. New York, NY: Scholastic.

Brisson, Pat. 1998. *The Summer My Father Was Ten.* Illustrated by Andrea Shine. Honesdale, PA: Boyds Mills Press.

Bunting, Eve. 1994. *Smoky Nights.* Illustrated by David Diaz. New York, NY: Harcourt Brace & Co.

Cisneros, Sandra. 1984. *Hairs: Pelitos.* Illustrated by Terry Ybanez. New York, NY: Dragonfly Books/Alfred A. Knopf.

Cline-Ransome, Lesa. 2000. *Satchel Paige.* Illustrated by James E. Ransome. New York, NY: Simon & Schuster Books for Young Readers.

Cooney, Barbara. 1988. *Island Boy.* New York, NY: Viking Penguin Inc.

Creech, Sharon. 2000. *Fishing in the Air.* Illustrated by Chris Raschka. New York, NY: HarperCollins Children's Books.

Crews, Donald. 1991. *Bigmama's.* New York, NY: Greenwillow Books.

———. 1992. *Shortcut.* New York, NY: Mulberry Paperback/William Morrow and Co.

Farris, Christine King. 2003. *My Brother Martin.* Illustrated by Chris Soentpiet. New York, NY: Simon & Schuster Books for Young Readers.

Fleischman, Paul. 1988. *Rondo in C.* New York, NY: Harper and Row.

Fox, Mem. 1985. *Wilfrid Gordon McDonald Partridge.* Illustrated by Julie Vivas. New York, NY: Kane/Miller.

Garza, Carmen Lomas. 1990. *Family Pictures.* San Francisco, CA: Children's Book Press.

Gray, Libby Moore. 1995. *My Mama Had a Dancing Heart.* Illustrated by Raul Colon. New York, NY: Orchard Books/Scholastic Inc.

Grimes, Nikki. 1997. *Come Sunday.* Illustrated by Michael Bryant. Grand Rapids, MI: Wm B. Erdman Publishing Co.

Heinz, Brian J. 2000. *Butternut Hollow Pond.* Illustrated by Bob Marstall. Brookfield, CT: The Millbrook Press, Inc.

Helldorfer, M. C. 1994. *Gather Up, Gather In.* New York, NY: Viking Penguin Inc.

Hesse, Karen. 1999. *Come On, Rain!* Illustrated by Jon J. Muth. New York, NY: Scholastic Inc.

Hest, Amy. 1990. *The Ring and the Window Seat.* Illustrated by Deborah Haeffele. New York, NY: Scholastic Inc.

———. 1995. *How to Get Famous in Brooklyn.* Illustrated by Linda Dalal Sawaya. New York, NY: Simon and Schuster.

Hobbs, Will. 1998. *Howling Hill.* Illustrated by Jill Kastner. New York, NY: Morrow Junior Books.

Houston, Gloria. 1992. *My Great-Aunt Arizona.* Illustrated by Susan Condie Lamb. New York, NY: HarperCollins.

Howard, Elizabeth Fitzgerald. 1991. *Aunt Flossie's Hats (and Crab Cakes Later).* Paintings by James Ransome. New York, NY: Houghton Mifflin.

Hundal, Nancy. 1999. *Prairie Summer.* Illustrated by Brian Deines. Toronto, Ontario, Canada: Fitzhenry and Whiteside.

———. 2002. *Camping.* Illustrated by Brian Deines. Allston, MA: Fitzhenry and Whiteside.

Isadora, Rachel. 1979. *Ben's Trumpet.* New York, NY: Greenwillow Books.

Johnson, Angela. 2001. *Those Building Men.* New York, NY: Scholastic Inc.

Jones, Rebecca C. 1995. *Great Aunt Martha.* Illustrated by Shelley Jackson. New York, NY: Dutton Children's Books.

Kaplan, Howard. 2000. *Waiting to Sing.* Illustrated by Herve Blondon. New York, NY: DK Publishing Inc.

Khalsa, Dayal Kaur. 1986. *The Tale of a Gambling Grandma.* New York, NY: Clarkson N. Potter Inc.

Kuskin, Karla. 1987. *Jerusalum, Shining Still.* Illustrated by David Frampton. New York, NY: Harper & Row.

Laminack, Lester L. 1998. *The Sunsets of Miss Olivia Wiggins.* Illustrated by Constance P. Bergum. Atlanta, GA: Peachtree.

Lessac, Frane. 1984. *My Little Island.* New York, NY: Harper and Row Publishers.

London, Jonathan. 1995. *Like Butter on Pancakes.* Illustrated by G. Brian Karas. New York, NY: Viking Press.

MacLachlan, Patricia. 1994. *All the Places to Love.* Illustrated by Mike Wimmer. New York, NY: HarperCollins.

———. 1995. *What You Know First.* Engravings by Barry Moser. New York, NY: Joanna Cotler Books.

Madenski, Melissa. 1995. *In My Mother's Garden*. Illustrated by Sandra Speidel. Boston, MA: Little, Brown and Co.

McCaughrean, Geraldine. 2002. *My Grandfather's Clock*. Illustrated by Stephen Lambert. Boston, MA: Houghton Mifflin Co.

McLerran, Alice. 1991. *The Legacy of Roxaboxen: A Collection of Voices*. Illustrated by Barbara Cooney. New York, NY: Scholastic Inc.

Miller, Debbie S. 2002. *The Great Serum Race: Blazing the Iditarod Trail*. Illustrated by Jan Van Zyle. New York, NY: Walker & Company.

Moss, Marissa. 1994. *Mel's Diner*. United States of America: BridgeWater Books.

———. 1995. *Amelia's Notebook*. New York, NY: Scholastic Inc.

Moss, Thylias. 1993. *I Want to Be*. Illustrated by Jerry Pinkney. New York, NY: Dial Press.

Nickens, Bessie. 1994. *Walking the Log: Memories of a Southern Childhood*. New York, NY: Rizzoli International.

Nolen, Jerdine. 1999. *In My Momma's Kitchen*. Illustrated by Colin Bootman. New York, NY: Lothrop, Lee & Shepard Books.

Nye, Naomi Shihab. 1997. *Sitti's Secrets*. Illustrated by Nancy Carpenter. New York, NY: Aladdin Paperbacks.

Pilkey, Dav. 1996. *The Paperboy*. New York, NY: Scholastic Inc.

Polacco, Patricia. 1992. *Chicken Sunday*. New York, NY: Philomel Books/Putnam and Grosset Group.

———. 2001. *Mr. Lincoln's Way*. New York, NY: Scholastic, Inc.

Pomerantz, Charlotte. 1989. *The Chalk Doll*. Illustrated by Frane Lessac. New York, NY: J. B. Lippincott.

Ringgold, Faith. 1991. *Tar Beach*. New York, NY: Crown Publishing Group/Random House.

Russo, Marisbinal. 1996. *Grandpa Abe*. New York, NY: Greenwillow Books.

Rylant, Cynthia. 1982. *When I Was Young in the Mountains*. New York, NY: Dutton.

———. 1985. *When the Relatives Came*. Illustrated by Stephen Gammell. New York, NY: Aladdin Paperbacks/ Simon and Schuster.

———. 1988. *All I See*. Illustrated by Peter Catalanotto. New York, NY: Orchard Books.

———. 1996. *An Angel for Solomon Singer*. Illustrated by Peter Castalanotto. New York, NY: Orchard Books/ Scholastic Books Inc.

———. 1996. *The Bookshop Dog*. New York, NY: Scholastic Inc.

———. 1998. *Tulip Sees America*. Illustrated by Lisa Desimini. New York, NY: Scholastic.

———. 2000. *In November*. Illustrated by Jill Kastner. New York, NY: Harcourt Publishing.

Saul, Carol P. 1995. *Someplace Else*. Illustrated by Barry Root. New York, NY: Simon and Schuster Books for Young Readers.

Schotter, Roni. 1999. *Nothing Ever Happens on 90th Street*. Illustrated by Kyrsten Brooker. New York, NY: Orchard Books/Scholastic Inc.

Smith Jr., Charles R. 1999. *Rimshots: Basketball Pix, Rolls, and Rhythms*. New York, NY: Puffin.

Soto, Gary. 1996. *Too Many Tamales*. Illustrated by Ed Martinez. New York, NY: Putnam and Grosset Group.

Spinelli, Eileen. 2001. *Sophie's Masterpiece: Spider's Tale*. Illustrated by Jane Dyer. New York, NY: Simon and Schuster Children's.

Stolz, Mary. 1988. *Storm in the Night*. Illustrated by Pat Cummings. New York, NY: Harper and Row.

Weidt, Maryann, and Henri Sorensen. 1995. *Daddy Played Music for the Cows*. New York, NY: Lothrop, Lee and Shepard.

Wild, Margaret. 1993. *Our Granny*. Illustrated by Julie Vivas. Boston, MA: Houghton Mifflin.

Williams, Karen Lynn. 1990. *Galimoto*. Illustrated by Karen Stock. New York, NY: Lothrop, Lee and Shepard Books.

Williams, Vera B. 1983. *A Chair for My Mother*. New York, NY: William Morrow and Co.

Wyeth, Sharon Dennis. 1998. *Something Beautiful*. Illustrated by Chris K. Soentpiet. New York, NY: Bantam Doubleday.

Yolen, Jane. 1987. *Owl Moon*. Illustrated by John Schoenherr. New York, NY: Philomel Books.

———. 1994. *Grandad Bill's Song*. Illustrated by Melissa Bay Mathis. New York, NY: Philomel.

———. 1997. *Nocturne*. New York, NY: Harcourt Brace and Co.

Zolotow, Charlotte. 1974. *My Grandson Lew*. Pictures by William Pene du Bois. Mexico City, Mexico: Harper/Trophy.

———. 1993. *The Moon Was the Best*. Photography by Tana Hoban. New York, NY: Greenwillow.

Books Containing Short Texts

Cisneros, Sandra. 1991. *House on Mango Street*. New York, NY: Alfred A. Knopf.

———. 1992. *Woman Hollering Creek and Other Stories*. New York, NY: Vintage Books.*

Greenfield, Eloise.1992. *Childtimes: A Three Generation Memoir*. Illustrated by Lessie Jones Little and Jerrie Pinkney. New York, NY: HarperCollins.

Little, Jean. 1991. *Hey World, Here I Am*. Illustrated by Sue Truesdell. New York, NY: HarperCollins Children's Books.

Kitchen, Judith, Editor, and Mary Paumier Jones, Introduction. 1996. *In Short: A Collection of Brief Creative Nonfiction*. New York, NY: W. W. Norton and Co.

———. 1999. *In Brief: Short Takes on the Personal*. New York, NY: W.W. Norton and Co.

Rosen, Michael J., Editor. 1992. H*ome: A Collaboration to Aid the Homeless*. New York, NY: HarperCollins.

Reading Is Fundamental. 1991. *To Ride A Butterfly: Original Pictures, Stories, Poems & Songs for Children*. New York, NY: Bantam Doubleday Dell.

* We recommend the story "Eleven" from this collection. Some of the other entries are not appropriate for the elementary level.

Index

The Year at a Glance: *From Notebook to Published Work*

BEGINNING OF YEAR →

Setting Up the Writing Workshop

- Understanding the writing process
- Understanding what goes in a notebook
- Rehearsing for writing
- Initiating flip books
- Warming up through storytelling
- Getting started in the notebook
- Building stamina for writing
- Managing the notebook
- Gathering a variety of entries
- Learning how to use the right side of the notebook
- Using mentor texts to scaffold the writing
- Learning to use organizing tools to scaffold writing
- Learning to use assessment tools to reflect and set goals
- Understanding the components of the publishing process
- Learning to apply simple revision strategies to drafts
- Learning to peer edit/self-edit

Lifting the Quality of the Writing

- Broadening the strategies for getting ideas
- Continuing to broaden the variety of entries
- Practicing taking different perspectives
- Rereading the notebook to extend the thinking
- Deepening the thought—deciding what you really want to say
- Organizing ideas for drafting—using flow charts
- Refining revision strategies/crafting techniques to lift the quality of drafts
- Increasing focus on peer editing and self-editing

GOALS FOR WRITERS

The Writing Cycle:

1. Generating Notebook Entries
   ↓
2. Choosing an Idea
   ↓
3. Developing the Idea
   ↓
4. Drafting
   ↓
5. Revising
   ↓
6. Editing

and then...

POSSIBLE FORMS OF PUBLISHING

Published after 4 to 5 weeks:

Personal Narratives
Poems
Letters

Published in 4- to 5-week cycles:

Personal Narratives

Letters

Poems

7. Publishing!

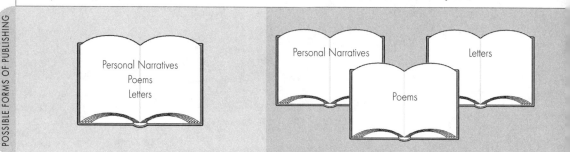

Forms of Writing Generated by the Reading Workshop

- Reading response to literature (in a reading journal)
  - Comparison to other texts
  - Character analysis
  - Response to big ideas found in the text
- Essay writing
- Book reviews
- Book recommendations
- Jottings on sticky notes in the book
- Letters to the Authors/Editors
- Critique
- Writing in preparation for book talk
- Writing to answer questions about the text
- Summarizing or retelling
- Writing to express a point of view
- Writing in preparation for city- and statewide tests
- E-mails